Freedom of Speech, Press, and Assembly

Exploring the Constitution Series

by Darien A. McWhirter

The Separation of Church and State
Freedom of Speech, Press, and Assembly
Search and Seizure
Equal Protection

Freedom of Speech, Press, and Assembly

by
Darien A. McWhirter

Exploring the Constitution Series
Darien A. McWhirter, Series Editor

Oryx
1994

The rare Arabian Oryx is believed to have inspired the myth of the unicorn. This desert antelope became virtually extinct in the early 1960s. At that time several groups of international conservationists arranged to have 9 animals sent to the Phoenix Zoo to be the nucleus of a captive breeding herd. Today the Oryx population is nearly 800, and over 400 have been returned to reserves in the Middle East.

Copyright © 1994 by Darien A. McWhirter
Published by The Oryx Press
4041 North Central at Indian School Road
Phoenix, Arizona 85012-3397

Published simultaneously in Canada

Printed and Bound in the United States of America

∞ The paper used in this publication meets the minimum requirements of American National Standard for Information Science—Permanence of Paper for Printed Library Materials, ANSI Z39.48, 1984

This publication is designed to provide accurate and authoritative information in regard to the subject matter covered. It is sold with the understanding that the publisher is not engaged in rendering legal, accounting, or other professional services. If legal advice or other expert assistance is required, the services of a competent professional should be sought.
From a Declaration of Principles jointly adopted by a Committee of the American Bar Association and the Committee of Publishers.

Library of Congress Cataloging-in-Publication Data
McWhirter, Darien A. (Darien Auburn)
    Freedom of speech, press, and assembly / by Darien A. McWhirter.
        p. cm. — (Exploring the Constitution series)
    Includes bibliographical references and indexes.
    ISBN 0-89774-853-0 (acid-free paper)
    1. Freedom of speech—United States—History. 2. Freedom of the press—United States—History. 3. Assembly, Right of—United States—History. I. Title. II. Series.
KF4770.M39 1994
342.73'0853—dc20   94-4842
[347.302853]   CIP

CONTENTS

❋ ❋ ❋ ❋ ❋ ❋ ❋ ❋

SERIES STATEMENT

The Constitution of the United States is one of the most important documents ever written, but it is not just of historical interest. Over two centuries after its adoption, the Constitution continues to influence the lives of everyone in the United States. Many of the most divisive social issues, from abortion to free speech, have been and are being resolved by the U.S. Supreme Court through interpretation of the U.S. Constitution.

Yet much of what has been written about these Supreme Court decisions and the Constitution itself has served only to confuse people who would like to understand exactly what the Court has ruled and exactly what the Constitution means. So much of the discussion revolves around what the Constitution *should* mean that what the Constitution actually *does* mean is obscured.

The Exploring the Constitution Series provides a basic introduction to important areas of constitutional law. While the books in this series are appropriate for a general audience, every effort has been made to ensure that they are especially accessible to high school and college students.

Each volume contains a general introduction to a particular constitutional issue combined with excerpts from significant Supreme Court decisions in that area. The text of the Constitution, a chronological listing of the Supreme Court justices, and a glossary of legal terms are included in each volume. Every effort has been made to provide an objective analysis of the Court's interpretation of constitutional issues with an emphasis on how that interpretation has evolved over time.

PREFACE

❀ ❀ ❀ ❀ ❀ ❀ ❀ ❀ ❀

No area of constitutional decision making has generated more public interest and media attention than the right of free speech. In decisions involving everyone from Nazis to anti-abortion protesters, the Supreme Court has been called upon to articulate the rules that control much of what the average American can see and hear. Issues such as how to define obscenity and what constitute speech have kept the Supreme Court busy over the course of many decades. As one free speech issue appears to leave center stage another one rises to take its place.

PURPOSE

While this volume is written for everyone, every effort has been made to make the discussion interesting and accessible to high school and college students. Issues and Supreme Court decisions have been chosen with an eye to what students might find interesting. Cases involving schools, both public and private, have been included whenever appropriate.

This volume is intended to be useful both as a reference work and as a supplement to the standard textbook in social studies, history, government, political science, and law courses. The Supreme Court decisions reprinted here were chosen because of their importance and the likelihood that they would stimulate discussion about the issues presented in this volume. Teachers should consider having students read only the actual Court decisions in preparation for class discussion, and then having students read the discussion material following the class discussion.

In addition to the actual texts of some of the most important Supreme Court decisions in this area, this volume provides the reader with discussions that place those decisions into their legal and historical context. While other sources provide either analysis or the text of actual Court decisions, this volume attempts to provide both in a format that will both stimulate thinking and provide a general overview of this important area of constitutional law. Both the discussion and the decisions are necessary for anyone who is really interested in understanding how the Supreme Court has interpreted the free speech section of the First Amendment. It is assumed, however, that readers have a general understanding of how the American legal system works and the role of the U.S. Supreme Court in that system.

Other sources have discussed some of the material presented here, but such discussions usually present only one side of the free speech debate. This volume attempts to explain as objectively as possible what the Supreme Court has ruled in this area. Supreme Court decisions are criticized here to the extent that they do not logically follow from earlier decisions, not because they fail to live up to the author's personal beliefs about what the Court should rule in this complex area of constitutional law.

ARRANGEMENT

This volume discusses seven major free speech issues that the Supreme Court has addressed. Chapter 2 examines the Court's decisions about what constitutes speech and the limits of what is protected by the right of free speech. Chapter 3 examines the complex area of where people have a right to speak and what types of public property may serve as a forum for the expression of opinion. Chapter 4 looks at what some consider to be the core of the right of free speech—the right to speak about political issues. During the course of the twentieth century, the Supreme Court has tried to develop the idea that political speech may only be limited if it poses a "clear and present danger" of violence or revolution.

Chapter 5 explores the right to engage in entertainment speech and the problem of defining what is and what is not obscenity. Chapter 6 looks at the issue of commercial speech and the extent to which the right of free speech protects commercial speech. Chapter 7 examines the right of a free press to gather and disseminate information. Chapter 8 looks at the right of the people to assemble and petition government and how this right has evolved over the course of many decades.

Each of the seven substantive chapters (2 through 8) is divided into three parts. The first part, "Discussion," provides an overview of the important Supreme Court decisions in a particular area to show the development of the Supreme Court's thinking over time. Each of the substantive chapters also contains excerpts from the text of Supreme Court decisions that illustrate the major issues under discussion and the logic behind the Court's thinking in

each area. Discussion questions at the end of each of these chapters are
intended to stimulate thought and discussion.

The table of cases provides references to all of the Supreme Court decisions discussed in the text. Anyone wishing to read the actual decisions may
find them by showing the reference to a librarian in a library that contains the
Supreme Court's decisions. The citation 374 U.S. 203 (1963), for example,
tells us that the decision was made in 1963, and that the text of the decision
is contained in volume 374 of the United States Reports at page 203.

The glossary is included to provide a ready reference, but readers may wish
to research some of the terms further. Not every term found in the glossary
will be found in each volume of this series.

This volume contains two appendixes. Appendix A contains the complete
text of the Constitution. Appendix B contains a chronological listing of all
the justices who have sat on the U.S. Supreme Court.

When James Madison wrote the first draft of what would be the First
Amendment, he placed the freedoms of speech, press, and assembly in a
position of prominence in the Bill of Rights, where they have remained ever
since. Many consider the right of free speech to be the most important right
and the right most fundamental to the process of democracy itself. Over the
past two centuries, the right of free speech has expanded as the United States
has become more secure in its democracy. It is only by reading the Court's
actual decisions and understanding the legal and historical context of those
decisions that any citizen can begin to understand what the law is in this area
and why it is what it is. It is to that end that this volume was written and it is
to the education of those citizens that this volume is dedicated.

Darien A. McWhirter
San Jose, California
February 1994

TABLE OF CASES
CITED IN THE TEXT

❋ ❋ ❋ ❋ ❋ ❋ ❋ ❋

CHAPTER
one
✸ ✸ ✸ ✸ ✸ ✸ ✸ ✸

Introduction

A discussion of free speech in the United States is concerned with the meaning of 33 words in the First Amendment to the U.S. Constitution. The First Amendment states that

> Congress shall make no law . . . abridging the freedom of speech, or of the press; or the right of the people peaceably to assemble, and to petition the Government for a redress of grievances.

While all aspects of the rights protected by this part of the First Amendment are interrelated, for the purposes of discussion we will consider that three different rights are protected:

1. The right of free speech
2. The right of a free press
3. The right to peaceably assemble to petition government

Before we can discuss what these words mean today, it is important to consider their history.

When the Constitution was first proposed, many states said that they would not approve a constitution without a bill of rights. These states approved the Constitution only after assurances that a bill of rights would soon be added. When the first Congress assembled after the Constitution was adopted, James Madison proposed the addition of 12 amendments. Ten were ultimately passed by Congress and ratified by the states. It is generally accepted that the rights considered most important were placed in the First Amendment. We have discussed the right to freely exercise religion in the first volume of this series, *The Separation of Church and State*. The rest of the First Amendment is concerned with the rights of free speech, press, and assembly. At the time these words were placed in the Constitution, there was very little debate about their meaning; the U.S. Supreme Court did not begin to define these rights until the twentieth century. During the nineteenth century, one philosopher above all others spoke about the right of free speech, John Stuart Mill.

JOHN STUART MILL

John Stuart Mill was born in London in 1806, the son of the well-known economist and philosopher James Mill. In order to give his son the best possible education as early as possible, James Mill acted as John's personal tutor. John Stuart Mill could read English, Greek, and Latin before most children even begin to read. At the age of 17, Mill began work as a bureaucrat with the East India Company, which was the main source of his income for most of his life.

John Stuart Mill did not just write that ideas should be discussed and that the best way to the truth is through vigorous debate; he formed debating societies and study groups. A typical day for Mill began with a breakfast discussion group on economics and ended with a session at a debating society. An active participant in British politics, he ran for and was elected to Parliament.

John Stuart Mill and his father were followers of the philosopher Jeremy Bentham. Most political philosophers of the eighteenth century had argued that liberty and democracy were things to be valued in and of themselves, but Jeremy Bentham wrote that liberty and democracy only deserved the support of society to the extent that they tended to bring about the greatest happiness for the greatest number of people. Things were to be judged by their "utility" for the society as a whole. Bentham's philosophy came to be called utilitarianism.

The key question for utilitarians is: How should society decide what will bring about the greatest happiness for the greatest number? According to Bentham, a free and fair election would be the first step. The rights of free speech, free press, and assembly would be necessary so that people could freely discuss all ideas before the election. The freely elected legislature would then decide what was best for the society. Such a legislature might decide that guaranteeing other kinds of liberty was best for the society, or it might decide that repression of liberty was in the best interest of the society. While some philosophers had argued that liberty was a good to be valued for itself, Bentham valued liberty only to the extent that it brought about the greatest happiness for the greatest number of people. However, what we might call the democratic liberties—free speech, free press, and assembly—occupied a special place in Bentham's scheme because they were necessary to guarantee that the legislature would actually reflect the will of the informed majority.

While John Stuart Mill read and listened to Bentham, he also read other important writers of his day. Auguste Comte's *Système de Politique Positive* horrified Mill. Comte argued that the people could not be trusted to elect leaders who would make decisions for the good of the whole society. Instead of a parliament, Comte argued that a group of philosophers should make all the major decisions for the society. Only philosophers concerned with the well-being of the entire society could be trusted to see clearly the best course for the society. As John Stuart Mill saw it, Comte's outline of the perfect society consisted of a system of "spiritual and temporal despotism" where a group of "spiritual teachers" would rule supreme over every thought and action in the name of the greater good of society. John Stuart Mill saw in Comte's writings where a total faith in utilitarianism might lead without both democracy and liberty.

John Stuart Mill came to believe that liberty must be protected, but he did not accept the idea that liberty was simply something to be valued for its own sake. He finally outlined his views in his book *On Liberty*, published in 1859. What reasons did Mill put forward to support individual liberty? First, Mill rejected the idea that Bentham's freely elected legislature would always bring about the greatest happiness for the greatest number of people. Mill's own experience in Parliament had shown him that a legislature was just as likely to bring about the greatest happiness for a vocal and active minority, leaving the rest of society to suffer. At the same time, he did not trust Comte's philosophers to do any better. He had seen for himself the negative results that often flow from well-meaning but misguided leaders. Whenever possible, Mill believed, individuals should be free to decide for themselves what brings them the most happiness. Mill's critics argued that a society where everyone was free to do anything he or she wanted to do would soon result in chaos and harm to others. Mill responded with what is the most famous statement on the legitimate limits of liberty ever written:

> the sole end for which mankind are warranted, individually or collectively, in interfering with the liberty of action of any of their number, is self-protection. . . . the only purpose for which power can be rightfully exercised over any member of a civilized community, against his will, is to prevent harm to others. His own good, either physical or moral, is not a sufficient warrant. He cannot rightfully be compelled to do or forbear because it will be better for him to do so, because it will make him happier, because, in the opinions of others, to do so would be wise, or even right. These are good reasons for remonstrating with him, or reasoning with him, or persuading him, or entreating him, but not for compelling him, or visiting him with any evil in case he do otherwise.

The idea that philosophers or politicians would somehow know better than the people themselves what made the people happy was rejected by Mill as utopian and even dangerous.

But what good is liberty to society as a whole? Mill had an answer for that too. Society needs progress. The history of the improvement of mankind has been a history of progress out of ignorance toward reason and knowledge, but progress means change. How can a society change if everyone thinks alike, acts alike, and says the same things? It is only when individuals speak out against some aspects of society and experiment with different ways of living that society moves forward. It is by the example of these individuals that progress occurs. Mill used the life of Jesus to make his point. Jesus said and did things that did not fit into the society of his time. Mill assumed that most of his readers would accept the idea that the world was better off because Jesus had been able to speak and act differently from those around him. Only by allowing people to express different ideas and to live different lifestyles would society be able to move forward, Mill argued. Although Mill agreed that most of the ideas spoken and lifestyles lived would probably not directly help society progress, if they did no real harm, and if they allowed the ideas and lifestyles that would change society for the better to come to light, then what reason could be advanced to suppress them? Mill argued that social progress needs genius, but

> Genius can only breathe freely in an *atmosphere* of freedom. Persons of genius are, *ex vi termini* [because of their inner force], *more* individual than other people—less capable, consequently, of fitting themselves, without hurtful compression, into any of the small number of moulds which society provides in order to save its members the trouble of forming their own character.

Mill also believed that one of the goals of society should be the development of the individuals within the society. A society can only be great, he argued, if it has great people within it, but a society dedicated to conformity will not create great people. In Mill's opinion, it was better to leave individual development up to the individuals rather than have leaders decide how people should develop.

Part 2 of *On Liberty* is concerned with the particular question of the "liberty of thought and discussion." Why should a society allow freedom of speech? Mill began his discussion by saying that "the time, it is to be hoped, is gone by, when any defense would be necessary of the 'liberty of the press' as one of the securities against corrupt or tyrannical government." A free press serves an important function, fighting corruption and tyranny by exposing it to public view, even in a democracy. But what about speech in general? Speech should not be suppressed, Mill argued, because we can never know what the truth is without free discussion. Mill outlined three reasons why freedom of speech is important. First, if any opinion is suppressed, it is always possible that that opinion was true. Second, even if the opinion was not totally true, it might have helped guide us to truth through discussion. Third, even if the opinion is totally false, only through vigorous discussion will we come to realize that the opinion is false and that some other idea is true.

Although he advocated freedom of speech, Mill accepted that there must be limitations to debate. Speech could be suppressed, he believed, if it would bring about some "mischievous act":

> An opinion that corn-dealers are starvers of the poor, or that private property is robbery, ought to be unmolested when simply circulated through the press, but may justly incur punishment when delivered orally to an excited mob assembled before the house of a corn-dealer, or when handed about among the same mob in the form of a placard.

In Mill's opinion, speech that was likely to bring about immediate violence could be controlled.

Mill did not accept the idea that free speech should be allowed only because, and to the extent that, it makes for a better-functioning democracy. Free speech allows people to develop as individuals; to discover truth unrelated to politics, such as religious truth; and to make more informed decisions about their private lives. Freedom of speech is part of an atmosphere of freedom that allows genius to develop and new lifestyles to be experimented with. Freedom of speech sets the stage for progress and allows great individuals to develop, who ultimately are an indispensable part of any great society.

THE SUPREME COURT AND MILL'S IDEAS

In the Supreme Court's early decisions there was little effort to spell out a "philosophy" of free speech. At the beginning of the twentieth century the Court had a fairly limited idea of what was protected by the rights of free speech, free press, and assembly and did not fully accept the ideas of John Stuart Mill. Over time, however, the Court's concept of what these rights encompassed expanded. Decade after decade the Court changed its mind, and what was not worthy of protection under the First Amendment a few years before was suddenly found to be covered by the amendment.

At first the Court believed that mainly political speech was protected by the First Amendment, and that even political speech could be suppressed if it posed any threat to the government. Over the years the Court was willing to allow more and more vigorous political debate. The Supreme Court decided later that art and entertainment were also covered by the First Amendment. Still later the Court expanded the right of free speech further to cover commercial speech, speech about products and services by people trying to sell something. The rights of free press and assembly also expanded over time. Early in the century, the right of a free press to expose "corruption and tyranny" and the right to assemble were not given much protection, but today these rights are highly protected.

CONSTITUTIONAL DECISION MAKING

The Supreme Court has developed a number of approaches to use in making decisions about constitutional provisions. The justices may use one, or more than one, approach in any one case. First, they may try to figure out what the authors of a particular provision had in mind when they wrote it. This approach is difficult to use to interpret the Bill of Rights. The amendments that make up the Bill of Rights were voted on not only by Congress but also by the many state legislatures, and it is not easy to determine what all of those people had in mind when they cast their votes.

Second, constitutional decision making often involves drawing a line. The Court decides that one type of behavior is protected from governmental interference by a particular provision of the Bill of Rights, and another type of behavior is not.

Third, the Court may try to balance governmental goals against individual rights. In evaluating a case, the Court must weigh the importance of the goals government is trying to achieve by passing a particular law or by engaging in a particular action against the damage the law or action appears to do to the individual rights of citizens. Often the Supreme Court asks how "compelling" is the goal government is trying to achieve. Then the Court tries to balance that against the importance of the right that is being infringed upon.

When dealing with free speech issues, the Supreme Court tried to use both line drawing and balancing. The Court first asked: Is this the kind of speech that is protected by the First Amendment? If the answer was no, and the answer was often no in the early cases, then that ended the discussion. If the answer was yes, then the Court weighed the goal government was trying to achieve by interfering with free speech against the kind of speech being interfered with. Past decisions were of little help to the Court as the century progressed, however, because later Courts moved the line and expanded the protection of the First Amendment to include more and more kinds of speech. Also, the weight given to the right of free speech went up over time, so that government's reasons for interfering with this right had to be more and more compelling in order to outweigh the right of free speech enjoyed by the people. The balance struck in one decade no longer applied in a later decade as the Court decided the right protected was more important than originally thought.

When the first free speech decisions were handed down, America was still feeling the devastating effects of the Civil War. The need to protect the integrity of the U.S. government was very compelling. By the 1960s no one really feared that the fabric of American society might be torn apart by the exercise of free speech. The experiences of World War II had solidified America into a unified nation with little possibility of disintegration.

THE SUPREME COURT OVER TIME

Generally people divide the history of the Supreme Court into three major eras: before the Civil War; between the Civil War and the Great Depression; and the modern era. The modern era can be broken up further into the New Deal Court (1941–53), the Warren Court (1953–69), the Burger Court (1969–86), and the Rehnquist Court (1986–present).

Pre–Civil War to the Great Depression

Before the Civil War the Supreme Court spent very little time on the meaning of the Bill of Rights. The Court decided that the Bill of Rights restricted only the federal government. State and local governments were free to do whatever they wanted, limited only by the bills of rights contained in state constitutions. Most of the governmental activities that touched people's lives were carried on by state governments, not by the federal government.

The Civil War was a great turning point in American history. With the victory of the Union army, two fundamental questions that had not been answered by the Constitution were well on their way to resolution. These were the question of the extent of the federal government's power to control the states and the question of slavery. After the Civil War, in the partnership between the states and the federal government, the federal government would be the more powerful partner, and slavery would be abolished in the United States. The Thirteenth, Fourteenth, and Fifteenth Amendments were then passed to make it clear to future generations who had won the Civil War and what should follow from that victory.

Between the Civil War and the Great Depression, the Supreme Court struggled to decide what these three amendments actually meant; the key question for the Court was the meaning of the Fourteenth Amendment. The Court decided that the amendment protected basic liberties of all Americans from infringement by state and local governments, but this raised another difficult question: What were the basic liberties that were protected? Between the Civil War and the Great Depression, the Court refused to be specific about this question. The Court simply took each case as it came and decided whether or not the freedoms involved were important enough to protect with the Fourteenth Amendment.

Critics of the Court argued that the members of the Court were simply using the Fourteenth Amendment as an excuse to overturn laws passed by the state legislatures because a majority of the justices did not agree with the laws, not because the laws violated any particular right. From the 1880s to the 1930s, 200 statutes were overturned by the Court. Most of these statutes attempted to regulate industry. For example, the Court overturned a New York law that limited bakers to a 60-hour work week. Other laws declared unconstitutional had attempted to protect a worker's right to join a labor union. While the Court argued that it was protecting the right of workers to work more than 60 hours a week and to not join labor unions, critics argued that the Court was mainly protecting the right of employers to exploit their employees.

The Modern Era

Beginning in the 1930s, the Court began to move away from this expansive idea and to develop the concept that the Fourteenth Amendment actually made most of the federal Bill of Rights applicable to state and local governments. This countered the critics and enabled the Court to give real substance to the Fourteenth Amendment's command that everyone should be able to enjoy liberty in the United States.

The composition of the Court was changing. By 1941 eight of the justices had been appointed by President Roosevelt. What had been a conservative court dominated by Republicans became a liberal court dominated by Democrats, the New Deal Court. As a practical matter, this meant that the Court spent less time trying to protect business from government and more time trying to protect the rights of individuals and minority groups.

In 1953 President Eisenhower appointed Earl Warren as chief justice of the Supreme Court, and in 1956 Eisenhower appointed William Brennan associate justice. These two justices turned out to be as concerned with the rights of individuals and minorities as the New Deal Court had been. The period from 1953 to 1969 is known as the Warren era in Supreme Court history, and many difficult issues concerning the meaning of the Bill of Rights and the relative power of the state and federal governments were decided during that time by the Warren Court.

In 1969 President Nixon appointed Warren Burger as chief justice; Burger was replaced by William Rehnquist in 1986. During this period, through the Burger Court and the Rehnquist Court, the Supreme Court is generally considered to have moved in a more conservative direction. That does not mean that the decisions of the New Deal and Warren Courts were simply overturned—far from it—but the tone and direction of the Court did change. The interests of the state and federal government were given greater emphasis, along with the needs of business.

Although the direction of the Court may change over time with the addition of new justices, the Court is limited by the doctrine of *stare decisis*.

This is a Latin phrase meaning "the decision must stand." In the American legal system, it means that generally a past decision of the Supreme Court will not be overturned except under exceptional circumstances.

In the area of free speech, the political and ideological affiliation of the justices has been a factor in helping to determine how they vote. For example, during the 1920s and 1930s the two most liberal justices, Justice Holmes and Justice Brandeis, often found themselves dissenting from the conservative majority and arguing in favor of more deference to the right of free speech. Even during periods of dominance by either liberal Democrats (the 1940s) or conservative Republicans (the 1980s), however, there has been a great deal of disagreement about how far the protection of freedom of speech should go. What has been true of the Court has also been true of American society in general. Some groups in society have been passionately committed to the idea of protecting free speech while others have argued just as passionately that other values such as respect for the American flag or standards of decency should be given greater weight.

CONCLUSION

This book discusses a difficult and divisive area of constitutional decision making—the right of free speech. Those of us who approach this issue today have the benefit of both hindsight and a century of Supreme Court decisions on the subject. We can see what questions and problems have resulted from particular decisions that could not have been anticipated by the justices who made those early decisions.

In no other area of constitutional decision making has the Court changed its collective mind so frequently. With each passing decade, decisions limiting the right of free speech have been overturned. This trend has continued regardless of the political affiliation of the justices.

No matter what a person's opinions are concerning the proper balance between the right of free speech and other important societal values, it is important to understand what the Court has ruled in this area and why. Disagreement based on ignorance is worthless. Reasoned argument based on understanding and facts is the most powerful weapon anyone can wield in a free society.

CHAPTER
two
❈ ❈ ❈ ❈ ❈ ❈ ❈ ❈

What Is Speech?

If Americans have a right of free speech, the first question is: What is speech? Or, more specifically, what kinds of communicative activities are protected by the right of free speech? For almost a century and a half after the First Amendment was added to the U.S. Constitution, it was generally agreed that speech included spoken and written words. The issue of what other kinds of potentially communicative activities might be included under the category of "speech" did not arise until 1931. Since then, the court has ruled that speech can be symbolic, that symbolic speech is protected by the First Amendment, and that the right to speak also includes the right not to speak.

RAISING THE RED FLAG

In the 1931 case of *Stromberg v. California*, a 19-year-old woman who worked as a camp counselor at a summer camp for working-class children was charged with the crime of "raising the red flag." Because the red flag is associated with revolution and communism, the state of California had made it a crime to display a red flag. Yetta Stromberg, a member of the Young Communist League, was teaching the children at the camp that all workers are of one blood and should unite to work for their common interests. She was convicted of raising the red flag, something this young woman did each morning at the summer camp. A majority of the members of the Court, with two dissenters, accepted the idea that raising the red flag was a type of speech, even though symbolic in nature, and therefore protected by the First Amendment.

The Court then tried to balance the right of free speech against the goal government was trying to achieve with this law. The state of California argued that it was trying to prevent violent revolution by outlawing the raising of the red flag. A majority of the justices could not see how simply raising a flag as a symbol of dissatisfaction with the American political and economic system could pose a significant threat to society. There was no evidence that this symbolic act had actually resulted in any kind of violence or harm to people or property. The Court ruled that raising the red flag was a symbolic speech act, protected by the First Amendment. Since the state could not put forward a good enough reason for suppressing this symbolic act, the Court overturned the California law. The next free speech case involved the right to refuse to speak when ordered to do so by government.

THE RIGHT NOT TO SPEAK

In the 1940 case of *Minersville School District v. Gobitis*, every justice but one agreed that a public school district had the power to force schoolchildren to say the Pledge of Allegiance to the American flag. In *Gobitis*, a group of children who were Jehovah's Witnesses refused to say the Pledge of Allegiance because they believed that their religion prohibited the worship of "graven images" and that the American flag qualified as a graven image. These children were willing to be expelled from public school rather than violate the teachings of their religion.

Eight of the nine justices believed that these children did not have the right under the Constitution to refuse to say the Pledge of Allegiance to the American flag. In writing the majority opinion, Justice Frankfurter pointed out that government had the power to force people to join the military in times of war and to require students at public colleges to take instruction in the military arts. He argued that "national unity is the basis of national security," and, that being the case, surely government also had the right to force schoolchildren to say the Pledge of Allegiance to the American flag as a way of creating national unity. Justice Frankfurter could have dealt with this case by saying that these were children and that children attending public school do not have the same rights as adults, but he did not. He accepted the idea that children have as much right to speak as adults, limited of course by the need to prevent the disruption of school activities. These children were not refusing to say their lessons; they were refusing to make a political statement that government required them to make and they were doing so because they believed it violated their most basic religious beliefs. Eight of the nine justices agreed that the right of free speech did *not* include the right not to speak when ordered to do so by a government official, in this case a schoolteacher.

Only Justice Stone dissented. In his dissenting opinion, he noted that the school district rules involved in the *Gobitis* case were special. These rules were not intended to keep children from doing disloyal things or from making disloyal statements but instead were intended to force the children to make a statement of loyalty they did not wish to make. Justice Stone believed the right to speak freely also included the right not to speak when ordered to do so by government. Put another way, what good is the right to speak if it does not include the right not to speak? If the right to speak is a right of the people to express their beliefs and opinions, then surely it includes the right not to express beliefs and opinions that they do not hold.

Justice Stone was the lone dissenter in 1940, but by 1943 major changes had taken place in the U.S. Supreme Court. Justice Stone had been elevated to chief justice by President Roosevelt. Two new justices had joined the Court after the former chief justice had retired along with another justice. Also, three members of the Court had thought about what now Chief Justice Stone had said in his dissenting opinion in *Gobitis* and were ready to change their minds and vote with him when given the chance. That chance came with the case of *Board of Education v. Barnette.*

After the Supreme Court's decision in *Gobitis*, many school boards around the country began to require students to salute the flag. The West Virginia State Board of Education ordered that the flag salute become "a regular part of the program of activities in the public schools." Jehovah's Witnesses brought suit in federal court to stop enforcement of this policy. This gave the Court a chance to reconsider its *Gobitis* decision. What had been eight to one in favor of forced Pledges of Allegiance became six to three against them; *Gobitis* was overturned.

Other changes contributed to the reversal of *Gobitis*. In 1943, when the Supreme Court considered *Board of Education v. Barnette*, the United States was fighting for democracy and freedom in both Europe and Asia. The standard way of saying the Pledge of Allegiance to the American flag in the 1940s involved having the children raise one arm in what we would call a "Heil Hitler" style salute. If the current government could force children to salute the flag in this way, could some future government force them to salute an American tyrant? The justices did not find that prospect very appealing. Also, Americans were being told they were fighting and dying to save freedom. Freedom to do what? Freedom to be forced to say things they did not believe or that they believed violated the teachings of their religion? The justices that voted to change the Court's collective mind argued that while government was free to force people to fight in the war if necessary, the Pledge of Allegiance was not in the same category with activities necessary to ensure the survival of the nation. They said:

> words uttered under coercion are proof of loyalty to nothing but self-
> interest. Love of country must spring from willing hearts and free minds,
> inspired by a fair administration of wise laws enacted by the people's

elected representatives within the bounds of express constitutional prohibitions.

These six justices could not see how the war effort depended on forcing "little children to participate in a ceremony which ends in nothing for them but a fear of spiritual condemnation." With the *Barnette* decision, the Court had decided that the right of free speech included the right not to speak.

THE *O'BRIEN* TEST

The next important decision concerning the protection of symbolic speech came 25 years later with the 1968 decision in *United States v. O'Brien*. This case involved the conviction of David Paul O'Brien and three others for burning their draft cards on the steps of the South Boston Courthouse as part of an anti-Vietnam War demonstration. David Paul O'Brien and his companions were convicted of violating a federal law that made it a crime for anyone to "knowingly" mutilate or destroy a draft card. While the Court agreed that some actions could be seen as symbolic speech, it ruled that government had a right to control such actions if the regulations were reasonable and fulfilled an important governmental function. In this case, the justices ruled in favor of the government. The Court believed that government had a right to run a draft system and could require people to keep their draft cards, which were an important part of that system. Chief Justice Warren, writing for the majority, said:

> We think it clear that a government regulation is sufficiently justified if it is within the constitutional power of the Government; if it furthers an important or substantial governmental interest; if the governmental interest is unrelated to the suppression of free expression; and if the incidental restriction on alleged First Amendment freedoms is no greater than is essential to the furtherance of that interest.

This statement came to be called the *O'Brien* test. The Court decided that the government regulation in the *O'Brien* case met this test.

The *O'Brien* test makes it clear that when government makes laws that restrict free speech, government must be trying to do something essential to the functions of government and must not have as its main goal the suppression of free speech. If government is furthering a "substantial" interest, its actions may have an incidental impact on free speech as long as that impact is kept to a minimum. While the Court did not talk about balancing, it was to some degree weighing the need for the government to engage in or prohibit a particular action against the degree of interference with the right of free speech. Since there are so many ways to communicate displeasure with the draft system besides burning draft cards, the Court did not think that the prohibition against burning draft cards would significantly interfere with the right to communicate about the draft system or the Vietnam War. Throughout the discussion, Chief Justice Warren accepted the idea that engaging in actions such as burning draft cards is a kind of symbolic speech that is entitled to some protection by the First Amendment. The next year, 1969, the Court would face two decisions in this area. One would be easy, the other would be very difficult.

SYMBOLIC SPEECH IN THE SCHOOLS

The easy case, *Tinker v. Des Moines School Dist.* (see p. 18), involved three students who were suspended from public school in Iowa because they came to school wearing black armbands as a protest against the Vietnam War. Justice Fortas wrote the opinion for the majority in this seven-to-two decision. He began with the principle that schoolchildren have constitutional rights just like adults, a principle that had already been established in the Pledge of Allegiance cases. He also accepted the idea that wearing a black armband is speech, even though symbolic; everyone involved in this case knew what the students were trying to communicate by wearing black armbands to school. There was no disruption of school activities or violence. Justice Fortas said that the "undifferentiated fear or apprehension of disturbance is not enough to overcome the right to freedom of expression." While any kind of speech could conceivably lead to disruption or even violence, he said, that was simply a risk a society bent on protecting the right of free speech had to take. In Justice Fortas's opinion, free speech contributed to our "national strength" and was an important part of the "vigor" of American life. He also pointed out that the Des Moines schools did not prevent all symbolic speech; students were allowed to wear political campaign buttons and other symbols to school. School officials should not be allowed to discriminate against those who wished to quietly express their opposition to the Vietnam War. In other words, while symbolic speech, like any speech, can be controlled for a good reason, it can not be restricted simply to prevent the communication of a message the government does not approve of.

Justice Black dissented, arguing that school officials should be given the power to control the school environment so that the primary function of schools—education—can go forward. He accepted the school officials' argument that the armbands took the student's minds off their schoolwork and made them think instead about the war many of them would soon be called upon to fight.

FLAG DESECRATION

The other 1969 decision concerned with symbolic speech, *Street v. New York*, was much more difficult. The case involved a New York law that made it a crime to "mutilate, deface, defile, or defy, trample upon, or cast contempt upon either by words or act" the flag of the United States. When Sidney Street, a black man living in New York City, heard that James Meredith, a civil rights leader, had been shot in Mississippi, he took an American flag, went to the corner of St. James Place and Lafayette Avenue, and set the flag on fire. There was no violence or disturbance. The police arrived to find him speaking to a small group saying: "Yes, that is my flag: I burned it. If they let that happen to Meredith we don't need an American flag."

In writing the opinion for the five-justice majority, Justice Harlan side-stepped the issue of symbolic speech. Because Sidney Street had been charged not just with burning the flag but also with "speaking" defiant words about the flag, the case involved spoken words as well as symbolic speech. The majority of justices believed that New York could not make it a crime to speak out on the issue of whether or not we "need" a flag. They did not think that New York's interest in preventing disrespect for the flag was strong enough to overcome the right of free speech. The majority of justices also did not think that the words spoken in this case could be seen as words likely to provoke a violent response from listeners. There was no real justification for interfering with the speech in this particular case, except perhaps that the state was not happy about the message conveyed, and that is not an acceptable reason for interfering with the right of free speech.

Four justices, Chief Justice Warren and Justices Black, White, and Fortas, dissented. The dissenting justices believed that Sidney Street had clearly been punished for his act of flag desecration, not for the words he said while doing it. In their opinion, the state of New York certainly had the power under the Constitution to punish this kind of activity. They did not think that the act of burning the flag could be classified as "symbolic speech" in the same way that wearing a black armband clearly could be.

In 1974 six justices voted to overturn the conviction of a man in Washington State for "improper use" of the flag (*Spence v. Washington*). What had he done? He had taped a large peace symbol to an American flag and hung it out the window of his apartment to protest the invasion of Cambodia by the United States and the killing of students at Kent State University by Ohio National Guard troops. In overturning his conviction, the Court pointed to several factors. This was a privately owned flag displayed on private property. There was no use of public property or disorderly conduct. There was no violence or breach of the peace. Everyone, including the state of Washington, conceded that this was a case of "speech," not "action." The Court also pointed out that the flag had not even been permanently disfigured or destroyed. In other words, there was no significant government interest to be weighed against the right of free speech in this case. Flying a flag with a peace symbol taped on it was clearly an act of communication and was protected by the First Amendment.

Justice Rehnquist dissented, joined by Chief Justice Burger and Justice White. They believed that the state had a valid interest in protecting the American flag as a "symbol of nationhood and unity," and that the act of using tape to place a peace symbol over the flag could and should be punished.

In 1989 the Court had to face the issue of flag desecration head-on. There was no question of removable tape or vaguely written statutes. In *Texas v. Johnson* (see p. 21), Gregory Lee Johnson was charged with publicly burning the American flag in front of the City Hall in Dallas, Texas, as part of a demonstration in conjunction with the Republican National Convention. As the flag burned the demonstrators chanted "America, the red, white, and blue, we spit on you." Johnson was charged with desecration of a venerated object and sentenced to one year in prison. The Texas Court of Criminal Appeals (the highest court of criminal review in Texas) overturned the conviction, believing that Johnson's right of free speech had been violated. The U.S. Supreme Court agreed with the Texas Court of Criminal Appeals by a vote of five to four.

Justice Brennan wrote the opinion for the majority of Supreme Court justices. Unlike Sidney Street, Gregory Lee Johnson clearly was convicted for an act—burning the flag—not for the words spoken while the act was being committed. This meant the Court had to face head-on the issues of whether or not this action amounted to speech and, if so, whether or not this speech was protected by the First Amendment. The Court ruled that the act of burning the flag was speech and that this speech was protected. The Court then weighed the interest of the government, which in this case was the desire to preserve the flag as a symbol of national unity, against the right of free speech and found the balance in favor of the right of free speech.

In a sense the issue was the same as that decided in the Pledge of Allegiance cases almost half a century before. In those cases the government had argued that it needed to protect national unity by forcing schoolchildren to say the Pledge of Allegiance. In *Texas v. Johnson* the government argued that it needed to protect national unity by protecting a symbol of that unity, the American flag. With both the Pledge of Allegiance and the flag burning cases, the Court ultimately ruled in favor of free speech and against the government.

Justice Brennan stated, "If there is a bedrock principle underlying the First Amendment, it is that the Government may not prohibit the expression of an idea simply because society finds the idea itself offensive or disagreeable." Justice Brennan viewed this act of flag burning as classic political speech in opposition to ideas held by the majority, the most important type of speech worthy of protection. In referring to the earlier flag cases, he pointed out that the right of free speech had been found superior in each case. In Justice Brennan's opinion, the flag's place of honor would be strengthened, not weakened, by this decision. He concluded:

> Our decision is a reaffirmation of the principles of freedom and inclusive-ness that the flag best reflects, and of the conviction that our toleration of criticism such as Johnson's is a sign and source of our strength. . . . The way to preserve the flag's special role is not to punish those who feel differently about these matters. It is to persuade them that they are wrong.

Justice Brennan was saying, as John Stuart Mill had said a century before, that the correct response to speech is not the repression of speech, but more speech. The principle that ideas should be freely discussed is what is being protected, not the content of any particular speech. Gregory Lee Johnson chose to convey his message in part through the use of a symbol, in this case the powerful symbol of a burning American flag, and government failed to come up with a good enough reason to justify stopping this kind of symbolic speech.

The four dissenting justices saw the issue quite differently. They believed that the government was not interfering with speech but with action. Justice Rehnquist said that the act of burning the flag conveyed no "particular idea" and was likely simply to "antagonize others." It was the destruction of a national symbol, not speech, that the state objected to, and Justice Rehnquist thought that the state had every right to do so. Justice Stevens in his dissenting opinion pointed to the unique place that the American flag holds in American society. He believed that the issue in this case was "disagreeable conduct" rather than "disagreeable ideas" and that the state should have the power to punish disagreeable conduct.

In response to this decision, Congress passed the Flag Protection Act of 1989, which was designed to overturn the Court's decision. The act was immediately violated on the steps of Congress, and the Court, with a five-to-four vote, declared the Flag Protection Act to be unconstitutional in 1990 (*United States v. Eichman*). This ruling made it clear that the only way to overturn the decision in *Texas v. Johnson* would be with a constitutional amendment. In June 1990 a proposed constitutional amendment that stated "The Congress and the States shall have power to prohibit the physical desecration of the flag of the United States" failed to receive the necessary two-thirds vote in both the House and Senate, although a majority voted for it in each house.

CONCLUSION

From the decision in 1931 in *Stromberg v. California* that people have a right to "raise the red flag" to the 1989 decision in *Texas v. Johnson* that people have a right to desecrate the American flag to make a political point, the Court has recognized that speech can be symbolic as well as verbal. In some cases actions speak louder than words, and if those actions are engaged in as part of speech, they are entitled to protection by the First Amendment. The Court has also accepted that the right of free speech includes the right not to speak when ordered to do so by government, at least in some circumstances. Government may not force people to express beliefs that they do not hold.

·· CASE DECISIONS ····································

The case of *Tinker v. Des Moines School Dist.*, decided in 1969, concluded that schoolchildren have a right of free speech that includes the right to engage in symbolic speech acts such as wearing black armbands to school to protest the Vietnam War. Justice Fortas wrote the opinion for the seven-justice majority, which is included here. Concurring opinions by Justices Stewart and White and dissenting opinions by Justices Black and Harlan are not included here.

The case that finally decided that people have the right to burn and alter the American flag as a symbolic statement of protest was *Texas v. Johnson*, decided in 1989. Justice Brennan wrote the opinion for the five-justice majority. Justice Kennedy wrote a brief concurring opinion, while Chief Justice Rehnquist and Justice Stevens wrote dissenting opinions. All four opinions are included here. Following are excerpts from the case decisions.

❀ ❀ ❀ ❀ ❀ ❀ ❀ ❀

TINKER v. DES MOINES SCHOOL DIST.
393 U.S. 503 (1969)

MR. JUSTICE FORTAS delivered the opinion of the Court.

Petitioner John F. Tinker, 15 years old, and petitioner Christopher Eckhardt, 16 years old, attended high schools in Des Moines, Iowa. Petitioner Mary Beth Tinker, John's sister, was a 13-year-old student in junior high school.

In December 1965, a group of adults and students in Des Moines held a meeting at the Eckhardt home. The group determined to publicize their objections to the hostilities in Vietnam and their support for a truce by wearing black armbands during the holiday season and by fasting on December 16 and New Year's Eve. Petitioners and their parents had previously engaged in similar activities, and they decided to participate in the program.

The principals of the Des Moines schools became aware of the plan to wear armbands. On December 14, 1965, they met and adopted a policy that any student wearing an armband to school would be asked to remove it, and if he refused he would be suspended until he returned without the armband. Petitioners were aware of the regulation that the school authorities adopted.

On December 16, Mary Beth and Christopher wore black armbands to their schools. John Tinker wore his armband the next day. They were all sent home and suspended from school until they would come back without their armbands. They did not return to school until after the planned period for wearing armbands had expired—that is, until after New Year's Day. . . .

First Amendment rights, applied in light of the special characteristics of the school environment, are available to teachers and students. It can hardly be argued that either students or teachers shed their constitutional rights to freedom of speech or expression at the schoolhouse gate. This has been the unmistakable holding of this Court for almost 50 years. . . .

The school officials banned and sought to punish petitioners for a silent, passive expression of opinion, unaccompanied by any disorder or disturbance on the part of petitioners. There is here no evidence whatever of petitioners' interference, actual or nascent, with the schools' work or of collision with the rights of other students to be secure and to be let alone. Accordingly, this case does not concern speech or action that intrudes upon the work of the schools or the rights of other students.

Only a few of the 18,000 students in the school system wore the black armbands. Only five students were suspended for wearing them. There is no indication that the work of the schools or any class was disrupted. Outside the classrooms, a few students made hostile remarks to the children wearing armbands, but there were no threats or acts of violence on school premises.

The District Court concluded that the action of the school authorities was reasonable because it was based upon their fear of a disturbance from the wearing of the armbands. But, in our system, undifferentiated fear or apprehension of disturbance is not enough to overcome the right to freedom of expression. Any departure from absolute regimentation may cause trouble. Any variation from the majority's opinion may inspire fear. Any word spoken, in class, in the lunchroom, or on the campus, that deviates from the views of another person may start an argument or cause a disturbance. But our Constitution says we must take this risk, *Terminiello v. Chicago*, 337 U.S. 1 (1949); and our history says that it is this sort of hazardous freedom—this kind of openness—that is the basis of our national strength and of the independence and vigor of Americans who grow up and live in this relatively permissive, often disputatious, society.

In order for the State in the person of school officials to justify prohibition of a particular expression of opinion, it must be able to show that its action was caused by something more than a mere desire to avoid the discomfort and unpleasantness that always accompany an unpopular viewpoint. Certainly where there is no finding and no showing that engaging in the forbidden conduct would "materially and substantially interfere with the requirements of appropriate discipline in the operation of the school," the prohibition cannot be sustained. . . .

It is also relevant that the school authorities did not purport to prohibit the wearing of all symbols of political or controversial significance. The record shows that students in some of the schools wore buttons relating to national political campaigns, and some even wore the Iron Cross, traditionally a symbol of Nazism. The order prohibiting the wearing of armbands did not extend to these. Instead, a particular symbol—black armbands worn to exhibit opposition to this Nation's involvement in Vietnam—was singled out for prohibition. Clearly, the prohibition of expression of one particular opinion, at least without evidence that it is necessary to avoid material and substantial interference with schoolwork or discipline, is not constitutionally permissible.

In our system, state-operated schools may not be enclaves of totalitarianism. School officials do not possess absolute authority over their students. Students in school as well as out of school are "persons" under our Constitution. They are possessed of fundamental rights which the State must respect, just as they themselves must respect their obligations to the State. In our system, students may not be regarded as closed-circuit recipients of only that which the State chooses to communicate. They may not be confined to the expression of those sentiments that are officially approved. In the absence of a specific showing of constitutionally valid reasons to regulate their speech, students are entitled to freedom of expression of their views. . . .

Under our Constitution, free speech is not a right that is given only to be so circumscribed that it exists in principle but not in fact. Freedom of expression would not truly exist if the right could be exercised only in an area that a benevolent government has provided as a safe haven for crackpots. The Constitution says that Congress (and the States) may not abridge the right to free speech. This provision means what it says. We properly read it to permit reasonable regulation of speech-connected activities in carefully restricted circumstances. But we do not confine the permissible exercise of First Amendment rights to a telephone booth or the four corners of a pamphlet, or to supervised and ordained discussion in a school classroom. . . .

We express no opinion as to the form of relief which should be granted, this being a matter for the lower courts to determine. We reverse and remand for further proceedings consistent with this opinion.

Reversed and remanded.

TEXAS v. JOHNSON
491 U.S. 397 (1989)

JUSTICE BRENNAN delivered the opinion of the Court.

After publicly burning an American flag as a means of political protest, Gregory Lee Johnson was convicted of desecrating a flag in violation of Texas law. This case presents the question whether his conviction is consistent with the First Amendment. We hold that it is not.

While the Republican National Convention was taking place in Dallas in 1984, respondent Johnson participated in a political demonstration dubbed the "Republican War Chest Tour." As explained in literature distributed by the demonstrators and in speeches made by them, the purpose of this event was to protest the policies of the Reagan administration and of certain Dallas-based corporations. The demonstrators marched through the Dallas streets, chanting political slogans and stopping at several corporate locations to stage "die-ins" intended to dramatize the consequences of nuclear war. On several occasions they spray-painted the walls of buildings and overturned potted plants, but Johnson himself took no part in such activities. He did, however, accept an American flag handed to him by a fellow protester who had taken it from a flag pole outside one of the targeted buildings.

The demonstration ended in front of Dallas City Hall, where Johnson unfurled the American flag, doused it with kerosene, and set it on fire. While the flag burned, the protesters chanted, "America, the red, white, and blue, we spit on you." After the demonstrators dispersed, a witness to the flag burning collected the flag's remains and buried them in his backyard. No one was physically injured or threatened with injury, though several witnesses testified that they had been seriously offended by the flag burning.

Of the approximately 100 demonstrators, Johnson alone was charged with a crime. The only criminal offense with which he was charged was the desecration of a venerated object in violation of Tex. Penal Code Ann. § 42.09(a)(3) (1989). After a trial, he was convicted, sentenced to one year in prison, and fined $2,000. The Court of Appeals for the Fifth District of Texas at Dallas affirmed Johnson's conviction, 706 S.W.2d 120 (1986), but the Texas Court of Criminal Appeals reversed, 755 S.W.2d 92 (1988), holding that the State could not, consistent with the First Amendment, punish Johnson for burning the flag in these circumstances. . . .

The First Amendment literally forbids the abridgment only of "speech," but we have long recognized that its protection does not end at the spoken or written word. While we have rejected "the view that an apparently limitless variety of conduct can be labeled 'speech' whenever the person engaging in the conduct intends thereby to express an idea," *United States v. O'Brien, supra,* at 376, we have acknowledged that conduct may be "sufficiently imbued with elements of communication to fall within the scope of the First and Fourteenth Amendments," *Spence, supra,* at 409.

In deciding whether particular conduct possesses sufficient communicative elements to bring the First Amendment into play, we have asked whether "[a]n intent to convey a particularized message was present, and [whether] the likelihood was great that the message would be understood by those who viewed it." 418 U.S., at 410–411. Hence, we have recognized the expressive nature of students' wearing of black armbands to protest American military involvement in Vietnam, *Tinker v. Des Moines Independent Community School Dist.,* 393 U.S. 503, 505 (1969); of a sit-in by blacks in a "whites only" area to protest segregation, *Brown v. Louisiana,* 383 U.S. 131, 141–142 (1966); of the wearing of American military uniforms in a dramatic presentation criticizing American involvement in Vietnam, *Schacht v. United States,* 398 U.S. 58 (1970); and of picketing about a wide variety of causes, see, *e.g., Food Employees v. Logan Valley Plaza, Inc.,* 391 U.S. 308, 313–314 (1968); *United States v. Grace,* 461 U.S. 171, 176 (1983).

Especially pertinent to this case are our decisions recognizing the communicative nature of conduct relating to flags. Attaching a peace sign to the flag, *Spence, supra,* at 409–410; refusing to salute the flag, *Barnette,* 319 U.S., at 632; and displaying a red flag, *Stromberg v. California,* 283 U.S. 359, 368–369 (1931), we have held, all may find shelter under the First Amendment. . . .

It remains to consider whether the State's interest in preserving the flag as a symbol of nationhood and national unity justifies Johnson's conviction.

As in *Spence,* "[w]e are confronted with a case of prosecution for the expression of an idea through activity," and "[a]ccordingly, we must examine with particular care the interests advanced by [petitioner] to support its prosecution." 418 U.S., at 411. Johnson was not, we add, prosecuted for the expression of just any idea; he was prosecuted for his expression of dissatisfaction with the policies of this country, expression situated at the core of our First Amendment values. See, *e.g., Boos v. Barry, supra,* at 318; *Frisby v. Schultz,* 487 U.S. 474, 479 (1988).

Moreover, Johnson was prosecuted because he knew that his politically charged expression would cause "serious offense." If he had burned the flag as a means of disposing of it because it was dirty or torn, he would not have been convicted of flag desecration under this Texas law: federal law designates burning as the preferred means of disposing of a flag "when it is in such condition that it is no longer a fitting emblem for display," 36 U.S.C. §176(k), and Texas has no quarrel with this means of disposal. Brief for Petitioner 45. The Texas law is thus not aimed at protecting the physical integrity of the flag in all circumstances, but is designed instead to protect it only against impairments that would cause serious offense to others. Texas concedes as much: "Section 42.09(b) reaches only those severe acts of physical abuse of the flag carried out in a way likely to be offensive. The statute mandates intentional or knowing abuse, that is, the kind of mistreatment that is not innocent, but rather is intentionally designed to seriously offend other individuals." *Id.*, at 44.

Whether Johnson's treatment of the flag violated Texas law thus depended on the likely communicative impact of his expressive conduct. Our decision in *Boos v. Barry, supra,* tells us that this restriction on Johnson's expression is content based. In *Boos,* we considered the constitutionality of a law prohibiting "the display of any sign within 500 feet of a foreign embassy if that sign tends to bring that foreign government into 'public odium' or 'public disrepute.'" *Id.*, at 315. Rejecting the argument that the law was content neutral because it was justified by "our international law obligation to shield diplomats from speech that offends their dignity," *id.*, at 320, we held that "[t]he emotive impact of speech on its audience is not a 'secondary effect'" unrelated to the content of the expression itself. *Id.*, at 321 (plurality opinion); see also *id.*, at 334 (Brennan, J., concurring in part and concurring in judgment).

According to the principles announced in *Boos,* Johnson's political expression was restricted because of the content of the message he conveyed. We must therefore subject the State's asserted interest in preserving the special symbolic character of the flag to "the most exacting scrutiny." *Boos v. Barry,* 485 U.S., at 321.

Texas argues that its interest in preserving the flag as a symbol of nationhood and national unity survives this close analysis. Quoting extensively from the writings of this Court chronicling the flag's historic and symbolic role in our society, the State emphasizes the "'special place'" reserved for the flag in our Nation. Brief for Petitioner 22, quoting *Smith v. Goguen,* 415 U.S., at 601, (Rehnquist, J., dissenting). The State's argument is not that it has an interest simply in maintaining the flag as a symbol of *something,* no matter what it symbolizes; indeed, if that were the State's position, it would be difficult to see how that interest is endangered by highly symbolic conduct such as Johnson's. Rather, the State's claim is that it has an interest in preserving the flag as a symbol of *nationhood* and *national unity,* a symbol with a determinate range of meanings. Brief for Petitioner 20–24. According to Texas, if one physically treats the flag in a way that would tend to cast doubt on either the idea that nationhood and national unity are the flag's referents or that national unity actually exists, the message conveyed thereby is a harmful one and therefore may be prohibited.

If there is a bedrock principle underlying the First Amendment, it is that the government may not prohibit the expression of an idea simply because society finds the idea itself offensive or disagreeable. . . .

We have not recognized an exception to this principle even where our flag has been involved. In *Street v. New York*, 394 U.S. 576 (1969), we held that a State may not criminally punish a person for uttering words critical of the flag. Rejecting the argument that the conviction could be sustained on the ground that Street had "failed to show the respect for our national symbol which may properly be demanded of every citizen," we concluded that "the constitutionally guaranteed 'freedom to be intellectually . . . diverse or even contrary,' and the 'right to differ as to things that touch the heart of the existing order,' encompass the freedom to express publicly one's opinions about our flag, including those opinions which are defiant or contemptuous." *Id.*, at 593, quoting *Barnette*, 319 U.S., at 642. Nor may the government, we have held, compel conduct that would evince respect for the flag. "To sustain the compulsory flag salute we are required to say that a Bill of Rights which guards the individual's right to speak his own mind, left it open to public authorities to compel him to utter what is not in his mind." *Id.*, at 634. . . .

We are fortified in today's conclusion by our conviction that forbidding criminal punishment for conduct such as Johnson's will not endanger the special role played by our flag or the feelings it inspires. To paraphrase Justice Holmes, we submit that nobody can suppose that this one gesture of an unknown man will change our Nation's attitude towards its flag. See *Abrams v. United States*, 250 U.S. 616, 628 (1919) (Holmes, J., dissenting). Indeed, Texas' argument that the burning of an American flag "is an act having a high likelihood to cause a breach of the peace,' " Brief for Petitioner 31, quoting *Sutherland v. DeWulf*, 323 F. Supp. 740, 745 (SD Ill. 1971) (citation omitted), and its statute's implicit assumption that physical mistreatment of the flag will lead to "serious offense," tend to confirm that the flag's special role is not in danger; if it were, no one would riot or take offense because a flag had been burned.

We are tempted to say, in fact, that the flag's deservedly cherished place in our community will be strengthened, not weakened, by our holding today. Our decision is a reaffirmation of the principles of freedom and inclusiveness that the flag best reflects, and of the conviction that our toleration of criticism such as Johnson's is a sign and source of our strength. Indeed, one of the proudest images of our flag, the one immortalized in our own national anthem, is of the bombardment it survived at Fort McHenry. It is the Nation's resilience, not its rigidity, that Texas sees reflected in the flag—and it is that resilience that we reassert today.

The way to preserve the flag's special role is not to punish those who feel differently about these matters. It is to persuade them that they are wrong. "To courageous, self-reliant men, with confidence in the power of free and fearless reasoning applied through the processes of popular government, no danger flowing from speech can be deemed clear and present, unless the incidence of the evil apprehended is so imminent that it may befall before there is opportunity for full discussion. If there be time to expose through discussion the falsehood and fallacies, to avert the evil by the process of education, the remedy to be applied is more speech, not enforced silence." *Whitney v. California*, 274 U.S. 357, 377 (1927) (Brandeis, J., concurring). And, precisely because it is our flag that is involved, one's response to the flag burner may exploit the uniquely persuasive power of the flag itself. We can imagine no more appropriate response to burning a flag than waving one's own, no better way to counter a flag burner's message than by saluting the flag that burns, no surer means of preserving the dignity even of the flag that burned than by—as one witness here did—according its remains a respectful burial. We do not consecrate the flag by punishing its desecration, for in doing so we dilute the freedom that this cherished emblem represents.

Johnson was convicted for engaging in expressive conduct. The State's interest in preventing breaches of the peace does not support his conviction because Johnson's conduct did not threaten to disturb the peace. Nor does the State's interest in preserving the flag as a symbol of nationhood and national unity justify his criminal conviction for engaging in political expression. The judgment of the Texas Court of Criminal Appeals is therefore

Affirmed.

Concurring Opinion JUSTICE KENNEDY, concurring.

I write not to qualify the words Justice Brennan chooses so well, for he says with power all that is necessary to explain our ruling. I join his opinion without reservation, but with a keen sense that this case, like others before us from time to time, exacts its personal toll. This prompts me to add to our pages these few remarks.

The case before us illustrates better than most that the judicial power is often difficult in its exercise. We cannot here ask another Branch to share responsibility, as when the argument is made that a statute is flawed or incomplete. For we are presented with a clear and simple statute to be judged against a pure command of the Constitution. The outcome can be laid at no door but ours.

The hard fact is that sometimes we must make decisions we do not like. We make them because they are right, right in the sense that the law and the Constitution, as we see them, compel the result. And so great is our commitment to the process that, except in the rare case, we do not pause to express distaste for the result, perhaps for fear of undermining a valued principle that dictates the decision. This is one of those rare cases.

Our colleagues in dissent advance powerful arguments why respondent may be convicted for his expression, reminding us that among those who will be dismayed by our holding will be some who have had the singular honor of carrying the flag in battle. And I agree that the flag holds a lonely place of honor in an age when absolutes are distrusted and simple truths are burdened by unneeded apologetics.

With all respect to those views, I do not believe the Constitution gives us the right to rule as the dissenting Members of the Court urge, however painful this judgment is to announce. Though symbols often are what we ourselves make of them, the flag is constant in expressing beliefs Americans share, beliefs in law and peace and that freedom which sustains the human spirit. The case here today forces recognition of the costs to which those beliefs commit us. It is poignant but fundamental that the flag protects those who hold it in contempt.

For all the record shows, this respondent was not a philosopher and perhaps did not even possess the ability to comprehend how repellent his statements must be to the Republic itself. But whether or not he could appreciate the enormity of the offense he gave, the fact remains that his acts were speech, in both the technical and the fundamental meaning of the Constitution. So I agree with the Court that he must go free.

Dissenting Opinion CHIEF JUSTICE REHNQUIST, with whom JUSTICE WHITE and JUSTICE O'CONNOR join, dissenting.

In holding this Texas statute unconstitutional, the Court ignores Justice Holmes' familiar aphorism that "a page of history is worth a volume of logic." *New York Trust Co. v. Eisner*, 256 U.S. 345, 349 (1921). For more than 200 years, the American flag has occupied a unique position as the symbol of our Nation, a uniqueness that justifies a governmental prohibition against flag burning in the way respondent Johnson did here. . . .

Our Constitution wisely places limits on powers of legislative majorities to act, but the declaration of such limits by this Court "is, at all times, a question of much delicacy, which ought seldom, if ever, to be decided in the affirmative, in a doubtful case." *Fletcher v. Peck*, 6 Cranch 87, 128 (1810) (Marshall, C.J.). Uncritical extension of constitutional protection to the burning of the flag risks the frustration of the very purpose for which organized governments are instituted. The Court decides that the American flag is just another symbol, about which not only must opinions pro and con be tolerated, but for which the most minimal public respect may not be enjoined. The government may conscript men into the Armed Forces where they must fight and perhaps die for the flag, but the government may not prohibit the public burning of the banner under which they fight. I would uphold the Texas statute as applied in this case.

Dissenting Opinion   JUSTICE STEVENS, dissenting.

As the Court analyzes this case, it presents the question whether the State of Texas, or indeed the Federal Government, has the power to prohibit the public desecration of the American flag. The question is unique. In my judgment rules that apply to a host of other symbols, such as state flags, armbands, or various privately promoted emblems of political or commercial identity, are not necessarily controlling. Even if flag burning could be considered just another species of symbolic speech under the logical application of the rules that the Court has developed in its interpretation of the First Amendment in other contexts, this case has an intangible dimension that makes those rules inapplicable.

A country's flag is a symbol of more than "nationhood and national unity." *Ante,* at 407, 410, 413, and n. 9, 417, 420. It also signifies the ideas that characterize the society that has chosen that emblem as well as the special history that has animated the growth and power of those ideas. The fleurs-de-lis and the tricolor both symbolized "nationhood and national unity," but they had vastly different meanings. The message conveyed by some flags—the swastika, for example—may survive long after it has outlived its usefulness as a symbol of regimented unity in a particular nation.

So it is with the American flag. It is more than a proud symbol of the courage, the determination, and the gifts of nature that transformed 13 fledgling Colonies into a world power. It is a symbol of freedom, of equal opportunity, of religious tolerance, and of good will for other peoples who share our aspirations. The symbol carries its message to dissidents both at home and abroad who may have no interest at all in our national unity or survival. . . .

The Court is therefore quite wrong in blandly asserting that respondent "was prosecuted for his expression of dissatisfaction with the policies of this country, expression situated at the core of our First Amendment values." *Ante,* at 411. Respondent was prosecuted because of the method he chose to express his dissatisfaction with those policies. Had he chosen to spray-paint—or perhaps convey with a motion picture projector—his message of dissatisfaction on the facade of the Lincoln Memorial, there would be no question about the power of the Government to prohibit his means of expression. The prohibition would be supported by the legitimate interest in preserving the quality of an important national asset. Though the asset at stake in this case is intangible, given its unique value, the same interest supports a prohibition on the desecration of the American flag.

The ideas of liberty and equality have been an irresistible force in motivating leaders like Patrick Henry, Susan B. Anthony, and Abraham Lincoln, schoolteachers like Nathan Hale and Booker T. Washington, the Philippine Scouts who fought at Bataan, and the soldiers who scaled the bluff at Omaha Beach. If those ideas are worth fighting for—and our history demonstrates that they are—it cannot be true that the flag that uniquely symbolizes their power is not itself worthy of protection from unnecessary desecration.

I respectfully dissent.

DISCUSSION QUESTIONS

1. Would it be constitutional to punish someone who burned an American flag in a public place for "having an open fire in a public place"? How would this be different from the decisions discussed in this chapter?

2. Suppose a group of students wore Nazi uniforms to public school, and this was very upsetting to other students. Suppose that several fights broke out. Could the school outlaw the wearing of such uniforms in the future? Would it make a difference if no fights had broken out?

3. The right not to speak at least includes the right not to express beliefs that a person does not hold. What else might it include? Would it also include the right to refuse to provide a government official with factual information that had nothing to do with a person's beliefs?

4. If a woman wears a dress made out of the American flag, what message do you think she is trying to communicate? Does it make any difference where she wears the dress or what she does and says while she is wearing the dress?

5. Wearing a black armband was considered by the Court to be a symbolic speech act. What other kinds of symbolic speech acts can you think of?

6. The Court ruled that the burning of draft cards could be outlawed because of the need to administer the draft system. What if government officials had testified that they never looked at the cards and that everything they needed to administer the system was contained in their computer data banks? Do you think the Court might have made a different decision?

7. Some states have mottoes on their license plates such as "Live Free or Die" or "Oklahoma is OK." What if people living in a state did not agree with such a statement? Could they refuse to place the license plates on their car even though license plates are needed to administer the automobile laws?

CHAPTER
three
❋ ❋ ❋ ❋ ❋ ❋ ❋

Where Can People Speak? The Public Forum Issue

.... DISCUSSION ....

The question of where people can exercise their right of free speech has been a difficult one. Everyone, including the Supreme Court, has simply taken for granted that the right of free speech protects the right of Americans to speak on their own private property. For example, it has been generally accepted that people are free to pass out leaflets at the edge of their own private property, put up a sign reflecting their political opinion in their own front yard, and have a group of friends over to discuss politics in their own living room. But to what extent are people free to engage in these and other types of free speech activities on public property? To deal with this question, the Court has developed the concept of the public forum and has gradually outlined when and how government may limit the right of free speech on public property.

LEAFLET DISTRIBUTION ON PUBLIC PROPERTY

In 1939 members of the Congress of Industrial Organizations (CIO), a labor union federation, passed out leaflets in Jersey City, New Jersey, in support of the rights of unions. They were arrested for violating a city ordinance that made the distribution of leaflets on public property such as parks and sidewalks a crime. Jersey City argued that because the city owned the property in question, it could control the property just like any other property owner. Five members of the Supreme Court did not agree (two justices did not take part in the decision, and two wrote dissenting opinions). Justice Roberts, writing for the Court in *Hague v. C.I.O.* (see p. 35) stated:

> Wherever the title of streets and parks may rest they have immemorially been held in trust for the use of the public and, time out of mind, have been used for purposes of assembly, communicating thoughts between citizens, and discussing public questions. Such use of the streets and public places has, from ancient times, been a part of the privileges, immunities, rights and liberties of citizens.

Ruling in favor of the C.I.O., the Court declared this Jersey City ordinance void as a violation of the First Amendment right of free speech.

With the decision in *Hague v. C.I.O.*, the Court began to develop the principle that the public has a right to use government property that has been historically used as a "public forum" to express ideas. This public forum property includes sidewalks, parks, and the front steps of the state capitol. Whether or not the public has a right to use other public property depends on the type of property and on whether or not the government has allowed that property to be turned into a public forum. The Court made it clear in *Hague v. C.I.O.* and other cases that what the government may not do is allow some groups (presumably those it agrees with) to use public property to express ideas and deny that right to other groups.

LIMITATIONS ON GOVERNMENT CONTROL OF PUBLIC PROPERTY

The difficult issue has been the extent to which government may outlaw all speech activities on a particular piece of public property. As a general rule the Court has said that government may not outlaw speech activity entirely from public property that has become a public forum. However, the government may enforce reasonable rules that control the time, place, and manner of the speech. In the 1938 case of *Lovell v. Griffin*, Alma Lovell, a Jehovah's Witness, was sentenced to 50 days in jail because she neglected to get a permit from the city manager before distributing her religious leaflets in the town of Griffin, Georgia. A unanimous Court overturned her conviction and threw out the ordinance requiring permits because it appeared to give the city manager total control over who could pass out leaflets in the town. The Court said that the city could control the "time, place and manner" of speech, but it could not outlaw speech activities altogether, and it could not regulate speech activities based on the content of the speech involved.

In 1939 the Court overturned ordinances of four New Jersey cities that completely forbade the passing out of leaflets on city sidewalks in an attempt to prevent littering (*Schneider v. State*). While government may limit the time, place, and manner of speech on public forum property, it may do so only for good reasons and the regulations must be reasonable. In this case, the desire to prevent litter was not a good enough reason to ban leaflet distribution, and a complete ban seemed particularly unreasonable. The distribution of political leaflets has a long history in the United States. Thomas Paine raised the political consciousness of a nation with his pamphlets during the American Revolution. Leaflet distribution does not make noise like other forms of speech. It does not threaten anyone or interfere with traffic the way a parade or demonstration might. The simple leaflet, passed out on the sidewalk or left at a front door, is in a way the purest form of political speech, and the Court has defended leafleting whenever it has been threatened, from 1939 to the present. The same can be said for the lone demonstrator with a large sign over the shoulder.

In 1983 the Court was faced with a federal statute that made it a crime to "display devices designed to bring public notice" in the Supreme Court building or on the Supreme Court grounds. Thaddeus Zywicki tried to pass out leaflets on the sidewalk in front of the U.S. Supreme Court building, but he was told by the guards that he had to move across the street. Then Mary Grace tried to walk on the sidewalk in front of the Supreme Court building with a four foot-by-two foot sign containing the text of the First Amendment. She was told she could not demonstrate in this way on the sidewalk in front of the Court. Both Zywicki and Grace sued to stop the guards from forcing them off the sidewalk. Justice White, writing for a seven-justice majority, ruled that the federal government could not prevent the peaceful distribution of leaflets on a public sidewalk, nor could it prevent a single person from carrying a sign on a public sidewalk, even if that sidewalk was in front of the Supreme Court building (*United States v. Grace*). These activities were protected by the First Amendment, and the public sidewalk was the ultimate public forum.

PUBLIC FORUMS: MORE THAN JUST SIDEWALKS

What else constitutes a public forum? The Court has ruled that some areas, such as sidewalks, are public forums by their very nature. It has not always been clear what is or is not a "natural" public forum. For example, in the 1966 case of *Adderley v. Florida*, a five-justice majority upheld the conviction of 32 college students for trespassing on public property. The students had gathered outside the county jail in Tallahassee, Florida, to protest the arrest of other students and refused to leave when ordered to do so by the sheriff. The five-justice majority believed that the area around a jail was not a public forum and the demonstrators had no right to use it for speech activities. The property was instead dedicated to the performance of an important public function—the incarceration of those accused of crime—and speech activities would clearly interfere with that function. Justice Douglas wrote a dissenting opinion joined by two other justices and Chief Justice Warren. Justice Douglas argued that areas outside of jails had been considered to be public forums throughout history, along with the steps in front of courthouses and state capitols.

In 1975 a six-justice majority ruled that a city theater in Chattanooga, Tennessee, was a public forum (*Southeastern Promotions v. Conrad*). Justice Black, writing for the majority, ruled that a city theater is clearly a public forum "designed for and dedicated to expressive activities." The expressive activity in this case was the rock musical "Hair," and the Supreme Court ordered the city to rent its auditorium for a production of the musical. The three dissenting justices thought that the city should have the right to "reserve its auditorium for productions suitable for exhibition to all the citizens of the city, adults and children alike."

In 1981 a five-justice majority upheld a regulation by the Minnesota State Fair that required that the sale or distribution of literature (or anything else) on the fairgrounds be from booths rented on a first-come–first-served basis (*Heffron v. Intern. Soc. for Krishna Consciousness*). The International Society for Krishna Consciousness wanted the right to sell and give away literature anywhere on the fairgrounds. The majority of justices rejected the idea that the state fairgrounds were a public forum. Because the fair had a daily attendance of over 100,000 people, the need to control the flow of people was obvious. The four dissenting justices agreed that the Minnesota State Fair could prevent the sale of items except in booths rented for that purpose, but they disagreed with the ban on the free distribution of literature on the fairgrounds. The dissenting justices believed that this distribution of literature should be allowed and that the fairgrounds should be considered to be a public forum for that purpose.

DISCRIMINATION AND PUBLIC FORUMS

The Court has found some areas to be public forums because they have traditionally been used by Americans for speech activities. Other areas have become public forums in some cities and states because governments in these cities and states have allowed speech activities to take place there. The one thing government may not do is allow one group to use an area for speech activities and deny access to other groups.

In the 1981 case of *Widmar v. Vincent*, the Court ruled that the University of Missouri at Kansas City did not have to make its facilities available to student groups for meetings, but, once the university did so, the campus became a public forum for students and the university could not discriminate against some student groups in favor of others. In this case, a group of students wished to use the university facilities for religious worship and religious teaching. Justice Powell, writing for the majority, ruled that once the state university had created a forum open to students, it could not exclude some groups because of the content of their speech. Justice White, the only dissenter, believed that state universities should be allowed to prevent religious worship on the campus to avoid possibly violating the Establishment Clause of the First Amendment, which commands that government may not promote religion.

In recent free speech decisions, the Court has made a distinction between government acting as the owner of traditionally accessible public property and government acting as the provider of public services. A majority of the Court has agreed that governments may prevent free speech activities on property that is used primarily to provide a public service. For example, a 1990 case, *United States v. Kokindo*, involved a post office regulation that prohibited the solicitation of money on post office property. A political group wanted to set up a table to ask for contributions near the sidewalk between a post office and the post office parking lot. Five justices agreed that the post office could prevent this. Justice O'Connor, in writing the majority opinion, pointed out that post office property has never been a public forum and is dedicated to getting the mail distributed efficiently, not to free speech activities. The four dissenting justices, in a dissenting opinion written by Justice Brennan, argued that a sidewalk on post office property should be considered a public forum just like any other sidewalk.

ARE AIRPORTS PUBLIC FORUMS?

A 1992 case, *Intern. Soc. for Krishna Consciousness v. Lee* (see p. 37), split the Court into three groups. The International Society for Krishna Consciousness wanted to solicit contributions and pass out literature at the major New York City airports. Four justices believed that the airports were not public forums and therefore could prevent both the solicitation of funds and the distribution of literature. Four other justices thought that the airports were public forums. Justice O'Connor was the swing vote. Although she accepted the idea that airports are not public forums, she pointed out that only part of the property in each airport terminal is dedicated to performing the essential functions of an airport. The rest of each airport is made up of restaurants and shops. To the extent that these airports are similar to government-owned shopping areas, Justice O'Connor argued, it is unreasonable to prevent all speech activities inside them. At the same time, it is not unreasonable to consider the special nature of these airport facilities. Busy travelers, rushing to catch a plane, would find it difficult to deal with a request for a financial contribution. Because of this, Justice O'Connor upheld the airport regulations banning all financial solicitation inside the airports. At the same time, she believed that the simple distribution of literature would not pose the same problem. Busy travelers could simply take the offered pamphlet and read it later. Also, she was willing to allow the airports to control the distribution of literature to keep high-traffic areas free from congestion.

CONCLUSION

Over the last 50 years the Court has developed a workable definition of what is and what is not a public forum. Areas traditionally used for speech activities, such as sidewalks and parks, are public forums and must be made available to the public for speech activities. At the same time, government may regulate that speech activity to serve important governmental goals such as limiting the level of noise in the city or preventing people from being disturbed at night. Government may not use regulations, however, to prevent those with opinions the government does not agree with from speaking out.

If the government property in question is not a public forum, the government has significant freedom to control and limit speech activities, as long as the limitations are reasonable and are not discriminatory. Government may prevent speech activities completely from areas such as the state fairgrounds, post office grounds, and the part of airports dedicated to air travel.

..............................CASE DECISIONS............................

With its 1939 decision in *Hague v. C.I.O.*, the Supreme Court decided that the American public has a right to use sidewalks and streets for speech activities. Justices Frankfurter and Douglas did not take part in the decision. Justice Roberts wrote the opinion for the Court, which is included here. Concurring opinions by Justice Stone and Chief Justice Hughes, and dissenting opinions by Justices McReynolds and Butler, are not included here.

In 1992, in *Intern. Soc. for Krishna Consciousness v. Lee*, the Court divided into three groups over whether or not the New York City airports could prevent the solicitation of funds and the distribution of literature. Four justices believed the airports were public forums and four did not. These justices wrote four opinions, which are not included here. Justice O'Connor wrote an opinion that found the airports not to be public forums but required them to allow the distribution of literature by the International Society for Krishna Consciousness. Her opinion is included here. Following are excerpts from the case decisions.

❀ ❀ ❀ ❀ ❀ ❀ ❀ ❀ ❀

HAGUE v. C.I.O.
307 U.S. 496 (1939)

MR. JUSTICE ROBERTS delivered an opinion in which MR. JUSTICE BLACK concurred:

We granted certiorari as the case presents important questions in respect of the asserted privilege and immunity of citizens of the United States to advocate action pursuant to a federal statute, by distribution of printed matter and oral discussion in peaceable assembly; and the jurisdiction of federal courts of suits to restrain the abridgment of such privilege and immunity. . . .

After trial upon the merits the District Court entered findings of fact and conclusions of law and a decree in favor of respondents. In brief, the court found that the purposes of respondents, other than the American Civil Liberties Union, were the organization of unorganized workers into labor unions, causing such unions to exercise the normal and legal functions of labor organizations, such as collective bargaining with respect to the betterment of wages, hours of work and other terms and conditions of employment, and that these purposes were lawful; that the petitioners, acting in their official capacities, have adopted and enforced the deliberate policy of excluding and removing from Jersey City the agents of the respondents; have interfered with their right of passage upon the streets and access to the parks of the city; that these ends have been accomplished by force and violence despite the fact that the persons affected were acting in an orderly and peaceful manner; that exclusion, removal, personal restraint and interference, by force and violence, are accomplished without authority of law and without promptly bringing the persons taken into custody before a judicial officer for hearing.

The court further found that the petitioners, as officials, acting in reliance on the ordinance dealing with the subject, have adopted and enforced a deliberate policy of preventing the respondents, and their associates, from distributing circulars, leaflets, or handbills in Jersey City; that this has been done by policemen acting forcibly and violently; that the petitioners propose to continue to enforce the policy of such prevention; that the circulars and handbills, distribution of which has been prevented, were not offensive to public morals, and did not advocate unlawful conduct, but were germane to the purposes alleged in the bill, and that their distribution was being carried out in a way consistent with public order and without molestation of individuals or misuse or littering of the streets. Similar findings were made with respect to the prevention of the distribution of placards. . . .

What has been said demonstrates that, in the light of the facts found, privileges and immunities of the individual respondents as citizens of the United States, were infringed by the petitioners, by virtue of their official positions, under color of ordinances of Jersey City, unless, as petitioners contend, the city's ownership of streets and parks is as absolute as one's ownership of his home, with consequent power altogether to exclude citizens from the use thereof, or unless, though the city holds the streets in trust for public use, the absolute denial of their use to the respondents is a valid exercise of the police power. . . .

Wherever the title of streets and parks may rest, they have immemorially been held in trust for the use of the public and, time out of mind, have been used for purposes of assembly, communicating thoughts between citizens, and discussing public questions. Such use of the streets and public places has, from ancient times, been a part of the privileges, immunities, rights, and liberties of citizens. The privilege of a citizen of the United States to use the streets and parks for communication of views on national questions may be regulated in the interest of all; it is not absolute, but relative, and must be exercised in subordination to the general comfort and convenience, and in consonance with peace and good order; but it must not, in the guise of regulation, be abridged or denied.

We think the court below was right in holding the ordinance . . . void upon its face. It does not make comfort or convenience in the use of streets or parks the standard of official action. It enables the Director of Safety to refuse a permit on his mere opinion that such refusal will prevent "riots, disturbances or disorderly asssemblage." It can thus, as the record discloses, be made the instrument of arbitrary suppression of free expression of views on national affairs, for the prohibition of all speaking will undoubtedly "prevent" such eventualities. But uncontrolled official suppression of the privilege cannot be made a substitute for the duty to maintain order in connection with the exercise of the right.

INTERN. SOC. FOR KRISHNA CONSCIOUSNESS v. LEE
112 S. Ct. 2701 (1992)

JUSTICE O'CONNOR, concurring in 91–155 and concurring in the judgment in 91–339.

In the decision below, the Court of Appeals upheld a ban on solicitation of funds within the airport terminals operated by the Port Authority of New York and New Jersey, but struck down a ban on the repetitive distribution of printed or written material within the terminals. 925 F.2d 576 (CA2 1991). I would affirm both parts of that judgment.

I concur in the Court's opinion in No. 91–155, and agree that publicly owned airports are not public fora. Unlike public streets and parks, both of which our First Amendment jurisprudence has identified as "traditional public fora," airports do not count among their purposes the "free exchange of ideas," Cornelius v. NAACP Legal Defense & Educational Fund, Inc., 473 U.S. 788, 800, 105 S. Ct. 3439, 3448, 87 L.Ed.2d 567 (1985); they have not "by long tradition or by government fiat . . . been devoted to assembly and debate;" Perry Education Assn. v. Perry Local Educators' Assn., 460 U.S. 37,

45, 103 S. Ct. 948, 954, 74 L.Ed.2d 794 (1983); nor have they "time out of mind, . . . been used for purposes of . . . communicating thoughts between citizens, and discussing public questions," *Hague v. CIO*, 307 U.S. 496, 515, 59 S. Ct. 954, 964, 83 L.Ed. 1423 (1939). Although most airports do not ordinarily restrict public access, "[p]ublicly owned or operated property does not become a 'public forum' simply because members of the public are permitted to come and go at will." *United States v. Grace*, 461 U.S. 171, 177, 103 S. Ct. 1702, 1707, 75 L.Ed.2d 736 (1983); see also *Greer v. Spock*, 424 U.S. 828, 836, 96 S. Ct. 1211, 1216, 47 L.Ed.2d 505 (1976). "[W]hen government property is not dedicated to open communication the government may—without further justification—restrict use to those who participate in the forum's official business." *Perry, supra*, 460 U.S. at 53, 103 S. Ct., at 959. There is little doubt that airports are among those publicly owned facilities that could be closed to all except those who have legitimate business there. See *Grace, supra*, 461 U.S. at 178, 103 S. Ct., at 1707. Public access to airports is thus not "inherent in the open nature of the locations," as it is for most streets and parks, but is rather a "matter of grace by government officials." *United States v. Kokinda*, 497 U.S. 720, 743, 110 S. Ct. 3115, 3128, 111 L.Ed.2d 571 (1990) (Brennan, J., dissenting). I also agree with the Court that the Port Authority has not expressly opened its airports to the types of expression at issue here, see 112 S. Ct., at 2706, and therefore has not created a "limited" or "designated" public forum relevant to this case.

For these reasons, the Port Authority's restrictions on solicitation and leafletting within the airport terminals do not qualify for the strict scrutiny that applies to restriction of speech in public fora. That airports are not public fora, however, does not mean that the government can restrict speech in whatever way it likes. "The Government, even when acting in its proprietary capacity, does not enjoy absolute freedom from First Amendment constraints." *Kokinda, supra*, at 725, 110 S. Ct., at 3119 (plurality opinion). For example, in *Board of Airport Commrs. of Los Angeles v. Jews for Jesus, Inc.*, 482 U.S. 569, 107 S. Ct. 2568, 96 L.Ed.2d 500 (1987), we unanimously struck down a regulation that prohibited "all First Amendment activities" in the Los Angeles International Airport (LAX) without even reaching the question whether airports were public fora. *Id.*, at 574–575, 107 S. Ct., at 2572. We found it "obvious that such a ban cannot be justified even if LAX were a nonpublic forum because no conceivable governmental interest would justify such an absolute prohibition of speech." *Id.*, at 575, 107 S. Ct., at 2572. Moreover, we have consistently stated that restrictions on speech in nonpublic fora are valid only if they are "reasonable" and "not an effort to suppress expression merely because public officials oppose the speaker's view." *Perry*, 460 U.S., at 46, 103 S. Ct., at 955; see also *Kokinda, supra*, 497 U.S. at 731, 110 S. Ct., at 312; *Cornelius, supra*, 473 U.S. at 800, 105 S. Ct., at 3448;

Lehman v. City of Shaker Heights, 418 U.S. 298, 303, 94 S. Ct. 2714, 2717, 41 L.Ed.2d 770 (1974). The determination that airports are not public fora thus only begins our inquiry.

"The reasonableness of the Government's restriction [on speech in a nonpublic forum] must be assessed in light of the purpose of the forum and all the surrounding circumstances." *Cornelius, supra*, 473 U.S. at 809, 105 S. Ct., at 3453. " '[C]onsideration of a forum's special attributes is relevant to the constitutionality of a regulation since the significance of the governmental interest must be assessed in light of the characteristic nature and function of the particular forum involved.' " *Kokinda, supra*, 497 U.S. at 732, 110 S. Ct., at 3122, quoting *Heffron v. International Soc. for Krishna Consciousness, Inc.*, 452 U.S. 640, 650–651, 101 S. Ct. 2559, 69 L.Ed.2d 298 (1981). In this case, the "special attributes" and "surrounding circumstances" of the airports operated by the Port Authority are determinative. Not only has the Port Authority chosen not to limit access to the airports under its control, it has created a huge complex open to travelers and nontravelers alike. The airports house restaurants, cafeterias, snack bars, coffee shops, cocktail lounges, post offices, banks, telegraph offices, clothing shops, drug stores, food stores, nurseries, barber shops, currency exchanges, art exhibits, commercial advertising displays, bookstores, newsstands, dental offices and private clubs. See 1 App. 183–185 (Newark); *id.*, at 185–186 (JFK); *id.*, at 190–192 (LaGuardia). The International Arrivals Building at JFK Airport even has two branches of Bloomingdale's. *Id.*, at 185–186.

We have said that a restriction on speech in a nonpublic forum is "reasonable" when it is "consistent with the [government's] legitimate interest in 'preserv[ing] the property . . . for the use to which it is lawfully dedicated.' " *Perry, supra*, 460 U.S. at 50–51, 103 S. Ct., at 958, quoting *United States Postal Service v. Council of Greenburgh Civic Assns.*, 453 U.S. 114, 129–130, 101 S. Ct. 2676, 2685, 69 L.Ed.2d 517 (1981) (internal quotation marks omitted). Ordinarily, this inquiry is relatively straightforward, because we have almost always been confronted with cases where the fora at issue were discrete, single-purpose facilities. See, *e.g.*, *Kokinda, supra* (dedicated sidewalk between parking lot and post office); *Cornelius v. NAACP Legal Defense & Educational Fund, Inc.*, 473 U.S. 788, 105 S. Ct. 3439, 87 L.Ed.2d 567 (1985) (literature for charity drive); *City Council of Los Angeles v. Taxpayers for Vincent*, 466 U.S. 789, 104 S. Ct. 2118, 80 L.Ed.2d 772 (1984) (utility poles); *Perry, supra* (interschool mail system); *United States Postal Service v. Council of Greenburgh Civic Assns., supra*, (household mail boxes); *Adderley v. Florida*, 385 U.S. 39, 87 S. Ct. 242, 17 L.Ed.2d 149 (1966) (curtilage of jailhouse). The Port Authority urges that this case is no different and contends that it, too, has dedicated its airports to a single purpose—facilitating air travel—and that the speech it seeks to prohibit is not consistent with that purpose. But the wide range of activities promoted by the Port Authority is no more directly related to facilitating air travel than are the types of activities in which ISKCON wishes to engage. See *Jews for Jesus, supra,* 482 U.S. at 576, 107 S. Ct., at 2573 ("The line between airport-related speech and nonairport-related speech is, at best, murky"). In my view, the Port Authority is operating a shopping mall as well as an airport. The reasonableness inquiry, therefore, is not whether the restrictions on speech are "consistent with . . . preserving the property" for air travel, *Perry, supra,* 460 U.S. at 50–51, 103 S. Ct., at 958 (internal quotation marks and citation omitted), but whether they are reasonably related to maintaining the multipurpose environment that the Port Authority has deliberately created.

Applying that standard, I agree with the Court in No. 91–155 that the ban on solicitation is reasonable. Face-to-face solicitation is incompatible with the airport's functioning in a way that the other, permitted activities are not. We have previously observed that "[s]olicitation impedes the normal flow of traffic [because it] requires action by those who would respond: The individual solicited must decide whether or not to contribute (which itself might involve reading the solicitor's literature or hearing his pitch), and then, having decided to do so, reach for a wallet, search it for money, write a check, or produce a credit card. . . . As residents of metropolitan areas know from daily experience, confrontation by a person asking for money disrupts passage and is more intrusive and intimidating than an encounter with a person giving out information." *Kokinda,* 497 U.S., at 733–734, 110 S. Ct., at 3123 (plurality opinion) (citations omitted); *id.,* at 739, 110 S. Ct., at 3126 (Kennedy, J., concurring in judgment) (accepting Postal Service's judgment that, given its past experience, "in-person solicitation deserves different treatment from alternative forms of solicitation and expression"); *Heffron, supra,* 452 U.S. at 657, 101 S. Ct., at 2568 (Brennan, J., concurring in part and dissenting in part) (upholding partial restriction on solicitation at fair grounds because of state interest "in protecting its fairgoers from fraudulent, deceptive, and misleading solicitation practices"); *id.,* at 665, 101 S. Ct., at 2573 (Blackmun, J., concurring in part and dissenting in part) (upholding partial restriction on solicitation because of the "crowd control problems" it creates). The record in this case confirms that the problems of congestion and fraud that we have identified with solicitation in other contexts have also proved true in the airports' experience. See App. 67–111 (affidavits). Because airports' users are frequently facing time constraints, and are traveling with luggage or children, the ban on solicitation is a reasonable means of avoiding disruption of an airport's operation.

In my view, however, the regulation banning leafletting—or, in the Port Authority's words, the "continuous or repetitive . . . distribution of . . . printed or written material"—cannot be upheld as reasonable on this record. I therefore concur in the judgment in No. 91–339 striking down that prohibition. While the difficulties posed by solicitation in a nonpublic forum are sufficiently obvious that its regulation may "rin[g] of common-sense,"*Kokinda, supra,* 497 U.S., at 734, 110 S. Ct., at 3124 (internal quotation marks and citation omitted), the same is not necessarily true of leafletting. To the contrary, we have expressly noted that leafletting does not entail the same kinds of problems presented by face-to-face solicitation. Specifically, "[o]ne need not ponder the contents of a leaflet or pamphlet in order mechanically to take it out of someone's hand. . . . 'The distribution of literature does not require that the recipient stop in order to receive the message the speaker wishes to convey; instead the recipient is free to read the message at a later time.' "*Ibid.* (plurality opinion), quoting*Heffron,* 452 U.S., at 665, 101 S. Ct., at 2573 (Blackmun, J., concurring in part and dissenting in part). With the possible exception of avoiding litter, see *Schneider v. State,* 308 U.S. 147, 162, 60 S. Ct. 146, 151, 84 L.Ed. 155 (1939), it is difficult to point to any problems intrinsic to the act of leafletting that would make it naturally incompatible with a large, multi-purpose forum such as those at issue here. . . .

Of course, it is still open for the Port Authority to promulgate regulations of the time, place, and manner of leafletting which are "content-neutral, narrowly tailored to serve a significant government interest, and leave open ample alternative channels of communication."*Perry, supra,* at 45, 103 S. Ct., at 955; *United States Postal Service,* 453 U.S., at 132, 101 S. Ct., at 2686. For example, during the many years that this litigation has been in progress, the Port Authority has not banned *sankirtan* completely from JFK International Airport, but has restricted it to a relatively uncongested part of the airport terminals, the same part that houses the airport chapel. Tr. of Oral Arg. 5–6, 46–47. In my view, that regulation meets the standards we have applied to time, place, and manner restrictions of protected expression. See *Clark v. Community for Creative Non-Violence,* 468 U.S. 288, 293, 104 S. Ct. 3065, 3069, 82 L.Ed.2d 221 (1984).

I would affirm the judgment of the Court of Appeals in both No. 91–155 and No. 91–339.

......................DISCUSSION QUESTIONS......................

1. The sidewalk in front of a school is a public forum. What regulations on speech activities do you think would be legal, given the need to prevent the disruption of school activities?
2. A city has sold advertising space on the walls of the city-owned ice-skating rink. Do you think the rink has now become a public forum?

3. A city allows anyone to rent the city-owned theater, but only for theatrical performances. Is the theater a public forum? May the city refuse to rent the theater to a political group to hold a meeting? Should it make any difference that the city has another auditorium that it rents for meetings?

4. Difficult public forum cases for the Supreme Court to decide have involved a state fairgrounds, post office grounds, and an airport. If the Court had decided that these areas were public forums, where could the Court have reasonably drawn the line between public forums and nonpublic forums?

5. If the Court had decided to distinguish between public and nonpublic forum property by drawing a line between the inside and outside of buildings, how would the decisions we have discussed been decided? What problems do you see with drawing the line in this way?

6. How would the life of the average American city be different if the Supreme Court had decided that the right of free speech only encompassed the right to speak on private property, with the permission of the property owner? Cities would be allowed to prevent speech activities in any public area, but they would not be allowed to discriminate between groups. Do you think most cities would still have parades and street-corner leafleteers?

7. What groups in society would be at the biggest disadvantage if the Supreme Court had not developed the concept of the public forum?

CHAPTER
four

❊ ❊ ❊ ❊ ❊ ❊ ❊ ❊

Political Speech: The Clear and Present Danger Test

······································· **DISCUSSION** ·······································

The U.S. Supreme Court did not really begin to discuss what kinds of speech the right of free speech does and does not protect until 1919. Before that time the Court examined several cases and found that the speech involved was clearly not the kind of speech worthy of protection by the First Amendment. These cases involved questions such as whether or not motion pictures fall under the First Amendment's protection. It seems clear that the Court had a very limited view of what kinds of speech the amendment protected. Specifically, most members of the Court seemed to believe that the amendment only protected discussions of politics and religion, and then only those discussions that posed no threat to the safety or security of the society. The Supreme Court developed the concept of clear and present danger to determine when government may limit free speech, and over the years the Court's view of clear and present danger has changed.

It is important to remember in reading these early decisions that they were made by men for whom social revolution was not just an abstract concept. Many of these men had personal memories of either the Civil War or its immediate aftermath. The author of the first three decisions that seriously discussed the right of free speech was Justice Oliver Wendell Holmes. As a young man, Holmes had served with the Massachusetts 20th Volunteers during the Civil War and had been wounded three times in some of the bloodiest battles of the war. He had lived through an America torn apart by Reconstruction and had seen the horror of the war and its consequences.

WARTIME AND CLEAR AND PRESENT DANGER

In 1919 the Court handed down four decisions concerned with the right of free speech. These decisions all involved interpretation of the Espionage Act of 1917. The Espionage Act not only outlawed revealing national security secrets to the enemy, but also made it illegal to do things that might hinder the war effort such as interfering with the recruitment of soldiers. In each case the Court upheld the convictions of people who were charged primarily with interfering with the recruitment of soldiers during wartime. The first three decisions were unanimous, with Justice Holmes writing the opinions for the Court. The fourth opinion found Justices Holmes and Brandeis dissenting.

The first decision, *Schenck v. United States* (see p. 54), may be the most famous opinion ever written by Justice Holmes. The defendant, Charles Schenck, was the general secretary of the American Socialist Party. He mailed out 15,000 leaflets during World War I arguing that the draft was a violation of the Thirteenth Amendment, which forbids involuntary servitude. One side of the leaflet presented Schenck's argument, that the draft violated the Thirteenth Amendment and that people should not "submit to intimidation." It called on everyone to petition Congress to repeal the draft laws. The other side of the leaflet said that "if you do not assert and support your rights, you are helping to deny or disparage rights which it is the solemn duty of all citizens and residents of the United States to retain." The leaflet argued that the government did not have the power to send Americans to "foreign shores" to "shoot up people of other lands" and ended by saying, "You must do your share to maintain, support, and uphold the rights of the people of this country." Schenck was convicted of violating a section of the Espionage Act that made it a crime to obstruct the recruitment of soldiers.

In the opinion he wrote for a unanimous Court, Justice Holmes considered the leaflet to be within the category of speech that would usually be subject to the protection of the First Amendment, presumably because it would be considered political speech. Justice Holmes also asserted that "in ordinary times" the defendant would be within his rights to publish such a leaflet. In other words, the right to speak freely depended on the circumstances. Justice Holmes penned the famous line that the right of free speech would certainly not protect "a man in falsely shouting fire in a theatre and causing a panic." He went on to say:

> The question in every case is whether the words used are used in such circumstances and are of such a nature as to create a clear and present danger that they will bring about the substantive evils that Congress has a right to prevent. It is a question of proximity and degree.

The key in the *Schenck* case was the fact that the United States was engaged in fighting World War I. In the midst of a war, such a leaflet could be seen as a "clear and present danger" to the war effort. In a very real sense the Court was weighing the right of free speech against the government's reason for restricting speech. In this case the government's reason was a very good one—the desire to protect the entire society in time of war. The Court felt that this leaflet posed a "clear and present danger" to that war effort and therefore could be banned by a society attempting to protect itself.

The second unanimous decision, *Frohwerk v. United States*, involved the publication of the newspaper the "Missouri Staats Zeitung." The newspaper's publisher, Jacob Frohwerk, had been sentenced to 10 years in prison for writing an article that suggested that World War I was caused by the capitalist trusts that controlled the world economy. He argued that it did not make sense to send Americans to die in France in order to make a few very rich people richer. He also argued that soldiers had a right of self-preservation and that America had been drawn into the war by a very successful propaganda campaign by Great Britain. The Court, with Justice Holmes writing the opinion, had no trouble upholding the 10-year prison sentence Frohwerk had been given for violating the Espionage Act. Justice Holmes pointed out that "the circulation of the paper was in quarters where a little breath would be enough to kindle a flame." Again, he and the other justices believed that society had every right to extinguish the match before it could grow into a raging fire.

The third unanimous decision, *Debs v. United States*, involved a speech delivered by Eugene V. Debs at the national convention of the American Socialist Party on June 16, 1918, in Canton, Ohio. Debs was convicted of violating the Espionage Act by interfering with the recruitment of soldiers and attempting to cause a mutiny in the armed forces. What had he said? First, he expressed his opposition to German militarism. Then he praised Kate O'Hara, who had been convicted of obstructing the enlistment of soldiers. Debs stated that the "master class has always declared the war and the subject class has always fought the battles." He also said that Americans were fit to be something better than "cannon fodder." The jury was charged to convict Debs only if they believed the "natural and intended effect" of his statements "would be to obstruct recruiting." The jury found Debs guilty of obstructing the recruitment of soldiers with these statements, and the Supreme Court upheld that verdict.

THE FREE TRADE OF IDEAS

The fourth case, *Abrams v. United States*, involved the conviction under the Espionage Act of a man who printed up and distributed leaflets in New York

City objecting to the presence of American troops in Russia and calling for a general strike. The leaflet argued that American bullets should be used on Germans, not Russians. While the majority of justices upheld the conviction, Justice Holmes wrote a dissenting opinion joined by Justice Brandeis. Holmes believed that the government had not proved that the defendant, Jacob Abrams, had intended to hurt the war effort. "Congress cannot forbid all effort to change the mind of the country," Holmes argued. He also did not think that the "surreptitious publishing of a silly leaflet by an unknown man" presented any real danger to the war effort. In other words, in this case, Holmes did not think the danger was "clear and present" enough to prosecute Abrams for passing out this leaflet. Also, the defendant had been sentenced to 20 years in prison, and Holmes believed that this sentence was extreme considering the only goal of the leaflet seemed to be to stop American intervention in Russia.

For three decades the Supreme Court had fought to uphold the ideals of capitalism, and Holmes tried to turn these ideals to the case at hand. He argued that there should be "free trade in ideas" and that every idea should be allowed to face the "competition of the market." A majority of the justices were not swayed by his argument. They thought that Abrams's comments were just as likely to impede the war effort as those of Schenck, Frohwerk, and Debs.

Holmes's dissenting opinion in the Abrams case was just as important to the development of the concept of free speech as his opinions for the Court in Schenck, Frohwerk, and Debs. In the decades to come, more liberal justices would join the ranks of the Supreme Court and look back to Holmes for guidance. Later Courts would begin to really explore the meaning of "clear and present danger" and gradually require that the danger be clearer and more present. Later justices would echo Holmes's defense of the "marketplace of ideas" as the prime reason for protecting the right of free speech in the first place.

MEMBERSHIP IN POLITICAL PARTIES THAT ADVOCATE REVOLUTION

In the 1925 case of Gitlow v. New York, Justices Holmes and Brandeis were again the only dissenters. Benjamin Gitlow had been convicted in New York of the crime of "criminal anarchy" because he belonged to the "left wing" of the American Socialist Party, which had in its manifesto that "humanity can be saved only by Communist Revolution." Gitlow had not been caught mixing explosives or planning revolution; he simply belonged to this particular political group. A majority of the justices thought that Gitlow's membership in the American Socialist Party was enough to justify sending him to prison. Justices Holmes and Brandeis did not believe that Gitlow posed a real threat to society; they did not see any "clear and present danger" of revolution in this case. The question was how close to actually plotting violent revolution someone had to come before the police could act. A majority of the justices believed that the police should not have to wait until preparations for revolution were at hand. In their opinion, joining a group that had revolution in its creed was enough to warrant police action.

Justice Holmes revealed in his dissenting opinion a belief that it should ultimately be left up to the people to decide where society should go, and that they should base their decision on their evaluation of all views. He said:

> The only difference between the expression of an opinion and an incitement in the narrower sense is the speaker's enthusiasm for the result. Eloquence may set fire to reason. But whatever may be thought of the redundant discourse before us it had no chance of starting a present conflagration. If in the long run the beliefs expressed in proletarian dictatorship are destined to be accepted by the dominant forces of the community, the only meaning of free speech is that they should be given their chance and have their way.

The majority of justices were not willing to let things get to the point where the people might actually experiment with "proletarian dictatorship."

CRIMINAL SYNDICALISM

In 1927 the Court considered two cases involving people convicted of violating criminal syndicalism laws. In *Fiske v. Kansas,* the conviction was based on a Kansas statute that defined criminal syndicalism as "the doctrine which advocates crime, physical violence, arson, destruction of property, sabotage, or other unlawful acts or methods, as a means of accomplishing or effecting industrial or political ends." Anyone who advocated criminal syndicalism was guilty of a felony. The defendants in *Fiske v. Kansas,* who belonged to the Industrial Workers of the World, had passed out leaflets arguing that workers should organize to abolish the wage system. The Court could not find anything in the leaflets that called for the violent overthrow of government, no "clear and present" danger to society, so the convictions had to be overturned. There had been no call to violence, no suggestion that armed revolution should follow. Also, in 1927 America was not engaged in war, so past decisions justified by the need to protect the war effort did not apply.

In the second case, *Whitney v. California,* the defendant had joined the Oakland, California, branch of the left wing of the Socialist Party and had helped to form the Communist Labor Party of America. These groups did advocate the use of criminal means to overthrow the government, so the Court upheld the defendant's conviction under California's criminal syndicalism laws. Justice Brandeis wrote a concurring opinion, joined by Justice

Holmes. In his opinion Justice Brandeis summarized what he believed the right of free speech encompassed. He said:

> Those who won our independence believed that the final end of the State was to make men free to develop their faculties; . . .They valued liberty both as an end and as a means. They believed liberty to be the secret of happiness and courage to be the secret of liberty. They believed that freedom to think as you will and speak as you think are means indispensable to the discovery and spread of political truth; that without free speech and assembly discussion would be futile; that with them, discussion affords ordinarily adequate protection against the dissemination of noxious doctrines; that the greatest menace to freedom is an inert people; that public discussion is a political duty; and that this should be a fundamental principle of the American government.

Brandeis's summary of why the Bill of Rights protects the right of free speech summarizes not only the thoughts of the founders of the United States but also the ideas of John Stuart Mill. Mill's ideas that free speech helps people to discover truth, secure happiness, and develop as members of society had finally become a part of the Court's thinking. The call for violent revolution did not contribute to any of these goals, therefore it was not entitled to the protection of the First Amendment, even in the opinion of Justice Brandeis.

CHANGING VIEWS OF CLEAR AND PRESENT DANGER

From 1919 to 1927 the Court had begun to develop a basic theory of the right of free speech. The Court decided that the Fourteenth Amendment made the First Amendment applicable to state and local governments as well as the federal government, and that people in general have a right to speak about political issues. Governments, however, have a right to prevent the violent overthrow of democracy and to prevent other "substantive evils." The real issue in these early cases was how close to actually doing something evil the speakers had to come before the government could send them to prison. The answer during those early years was not very close. Belonging to a political group that called for ultimate revolution in its literature was enough. Making a speech at a political convention praising someone who had been convicted of obstructing the recruitment of soldiers was enough. Passing out leaflets during wartime telling people that the draft was wrong or that American foreign policy was wrong was enough.

It is important to realize that the United States was still recovering from the Civil War during this time, and no one needed reminding how much damage a revolution can cause to society. The further the United States got from the reality of the Civil War, the more the members of the Supreme Court could entertain the idea that perhaps the possibility of revolution should have to be much "clearer" and much more "present" before speech could be suppressed.

In the late 1930s and early 1940s the Court continued to balance the right of free speech against the various evils the government was trying to prevent. Over the years, however, the value of free speech was clearly going up and the realistic danger of evil was clearly going down, at least in the minds of the justices. In a series of cases involving members of various political groups, a majority of the Court moved away from the idea that mere membership in such groups could justify arrest and imprisonment. Instead, the Court looked more closely at what the particular person was saying or doing.

In the 1937 case of *Herndon v. Lowry*, the Court decided with a vote of five to four to overturn the conviction of an 18-year-old black Communist Party organizer in Atlanta. The defendant had passed out leaflets that called for equal rights for blacks, but he had never actually called for the violent overthrow of the U.S. government. He had also argued that the government should confiscate land and give it to black farmers and that blacks should have the right to vote. The majority of justices ruled that there must be a "reasonable apprehension of danger" and that "the limitation upon individual liberty must have appropriate relation to the safety of the state." The fact that this man belonged to a group that accepted the dictates of the Communist Manifesto, which called for the ultimate resort to violent revolution at some indefinite time in the future, was not clear and present enough of a danger to the security of the state. While similar convictions had been upheld a few years before, in *Gitlow*, for example, by the late 1930s the Court thought that the United States was secure enough from revolution to allow people to belong to these kinds of political groups.

This decision marked a significant change for the Court. The four dissenting justices argued that what the Georgia statute outlawed was an attempt to create "forcible resistance" to lawful authority. They believed that one only had to read the literature of the Communist Party to find ample evidence of its desire to create forcible resistance to lawful authority. While this evidence had been enough to send people to prison in 1927, it was not enough by 1937. New justices were being added to the Court who had sympathy with the goals of organized labor and civil rights groups. These justices could not allow this conviction to stand without putting many other people at risk of arrest and conviction who were not Communists. The Court was beginning to face the fact that in order to protect the speech of those we agree with, we have to protect the speech of those we disagree with.

Also in 1937, a unanimous Court overturned a conviction under Oregon's criminal syndicalism law in *De Jonge v. Oregon*. The defendant was a member of the Communist Party who spoke at a public meeting in Portland, Oregon, held to protest the shooting of striking longshoremen. He did not advocate violence or revolution at the meeting. The Court ruled that "peaceable assembly" and "lawful discussion" cannot be made crimes as long as the First Amendment protects the right to speak and assemble. Again, the mere fact that the defendant belonged to the Communist Party was not enough to justify his conviction.

In 1944 and 1945 the Court was faced with more convictions under the Espionage Act of 1917, only by then America was fighting World War II. One case, *Hartzel v. United States*, involved a man who wrote articles attacking the English and the Jews and calling for America to side with Germany in the war. The other case, *Keegan v. United States*, involved 25 people who belonged to the German-American Bund, an organization that endorsed the Nazi movement in Germany. In both cases five members of the Court thought that the speech of these defendants did not present a "clear and present" danger; the majority of justices did not think that people would refuse to serve in the military after hearing what the defendants had to say. In both cases four justices dissented, arguing that in time of war government had to be given greater leeway to prevent insurrection and maintain the recruitment effort of the armed forces.

FIGHTING WORDS

In the 1942 case of *Chaplinsky v. New Hampshire*, a Jehovah's Witness was convicted of violating a New Hampshire law that made it illegal to "address any offensive, derisive or annoying word to any other person who is lawfully in any street or other public place," or "call him by any offensive or derisive name." The judges of New Hampshire had interpreted this statute to forbid the use of words that when addressed to a particular person would probably cause that person to start a fight. Walter Chaplinsky, a Jehovah's Witness distributing leaflets on the streets of Rochester, New Hampshire, had attracted a crowd by calling all religion a "racket." When the police believed that violence was about to erupt, they tried to escort Chaplinsky away. When a city marshal arrived, Chaplinsky asked him to arrest the people he thought were really responsible for the disturbance. When the marshal refused, Chaplinsky called him a "God damned racketeer" and "a damned Fascist." Chaplinsky was convicted of saying fighting words to the marshal, and a unanimous Supreme Court upheld his conviction. Justice Murphy, in his opinion for the Court, argued that these kinds of statements were clearly the sort of statements that might lead the average person to breach the peace. Justice Murphy went on to say:

> It is well understood that the right of free speech is not absolute at all times and under all circumstances. There are certain well-defined and narrowly limited classes of speech, the prevention and punishment of which have

never been thought to raise any Constitutional problem. These include the lewd and obscene, the profane, the libelous, and the insulting or 'fighting' words—those which by their very utterance inflict injury or tend to incite an immediate breach of the peace. It has been well observed that such utterances are no essential part of any exposition of ideas, and are of such slight social value as a step to truth that any benefit that may be derived from them is clearly outweighed by the social interest in order and morality.

Justice Murphy's list of types of speech that are not protected by the right of free speech has been modified by the Court over time. Later Courts have found it necessary to protect much of the speech he listed, including the profane and the libelous. At the same time, the Court has not changed its mind about "'fighting' words." Words that are likely to cause an immediate breach of the peace can be controlled by the government.

By the 1960s and 1970s the Court was prepared to take the "clear and present" danger doctrine to its outer limit. In the 1969 case of *Brandenburg v. Ohio* (see p. 56), a unanimous Court overturned the conviction of a leader of the Ku Klux Klan under the Ohio criminal syndicalism statute that made it a crime to "advocate the duty, necessity, or propriety of crime." The leader had conducted a Ku Klux Klan meeting on a private farm in Ohio, complete with a burning cross and derogatory comments about blacks and Jews. As already discussed, during the early 1900s, criminal syndicalism laws had been used in *Fiske* and *Whitney*, with the permission of the Supreme Court, to put people who expressed unpopular ideas in prison. In this case the conviction was overturned. The Court said that the right of free speech does not allow a state to outlaw the "advocacy of the use of force or of law violation except where such advocacy is directed to inciting or producing imminent lawless action and is likely to incite or produce such action." The Court went on to say that the "mere abstract teaching" of the "necessity for a resort to force and violence is not the same as preparing a group for violent action and steeling it to such action." The Supreme Court believed that the Ohio criminal syndicalism law swept too broadly and was therefore unconstitutional. In 1927, an Oakland, California, resident was sent to prison for violating the California criminal syndicalism laws simply because she belonged to the left wing of the Socialist Party. In 1969, in *Brandenburg v. Ohio*, this decision was explicitly over-turned.

In the 1970 case of *Bachellar v. Maryland*, a unanimous Court overturned the convictions of a group of anti-Vietnam War demonstrators who had staged a demonstration both inside and in front of an Army recruiting station. They then staged a sit-in on the sidewalk in front of the station and were arrested by police under a law that made it a crime to "do or say" anything that disturbs the peace. While the convictions might have been based on the fact that these demonstrators had obstructed the sidewalk, the jury could have based their conviction on the fact that the demonstrators "said" things that were offensive to some people. The reasons for the conviction were not stated. Because the convictions might have been based on speech rather than action, they had to be overturned. The Court ruled that the demonstrators could be convicted for obstructing the sidewalk, but not for speaking in opposition to the Vietnam War, not even for speaking in opposition to the war in front of a recruiting station.

This decision demonstrates how far the Court's thinking had evolved. Eugene V. Debs was sentenced to 10 years in prison for making a speech at the national convention of the American Socialist Party in which he praised a woman who had obstructed the recruitment of soldiers. In 1919 this was enough for the Court to uphold his conviction with a unanimous decision. Fifty-one years later, the conviction of demonstrators who actually did disrupt the recruitment of soldiers was overturned by a unanimous Court because the conviction might have been based on the exercise of the right of free speech.

FREE SPEECH AND HATE CRIMES

The evolution of the Court's thinking in this area is also illustrated by the unanimous decision of the Supreme Court in the 1992 case of *R.A.V. v. St. Paul*. This case involved the conviction of a group of teenagers who had burned a crude cross across the street from a house where a black family had once lived. These teenagers were convicted under the city's "bias motivated crime" ordinance (commonly known as a hate crime law), which increased the penalty for any crime motivated by racial, religious, or sexual bias. Justice Scalia, writing for the Court, found this ordinance to be a violation of the right of free speech. He ruled that these kinds of ordinances are designed to punish people for expressing ideas the majority does not agree with; therefore these kinds of ordinances violate the First Amendment. While crimes may certainly be punished, the punishment cannot be increased because the crime is committed in a way that communicates an idea the majority does not agree with.

Justice Scalia pointed out that in this case the majority of St. Paul citizens did not like displays such as burning crosses that might insult people on the basis of "race, color, creed, religion or gender." Other displays would be permitted, no matter how vicious or severe, unless they were addressed to one of these "disfavored topics." St. Paul argued that only an ordinance based on the "content" of the ideas expressed by certain displays and actions would convey to minority groups that the majority did not condone "group hatred." Justice Scalia said that "the point of the First Amendment is that majority preferences must be expressed in some fashion other than silencing speech on the basis of its content." He concluded by saying that he and the other justices also found cross burning "reprehensible," but "St. Paul has sufficient means at its disposal to prevent such behavior without adding the First Amendment to the fire."

The idea of hate crimes, crimes performed in a way that suggests the crime is motivated by hatred based on race, religion, or sex, has found its way into the laws of many states. Of course, assaults on anyone, as well as the setting of fires or the destruction of property, can be punished by the criminal law. The difficult question is: Can the penalty be increased because the defendant says something the community does not like while committing the crime, or because the crime is clearly motivated by group, as opposed to individual, hatred? The answer from the Supreme Court appears to be no. Today, the right of free speech is too important to be subject to the criminal law, even if the speech is uttered during the commission of a crime. That idea is quite different from the Court's original conception of the reach of the First Amendment.

CONCLUSION

It is clear today that no constitutional right is more important than the right to speak, particularly the right to speak out on political issues. As the value of this right has gone up in the collective mind of the Court, the importance of other goals that could be put forward to justify interfering with this right has gone down. While Justice Holmes's statement that the right of free speech may only be interfered with if there is a "clear and present danger" of evil has been the stated standard throughout the century, the Court has required that the danger be much clearer and more present with each passing decade.

The right to speak about political issues has been expanding steadily during the twentieth century. In viewing this expansion, however, keep in mind the effects of history on the Court's interpretations. The Communist and Fascist revolutions the United States feared in the early 1900s never occurred, and American democracy was able to withstand two world wars and a great depression in the span of one generation. As the threat of revolution became more remote, the justices were able to focus more on the right of free speech and less on the need for government control.

Also, allowing people who belong to so-called subversive groups to speak out has had interesting benefits for law enforcement. Law-enforcement people in plain clothes attend anti-government rallies and take pictures of people and license plates; invaluable information can be gathered while people speak that would not be available if such groups could only meet in secret. Allowing people to speak and assemble may well be less dangerous than forcing them to vent their feelings only with violence.

While the Court acknowledges the right of government to limit the freedom of speech in order to prevent revolution and violence, the revolution must be imminent and the potential for violence very real before the right of free speech can be abridged.

....CASE DECISIONS..

The 1919 decision that first raised the question of "clear and present danger" was *Schenck v. United States.* The unanimous decision, written by Justice Holmes, is included here.

The 1969 decision in *Brandenburg v. Ohio* severely limited the concept of "clear and present danger" to situations where the danger is very "clear and present." The Court issued a per curiam opinion, which is included here. Concurring opinions by Justices Black and Douglas are not included here. Following are excerpts from the case decisions.

❋ ❋ ❋ ❋ ❋ ❋ ❋ ❋

SCHENCK v. UNITED STATES
249 U.S. 47 (1919)

MR. JUSTICE HOLMES delivered the opinion of the court.

This is an indictment in three counts. The first charges a conspiracy to violate the Espionage Act of June 15, 1917, c. 30, § 3, 40 Stat. 217, 219, by causing and attempting to cause insubordination, &c., in the military and naval forces of the United States, and to obstruct the recruiting and enlistment service of the United States, when the United States was at war with the German Empire, to-wit, that the defendants willfully conspired to have printed and circulated to men who had been called and accepted for military service under the Act of May 18, 1917, a document set forth and alleged to be calculated to cause such insubordination and obstruction. The count alleges overt acts in pursuance of the conspiracy, ending in the distribution of the document set forth. The second count alleges a conspiracy to commit an offense against the United States, to-wit, to use the mails for the transmission of matter declared to be non-mailable by Title XII, § 2 of the Act of June 15, 1917, to-wit, the above mentioned document, with an averment of the same overt acts. The third count charges an unlawful use of the mails for the transmission of the same matter and otherwise as above. The defendants were found guilty on all the counts. . . .

According to the testimony Schenck said he was general secretary of the Socialist party and had charge of the Socialist headquarters from which the documents were sent. He identified a book found there as the minutes of the Executive Committee of the party. The book showed a resolution of August 13, 1917, that 15,000 leaflets should be printed on the other side of one of them in use, to be mailed to men who had passed exemption boards, and for distribution. Schenck personally attended to the printing. On August 20 the general secretary's report said "Obtained new leaflets from printer and started work addressing envelopes" &c.; and there was a resolve that Comrade Schenck be allowed $125 for sending leaflets through the mail. He said that he had about fifteen or sixteen thousand printed. There were files of the circular in question in the inner office which he said were printed on the other side of the one sided circular and were there for distribution. Other copies were proved to have been sent through the mails to drafted men. . . .

The document in question upon its first printed side recited the first section of the Thirteenth Amendment, said that the idea embodied in it was violated by the Conscription Act and that a conscript is little better than a convict. In impassioned language it intimated that conscription was despotism in its worst form and a monstrous wrong against humanity in the interest of Wall Street's chosen few. It said "Do not submit to intimidation," but in form at least confined itself to peaceful measures such as a petition for the repeal of the act. The other and later printed side of the sheet was headed "Assert Your Rights." It stated reasons for alleging that any one violated the Constitution when he refused to recognize "your right to assert your opposition to the draft," and went on "If you do not assert and support your rights, you are helping to deny or disparage rights which it is the solemn duty of all citizens and residents of the United States to retain." It described the arguments on the other side as coming from cunning politicians and a mercenary capitalist press, and even silent consent to the conscription law as helping to support an infamous conspiracy. It denied the power to send our citizens away to foreign shores to shoot up the people of other lands, and added that words could not express the condemnation such cold-blooded ruthlessness deserves, &c., &c., winding up "You must do your share to maintain, support and uphold the rights of the people of this country." Of course the document would not have been sent unless it had been intended to have some effect, and we do not see what effect it could be expected to have upon persons subject to the draft except to influence them to obstruct the carrying of it out. The defendants do not deny that the jury might find against them on this point.

But it is said, suppose that that was the tendency of this circular, it is protected by the First Amendment to the Constitution. Two of the strongest expressions are said to be quoted respectively from well-known public men. It well may be that the prohibition of laws abridging the freedom of speech is not confined to previous restraints, although to prevent them may have been the main purpose, as intimated in *Patterson v. Colorado*, 205 U.S. 454, 462. We admit that in many places and in ordinary times the defendants in saying all that was said in the circular would have been within their constitutional rights. But the character of every act depends upon the circumstances in which it is done. *Aikens v. Wisconsin*, 195 U.S. 194, 205, 206. The most stringent protection of free speech would not protect a man in falsely shouting fire in a theatre and causing a panic. It does not even protect a man from an injunction against uttering words that may have all the effect of force. *Gompers v. Bucks Stove & Range Co.*, 221 U.S. 418, 439. The question in every case is whether the words used are used in such circumstances and are of such a nature as to create a clear and present danger that they will bring about the substantive evils that Congress has a right to prevent. It is a question of proximity and degree. When a nation is at war many things that might be said in time of peace are such a hindrance to its effort that their utterance will not be endured so long as men fight and that no Court could regard them as protected by any constitutional right.

BRANDENBURG v. OHIO
395 U.S. 444 (1969)

Per Curiam.

The appellant, a leader of a Ku Klux Klan group, was convicted under the Ohio Criminal Syndicalism statute for "advocat[ing] . . . the duty, necessity, or propriety of crime, sabotage, violence, or unlawful methods of terrorism as a means of accomplishing industrial or political reform" and for "voluntarily assembl[ing] with any society, group, or assemblage of persons formed to teach or advocate the doctrines of criminal syndicalism." Ohio Rev. Code Ann. § 2923.13. He was fined $1,000 and sentenced to one to 10 years' imprisonment. The appellant challenged the constitutionality of the criminal syndicalism statute under the First and Fourteenth Amendments to the United States Constitution, but the intermediate appellate court of Ohio affirmed his conviction without opinion. The Supreme Court of Ohio dismissed his appeal, *sua sponte*, "for the reason that no substantial constitutional question exists herein." It did not file an opinion or explain its conclusions. Appeal was taken to this Court, and we noted probable jurisdiction. 393 U.S. 948 (1968). We reverse.

The record shows that a man, identified at trial as the appellant, telephoned an announcer-reporter on the staff of a Cincinnati television station and invited him to come to a Ku Klux Klan "rally" to be held at a farm in Hamilton County. With the cooperation of the organizers, the reporter and a cameraman attended the meeting and filmed the events. Portions of the films were later broadcast on the local station and on a national network.

The prosecution's case rested on the films and on testimony identifying the appellant as the person who communicated with the reporter and who spoke at the rally. The State also introduced into evidence several articles appearing in the film, including a pistol, a rifle, a shotgun, ammunition, a Bible, and a red hood worn by the speaker in the films.

One film showed 12 hooded figures, some of whom carried firearms. They were gathered around a large wooden cross, which they burned. No one was present other than the participants and the newsmen who made the film. Most of the words uttered during the scene were incomprehensible when the film was projected, but scattered phrases could be understood that were derogatory of Negroes and, in one instance, of Jews. . . .

The Ohio Criminal Syndicalism Statute was enacted in 1919. From 1917 to 1920, identical or quite similar laws were adopted by 20 States and two territories. E. Dowell, A History of Criminal Syndicalism Legislature in the United States 21 (1939). In 1927, this Court sustained the constitutionality of California's Criminal Syndicalism Act, Cal. Penal Code §§ 11400–11402, the text of which is quite similar to that of the laws of Ohio. *Whitney v. California*, 274 U.S. 357 (1927). The Court upheld the statute on the ground that, without more, "advocating" violent means to effect political and economic change involves such danger to the security of the State that the State may outlaw it. Cf. *Fiske v. Kansas*, 274 U.S. 380 (1927). But *Whitney* has been thoroughly discredited by later decisions. See *Dennis v. United States*, 341 U.S. 494, at 507 (1951). These later decisions have fashioned the principle that the constitutional guarantees of free speech and free press do not permit a State to forbid or proscribe advocacy of the use of force or of law violation except where such advocacy is directed to inciting or producing imminent lawless action and is likely to incite or produce such action. As we said in *Noto v. United States*, 367 U.S. 290, 297–298 (1961), "the mere abstract teaching . . . of the moral propriety or even moral necessity for a resort to force and violence, is not the same as preparing a group for violent action and steeling it to such action." See also *Herndon v. Lowry*, 301 U.S. 242, 259–261 (1937); *Bond v. Floyd*, 385 U.S. 116, 134 (1966). A statute which fails to draw this distinction impermissibly intrudes upon the freedoms guaranteed by the First and Fourteenth Amendments. It sweeps within its condemnation speech which our Constitution has immunized from governmental control. . . .

Accordingly, we are here confronted with a statute which, by its own words and as applied, purports to punish mere advocacy and to forbid, on pain of criminal punishment, assembly with others merely to advocate the described type of action. Such a statute falls within the condemnation of the First and Fourteenth Amendments. The contrary teaching of *Whitney v. California, supra*, cannot be supported, and that decision is therefore overruled.

Reversed.

DISCUSSION QUESTIONS

1. The author suggests that allowing revolutionary groups to exercise their right of free speech can have advantages for law enforcement. Do you agree? What are these advantages?
2. What do you think members of a revolutionary group would have to say before they could be arrested by the police under the current interpretation of clear and present danger?
3. People can be arrested for uttering "fighting words." What are "fighting words"? Is it possible that different words would qualify as fighting words in different parts of the country? What words do you think would qualify as fighting words where you live?
4. Justice Oliver Wendell Holmes wrote a book entitled *The Common Law*, which began with the line "The life of the law has not been logic, it has been experience." How would this line apply to the development of the "clear and present danger" doctrine?
5. Justice Holmes argued that the right of free speech was intended to protect the "marketplace of ideas" and that people should be able to go into the marketplace of ideas and pick and choose those ideas they agree with after listening to all the choices. Do you think this analogy is a good one? Are there any problems with the current marketplace of ideas?

CHAPTER
five

⊛ ⊛ ⊛ ⊛ ⊛ ⊛ ⊛ ⊛

Entertainment Speech: The Problem of Obscenity

Most of the early free speech cases concerned political and religious speech. What about all the speech activities that are primarily entertainment? Are these protected by the First Amendment? In 1915, in the case of *Mutual Film v. Ohio*, the Supreme Court's answer was no. This case involved a motion picture distributor who asked the Supreme Court to declare the movie censorship laws that had been recently passed in several states to be unconstitutional. A unanimous Court ruled that movies were not protected by the First Amendment because they were simply entertainment, like the "circus and all other shows and spectacles." The particular movie that was being censored at the time was D. W. Griffith's *The Birth of a Nation*. Many people thought its portrayal of the South during Reconstruction unfairly portrayed blacks as bad and glorified the Ku Klux Klan. The movie was not allowed to be exhibited in several states.

The Court's view of entertainment speech did not begin to change until 1948. Once the Court began to consider First Amendment protection of entertainment speech, however, it had to struggle with the issue of obscenity. What is obscene, and to what extent can government limit free speech to control obscenity?

CRIME STORIES

The 1948 case that concerned entertainment speech, *Winters v. New York*, involved a book dealer in New York who was convicted of selling obscene magazines. The magazines in question contained stories about crime and pictures of bloody crime scenes. Justice Reed, writing for the six-justice majority, ruled that the First Amendment does protect entertainment speech. He said that the "line between the informing and the entertaining is too elusive" for the Court to draw. He went on to say that "what is one man's amusement, teaches another's doctrine." The majority of justices thought that entertainment, like political leaflets, could be used to communicate ideas and therefore was deserving of some protection under the First Amendment.

At the same time, the majority of justices believed that New York should be able to control obscenity. This particular obscenity statute had to be thrown out, however, because it did not make clear exactly what was and what was not obscene. There is a general principle in American law that a criminal statute must be clear enough so that the average person reading the statute will have a good idea of what is and what is not prohibited by the law. If the law is not clear, it is thrown out as being too vague. That was the situation in this case. The reason for this general rule is that Americans have a right under the Fourteenth Amendment to due process of law. The right to due process means that those accused of crimes have the right to receive a fair process, including trial by jury and representation by an attorney. The right to due process also includes the right to have written criminal laws that people can understand spelling out what is and what is not illegal. If a statute concerned with speech is too vague, people will be inclined not to speak because they will not know what is and what is not forbidden. Because of this, vague statutes are a particular concern where speech is concerned. Also, if a statute is too broad, in that it appears to prevent protected as well as unprotected speech, it will also be thrown out by the Supreme Court as a violation of the right of free speech.

FIRST AMENDMENT PROTECTION OF MOVIES

In 1952, with *Joseph Burstyn, Inc. v. Wilson*, a unanimous Court overturned another New York law, which required anyone wishing to show a motion picture to get a license first and allowed a censor to refuse to issue a license for "sacrilegious" movies. The decision overturned the 1915 *Mutual Film* decision, which held that movies were not protected by the First Amendment. The *Joseph Burstyn, Inc.* case involved the Italian movie *The Miracle*. The movie told the story of a simple-minded country girl who, while tending her goats, sees a bearded stranger. She believes him to be St. Joseph and asks him to take her to heaven. The stranger plies her with wine and apparently "ravishes" her. This part of the story is only suggested. Eventually it is discovered that the girl is pregnant, which she believes to be the work of St. Joseph. She suffers abuse in the village and ultimately finds her way to a country church where she has her baby alone. Anna Magnani played the girl, Federico Fellini wrote the screenplay, and Roberto Rossellini produced the movie. The film was not banned in Italy. The New York censor refused to issue a license for *The Miracle* because he believed the movie was sacrilegious. The justices thought that a state could not prevent the showing of a motion picture for this reason. Justice Frankfurter, in his concurring opinion, pointed out that many ministers and priests did not object to this particular movie.

A DEFINITION OF OBSCENITY

For decades the Court had said that there were certain things the First Amendment did not protect, and obscenity was certainly on that list. Finally, in 1957, the Court made its first attempt to define obscenity in a case involving obscene material sent through the mail in violation of federal law. Justice Brennan wrote the decision for the Court in *Roth v. United States*. He confirmed that the First Amendment does not protect obscenity, as the Court had said many times, and he defined obscenity as something "the average person, applying contemporary community standards" finds to have a "dominant theme" that "appeals to prurient interest." Justice Brennan did not define exactly what he meant by the term "prurient." He went out of his way, however, to say that sex by itself is not obscene. He said:

> However, sex and obscenity are not synonymous. Obscene material is material which deals with sex in a manner appealing to prurient interest. The portrayal of sex, *e.g.*, in art, literature and scientific works, is not itself sufficient reason to deny material the constitutional protection of freedom of speech and press. Sex, a great and mysterious motive force in human life, has indisputably been a subject of absorbing interest to mankind through the ages; it is one of the vital problems of human interest and public concern.

The *Roth* case involved two convictions under obscenity laws. The majority used its new definition to uphold those convictions.

Justices Douglas and Black believed that both convictions should have been overturned. These justices did not think that government had any business limiting speech, even speech some believed to be obscene. They thought that it would be better to "give the broad sweep of the First Amendment full support," and that adults should be left to decide for themselves what to read and what to see in a movie theater. Essentially, Justices Douglas and Black argued that even obscenity should fall under the umbrella of the First Amendment.

CENSORSHIP OF MOVIES

In 1959 a unanimous Court overturned the refusal of the New York censor to license the movie *Lady Chatterley's Lover*. The license was refused because the censor believed that the movie suggested that adultery was a good idea (*Kingsley Pictures Corp. v. Regents*). The justices believed that a movie could not be censored because it contained an unpopular "idea," even an idea the majority of citizens believed to be immoral. Several justices chose to write their own concurring opinions in this case. Justice Frankfurter had seen *Lady Chatterley's Lover* and said that it did not offend him so it should not be censored. The majority of justices rested their decision on *Roth*; in their opinion, this movie was not obscene under the *Roth* definition and they thought that that should be the end of the discussion.

By 1964 the problem of what is and what is not obscene came back to haunt the Court in *Jacobellis v. Ohio*. The defendant was convicted of showing an obscene film, Louis Malle's *The Lovers*. The majority of justices thought that the conviction should be overturned. While they still said that the definition outlined in *Roth* controlled this decision, they added to the definition. To be obscene, the book or movie must be "utterly without redeeming social value." While six justices believed that the conviction should be overturned, they found it necessary to write five different opinions explaining what they thought about the law on obscenity. Chief Justice Warren wrote a dissenting opinion, which was joined by Justices Harlan and Clark, in which he objected to what he saw as a dangerous trend. Chief Justice Warren believed that the Court was setting itself up as the ultimate censor of what the nation could see in movie houses and read in magazines. He pointed to the part of the *Roth* obscenity definition that said something was obscene if it violated "community standards"; he thought that different communities should be allowed to set different standards for obscenity. The problem with this view is the problem the authors of the Constitution faced in deciding who should regulate interstate commerce. If different states had been allowed to regulate interstate commerce, trade between states would be impossible. If every community is allowed to decide what is and what is not obscene, how will publishers in New York and moviemakers in California know what they can and cannot produce for the national market?

A MOVIE CENSORSHIP SYSTEM

By the 1965 case of *Freedman v. Maryland*, all the justices except one could at least agree on how a movie censorship system could work without violating the First Amendment. The Court said that the censor must have the burden of proving that the movie in question is obscene and that the final decision must be made by an independent judge. Also, the process must not take very long. Justice Douglas, the lone dissenter, did not think that any form of government censorship of movies should be allowed.

In 1966 the Court tried again to define obscenity. The case, *Memoirs v. Massachusetts*, involved a book entitled *Memoirs of a Woman of Pleasure (Fanny Hill)*. The book had been banned in Boston as obscene. The Court divided into three groups of three justices each. Chief Justice Warren and Justices Brennan and Fortas believed that something could be called obscene if (1) its dominant theme appealed to prurient interests; (2) it was patently offensive to contemporary community standards; and (3) it was utterly without redeeming social value. These three justices did not think *Memoirs of a Woman of Pleasure* met that definition and voted to overturn the book banning. Justices Black, Stewart, and Douglas, agreed that the book banning should be overturned but did not wish to even discuss the definition of obscenity. They seemed to think that even obscenity should be allowed to be published and purchased by adults if it is in book form. Finally, Justices Clark, Harlan, and White believed that the book banning should be upheld in this case.

In *Interstate Circuit v. Dallas* eight justices agreed that the standards set for the Motion Picture Classification Board in Dallas were too vague. The case involved the movie *Viva Maria*, starring Brigitte Bardot and directed by Louis Malle. The board thought that the movie had too much "sexual promiscuity." The Dallas ordinance that set the standards for classifying motion pictures said the board could prevent children under the age of 16 from seeing movies with too much "sexual promiscuity." The Court did not think the phrase "sexual promiscuity" provided a clear standard for the board and overturned the ordinance. Soon after this decision, the motion picture industry began to regulate itself by classifying movies under the now familiar rating system that gives a movie a rating depending on its suitability for viewing by children. Local movie review boards basically became obsolete soon after this rating system was implemented. In June 1981 the Maryland Movie Censorship Board became the last state board to cease operation after 65 years of censoring movies.

During the 1960s, what the press called a "generation gap" was becoming apparent. The college-age generation believed that the right of free speech should protect every kind of speech, including speech that the older generation thought was obscene. The older generation was shocked at what it considered to be obscene filth in the movie theaters and on the bookstore shelves. The Supreme Court was caught in the middle. Many people hoped that the appointment in 1969 of Warren Burger as chief justice would bring an end to the controversy and clear the way for more control over obscenity. It would not be that simple.

In 1971 all the justices agreed that a newspaper could publish nude photographs as part of a news story (*Kois v. Wisconsin*). The justices agreed that nudity is not, in and of itself, obscene and that these pictures did not "appeal to prurient interests."

By 1972 conservative Justices Blackmun, Powell, and Rehnquist had been appointed to the Court in part to bring an end to this obscenity problem. In 1972 six of the nine justices agreed that California could have a regulation that limited the exhibition of live adult entertainment in places that also served liquor. The majority of justices believed that the Twenty-first Amendment, which had repealed Prohibition, gave the states extraordinary powers to regulate liquor sales and this was simply a regulation of liquor sales, not a limitation on free speech (*California v. LaRue*).

REDEFINING OBSCENITY

In 1973 a five-justice majority tried to redefine obscenity in two cases, *Miller v. California* (see p. 70) and *Paris Adult Theatre I v. Slaton* (see p. 73). The new definition was an attempt by the new conservative majority to get back to the *Roth* definition. Whether or not something was obscene would be decided by "contemporary community standards." If the work "appeals to prurient interests, is patently offensive and lacks serious literary, artistic, political or scientific value," it can be considered to be obscene. The majority said that the standard that had been applied in *Memoirs v. Massachusetts*, which stated that something had to be "utterly without redeeming social value," was being overturned. The majority of justices clearly thought that by modifying the definition in this way they were expanding the amount of material that could now be called obscene because many movies and books that "lack serious literary, artistic, political or scientific value" could not be said to be "utterly without redeeming social value."

Justice Brennan wrote a dissenting opinion in which he chronicled the long and twisted history of the Court's attempts to deal with obscenity. He could not see how the "new" definition was significantly different from the "old" definition. He pointed to the significant differences within the Court over the years concerning the obscenity issue. Justices Black and Douglas had consistently maintained that government should not be allowed to control speech at any time in the name of limiting the obscene. Justice Harlan, on the other hand, had argued that the states should be given great freedom to deal with obscenity. Justice Stewart believed that only "hard core pornography" could be controlled, but it was not exactly clear what qualified as "hard core pornography" (he knew it when he saw it). Because of the different views among the justices, Justice Brennan tells us, in 1967 the Court began to summarily overturn obscenity convictions if five justices, using their own individual standards, thought the convictions should be overturned. Justice Brennan believed that this method of dealing with obscenity cases confused lower courts, and he did not think the "new" definition stated in the *Miller* and *Paris Adult Theatre I* cases would solve the problem. In Justice Brennan's opinion, adults should be allowed to purchase and view anything they like, and the law could only be justified in limiting speech if it protected juveniles and prevented "offensive exposure to unconsenting adults."

Of course, the actual words in the new obscenity definition looked a lot like the words in the old definition. People assumed, however, that the new "conservative" majority of justices would be more willing to allow local communities to set obscenity standards. This assumption did not last long.

In the 1974 case of *Jenkins v. Georgia* (see p. 79), the Court was faced with the ruling in Georgia that the movie *Carnal Knowledge* was obscene. A unanimous Supreme Court disagreed with the ruling. Here was a movie by a major motion picture studio with a famous cast that included Ann Margaret, Art Garfunkel, and Jack Nicholson, directed by Mike Nichols. The members of the Court viewed the movie and did not find it to be "patently offensive." There were no "genitals" shown during the "sex scenes" and while there was "occasional nudity" the Court had already said that nudity alone is not obscene.

It is ironic that the year after the new conservative majority announced the new definition of obscenity a decision on obscenity by a local community came along that not one member of the Court could accept. Many people had assumed that the key to the new obscenity definition articulated in 1973 was that each community was supposed to decide for itself what was obscene. By the end of 1974, it was clear that the Court was not willing to live with the implications of that interpretation.

Soon after this decision, many states and cities gave up trying to eliminate obscenity from their movie theaters and bookstores. Instead they allowed obscenity but subjected it to a variety of regulations designed to further a number of interests, including the protection of children and public safety. Some cities required all "adult entertainment" to be located in one area. Boston did this when it set up what has come to be called the "Combat Zone." Other cities required adult entertainment to be spread out around the city to prevent too much impact on any one neighborhood.

ZONING LAWS AND ADULT ENTERTAINMENT

In 1976 the Court decided that the city of Detroit could use an "anti-skid row" ordinance to control the location of "adult theaters" (*Young v. American Mini Theaters*). The city ordinance said that an adult theater could not be located within 500 feet of a residence or within 1,000 feet of another "regulated" location. Other regulated locations included businesses such as adult bookstores and bars. Five justices thought that this ordinance was simply a valid regulation of commercial enterprises and did not violate the First Amendment. Four justices dissented, arguing that businesses that deal in free speech are different and should not be subject to this kind of zoning law.

In 1981 the Court overturned a zoning law in Mt. Ephraim, New Jersey, because it outlawed all "live entertainment" in the entire town (*Schad v. Mt. Ephraim*). The ordinance had been passed to keep the local adult bookstore from putting in coin-operated machines that allowed customers to see a live nude dancer for a fixed period of time. The seven-justice majority ruled that "live nude dancing" is protected by the First Amendment, and that while towns could use zoning laws to regulate the location of such establishments, they could not outlaw live nude dancing completely. Chief Justice Burger and Justice Rehnquist dissented. They pointed out that Mt. Ephraim was a small town between the cities of Camden and Philadelphia, and that anyone who wanted to see live nude dancing could simply drive down the road a short distance to either of those cities. The dissenting justices believed the desire of the people of Mt. Ephraim to protect the tranquillity of their small town should be respected.

SECONDARY EFFECTS OF ADULT ENTERTAINMENT

The 1991 case of *Barnes v. Glen Theatre* involved an Indiana law that required nude dancers to wear pasties and a G-string at clubs such as the Kitty Kat Lounge and the Glen Theatre. This was a difficult case because the state of Indiana said that it never applied this law to "real" art such as operas, ballet, or plays. A five-justice majority upheld the Indiana law. These justices saw the law simply as a regulation of an "adult entertainment" business and did not find it to be unreasonable. Justice Souter wrote a concurring opinion, in which he accepted the idea that the state had an interest in controlling and combating the secondary effects of adult entertainment, such as various kinds of criminal activity. He did not make clear exactly how "pasties and a G-string" would combat those secondary effects. Four justices dissented, pointing out that the Court had consistently ruled that nudity was not, by itself, obscene. The dissenters also were disturbed by Indiana's admission that it did not apply the law to "real" art because they thought the whole purpose of the First Amendment was to take the decision concerning what constitutes "real" art out of the hands of government officials and place it in the hands of the people.

CHILDREN AND OBSCENITY

In the 1982 case of *New York v. Ferber*, the Court was faced with the problem of child pornography for the first time. This case involved the conviction of a bookstore owner who sold movies showing young boys masturbating. The New York law made it a crime to show children engaged in sexual conduct and defined sexual conduct to include sexual intercourse, masturbation, deviate sexual behavior, and the lewd exhibition of genitals. A unanimous Court accepted the state's argument that child pornography was a serious menace to society and ruled that states should be given substantial power to root out this menace.

In 1986 the Court made it clear how far it was willing to go to allow government to protect children in *Bethel School District v. Fraser*. On April 26, 1983, Matthew N. Fraser made a speech before the student body nominating his friend for elective student office. There were 600 students in the auditorium as Matthew said:

> I know a man who is firm—he's firm in his pants, he's firm in his shirt, his character is firm—but most . . . of all, his belief in you, the students of Bethel, is firm. Jeff Kuhlman is a man who takes his point and pounds it in. If necessary, he'll take an issue and nail it to the wall. He doesn't attack things in spurts—he drives hard, pushing and pushing until finally—he succeeds. Jeff is a man who will go to the very end—even the climax, for each and every one of you. So vote for Jeff for A.S.B. vice-president— he'll never come between you and the best our high school can be.

After the speech Matthew Fraser was suspended from school for three days and told he would not be allowed to make one of the student speeches at the high school graduation ceremony. The seven-justice majority thought that this case was very different from *Tinker v. Des Moines School Dist.*, where the right of students to wear black armbands to protest the Vietnam War had been upheld. The majority of justices believed that the speech in this case was "plainly offensive" and that government must be allowed to protect children from such offensive speech. Justices Marshall and Stevens dissented. Justice Marshall pointed out that there was no disruption of school activities and therefore the right of free speech should be protected. Justice Stevens was concerned that the student in this case could not have known by reading the school policy that what he was going to say was a violation of school rules. Without clear rules, his right to speak should be protected.

After three decades of dealing with the problem of obscenity most cities and states had developed a workable strategy. Given the expense of having to take every obscenity case up through the legal system, many locations decided to use the power of regulation to control "adult entertainment" instead of trying to ban obscenity. While no one knew what qualified as "obscenity," everyone could agree on what constituted "adult entertainment." The only exception to this approach was in the area of child pornography where states and cities enjoyed a great deal of freedom to deal with a serious social problem.

How much freedom was illustrated by two decisions handed down in 1989 and 1990.

In the 1989 case of *Massachusetts v. Oakes*, Douglas Oakes was convicted and sentenced to 10 years in prison for taking pictures of his 14-year-old "physically mature" stepdaughter nude from the waist up. The pictures were sent to a modeling school as part of her application for admission. A majority of the justices ruled that this conviction could stand without offending the First Amendment. Justices Brennan, Marshall, and Stevens dissented, pointing out that nudity alone is not obscene. The other justices apparently thought that the goal of eliminating child pornography was important enough to allow this kind of activity to result in a long prison sentence.

In the 1990 case of *Osborne v. Ohio*, the defendant was convicted of having child pornography, in this case pictures of nude children, in his possession. Six justices upheld the conviction. Three justices dissented because they thought that this Ohio law was too broad and that too much fell under the definition of child pornography. A majority of the justices were simply not going to get into the "definition game" where child pornography was concerned.

The rapid spread of videocassette players during the 1980s had a profound effect on the whole question of obscenity. With these machines there was no longer any need to attend an adult theater. Someone who wanted to see an adult movie could simply rent or buy it at the local video store. Most of the "secondary" effects of adult theaters did not apply to videocassette rentals and sales. The problem of limiting the exposure of children could be controlled by allowing adult movies to be rented or sold only to adults.

STATE PROSECUTION OF OBSCENITY

Even though many states have decided to regulate rather than eliminate obscenity, the Court has made it clear that states may prosecute obscenity if they wish to. In the 1987 case of *Pope v. Illinois*, the Court upheld the conviction of two part-time clerks at an adult bookstore in Rockford, Illinois, for selling an obscene magazine to an undercover policeman. The majority of justices approved of the definition of obscenity contained in the Illinois statute, which said something is obscene if:

> (1) the average person, applying contemporary community standards, would find that, taken as a whole, it appeals to prurient interest; and
> (2) the average person, applying contemporary community standards, would find that it depicts or describes, in a patently offensive way, ultimate sexual acts or sadomasochistic sexual acts, whether normal or perverted, actual or simulated, or masturbation, excretory functions or lewd exhibitions of the genitals, and (3) taken as a whole, it lacks serious literary, artistic, political or scientific value.

Justices Brennan, Marshall, and Stevens dissented. Justice Brennan argued that the concept of obscenity cannot be defined with "sufficient specificity and clarity to provide fair notice to persons who create and distribute sexually oriented material." Therefore, in his opinion, obscenity could not be the basis of a criminal conviction without violating the concept of due process of law.

Justice Stevens went further, arguing that the state of Illinois could not criminalize the sale of any magazine to an adult without violating the First Amendment "absent some connection to minors or obtrusive display to unconsenting adults." He ended his dissent by saying: "In the end, I believe we must rely on the capacity of the free marketplace of ideas to distinguish that which is useful or beautiful from that which is ugly or worthless."

CONCLUSION

The Supreme Court began the twentieth century with the idea that the right of free speech mainly protected a limited amount of political and religious speech and that entertainment speech was not protected by the First Amendment. From the 1940s onward the Court expanded this idea to include most forms of entertainment, including nude dancers at a nightclub, adult magazines, books, and movies. While some justices have objected that nude dancers are not communicating an "idea" and therefore are not worthy of constitutional protection, a majority of justices have not been willing to draw a line between dancing that does and dancing that does not convey ideas.

The Court attempted to draw a line between the obscene and the acceptable, but that line proved elusive. It was particularly difficult to come up with a definition of "obscenity" that conveyed anything of substance to people reading it. What does "prurient" mean? How can people know if something has "serious literary, artistic, political or scientific" value? What kinds of sexual conduct are "patently offensive"? Which "community standards" will be acceptable to the members of the Supreme Court?

Because of these difficulties, states have moved away from trying to define obscenity and have focused on outlawing "child pornography." Child pornography could be broadly defined without running into First Amendment issues. Certainly the right of free speech does not include the right to make, sell, or own child pornography. By allowing cities and states to regulate "adult entertainment," the Court has been able to create a legal system that both recognizes the right of adults to view adult material and acknowledges that cities and states have a legitimate interest in maintaining order and preventing crime.

At the same time, a majority of justices continue to believe that cities and states may prosecute people who sell obscene magazines or exhibit obscene movies to adults if cities and states choose to do so. A majority of justices also believe that definitions of obscenity such as the one found in the Illinois statute discussed in *Pope v. Illinois* do provide people with fair notice concerning what they can and cannot sell or show to adults.

CASE DECISIONS

On the same day in 1973, the Court handed down two obscenity decisions with *Miller v. California* and *Paris Adult Theatre I v. Slaton*. Chief Justice Burger wrote the opinions for the five-justice majority in both cases, and both of his opinions are included here. Justices Douglas and Brennan wrote dissenting opinions in both cases. Their dissenting opinions in *Paris Adult Theatre I v. Slaton* are included here.

In 1974 a unanimous Court agreed in *Jenkins v. Georgia* that the movie *Carnal Knowledge* was not obscene, contrary to the opinion of the Georgia Supreme Court and a Georgia jury. The Court's opinion, written by Justice Rehnquist, is included here. Following are excerpts from the case decisions.

❈ ❈ ❈ ❈ ❈ ❈ ❈ ❈

MILLER v. CALIFORNIA
413 U.S. 15 (1973)

MR. CHIEF JUSTICE BURGER delivered the opinion of the Court.

This is one of a group of "obscenity-pornography" cases being reviewed by the Court in a re-examination of standards enunciated in earlier cases involving what Mr. Justice Harlan called "the intractable obscenity problem." *Interstate Circuit, Inc. v. Dallas*, 390 U.S. 676, 704 (1968) (concurring and dissenting).

Appellant conducted a mass mailing campaign to advertise the sale of illustrated books, euphemistically called "adult" material. After a jury trial, he was convicted of violating California Penal Code § 311.2 (a), a misdemeanor, by knowingly distributing obscene matter, and the Appellate Department, Superior Court of California, County of Orange, summarily affirmed the judgment without opinion. Appellant's conviction was specifically based on his conduct in causing five unsolicited advertising brochures to be sent through the mail in an envelope addressed to a restaurant in Newport Beach, California. The envelope was opened by the manager of the restaurant and his mother. They had not requested the brochures; they complained to the police.

The brochures advertise four books entitled "Intercourse," "Man-Woman," "Sex Orgies Illustrated," and "An Illustrated History of Pornography," and a film entitled "Marital Intercourse." While the brochures contain some descriptive printed material, primarily they consist of pictures and drawings very explicitly depicting men and women in groups of two or more engaging in a variety of sexual activities, with genitals often prominently displayed. . . .

The dissent of Mr. Justice Brennan reviews the background of the obscenity problem, but since the Court now undertakes to formulate standards more concrete than those in the past, it is useful for us to focus on two of the landmark cases in the somewhat tortured history of the Court's obscenity decisions. In *Roth v. United States*, 354 U.S. 476 (1957), the Court sustained a conviction under a federal statute punishing the mailing of "obscene, lewd, lascivious or filthy . . ." materials. The key to that holding was the Court's rejection of the claim that obscene materials were protected by the First Amendment. Five Justices joined in the opinion stating:

> "All ideas having even the slightest redeeming social importance— unorthodox ideas, controversial ideas, even ideas hateful to the prevailing climate of opinion—have the full protection of the [First Amendment] guaranties, unless excludable because they encroach upon the limited area of more important interests. But implicit in the history of the First Amendment is the rejection of obscenity as utterly without redeeming social importance. . . . This is the same judgment expressed by this Court in *Chaplinsky v. New Hampshire*, 315 U.S. 568, 571–572:
>
> " '. . . There are certain well-defined and narrowly limited classes of speech, the prevention and punishment of which have never been thought to raise any Constitutional problem. *These include the lewd and obscene. . . . It has been well observed that such utterances are no essential part of any exposition of ideas, and are of such slight social value as a step to truth that any benefit that may be derived from them is clearly outweighed by the social interest in order and morality. . . .*' [Emphasis by Court in *Roth* opinion.]
>
> "We hold that obscenity is not within the area of constitutionally protected speech or press." 354 U.S., at 484–485 (footnotes omitted).

Nine years later, in *Memoirs v. Massachusetts*, 383 U.S. 413 (1966), the Court veered sharply away from the *Roth* concept and, with only three Justices in the plurality opinion, articulated a new test of obscenity. The plurality held that under the *Roth* definition

> "as elaborated in subsequent cases, three elements must coalesce: it must be established that (a) the dominant theme of the material taken as a whole appeals to a prurient interest in sex; (b) the material is patently offensive because it affronts contemporary community standards relating to the description or representation of sexual matters; and (c) the material is utterly without redeeming social value." *Id.*, at 418.

The sharpness of the break with *Roth*, represented by the third element of the *Memoirs* test and emphasized by Mr. Justice White's dissent, *id.*, at 460–462, was further underscored when the *Memoirs* plurality went on to state:

> "The Supreme Judicial Court erred in holding that a book need not be 'unqualifiedly worthless before it can be deemed obscene.' A book cannot be proscribed unless it is found to be *utterly* without redeeming social value." *Id.*, at 419 (emphasis in original).

While *Roth* presumed "obscenity" to be "utterly without redeeming social importance," *Memoirs* required that to prove obscenity it must be affirmatively established that the material is *"utterly* without redeeming social value." Thus, even as they repeated the words of *Roth*, the *Memoirs* plurality produced a drastically altered test that called on the prosecution to prove a negative, *i.e.*, that the material was *"utterly* without redeeming social value"—a burden virtually impossible to discharge under our criminal standards of proof. Such considerations caused Mr. Justice Harlan to wonder if the *"utterly* without redeeming social value" test had any meaning at all. See *Memoirs v. Massachusetts, id.*, at 459 (Harlan, J., dissenting). See also *id.*, at 461 (White, J., dissenting); *United States v. Groner*, 479 F.2d 577, 579–581 (CA5 1973)....

This much has been categorically settled by the Court, that obscene material is unprotected by the First Amendment. *Kois v. Wisconsin*, 408 U.S. 229 (1972); *United States v. Reidel*, 402 U.S., at 354; *Roth v. United States, supra*, at 485. "The First and Fourteenth Amendments have never been treated as absolutes [footnote omitted]." *Breard v. Alexandria*, 341 U.S., at 642, and cases cited. See *Times Film Corp. v. Chicago*, 365 U.S. 43, 47–50 (1961); *Joseph Burstyn, Inc. v. Wilson*, 343 U.S., at 502. We acknowledge, however, the inherent dangers of undertaking to regulate any form of expression. State statutes designed to regulate obscene materials must be carefully limited. See *Interstate Circuit, Inc. v. Dallas, supra*, at 682–685. As a result, we now confine the permissible scope of such regulation to works which depict or describe sexual conduct. That conduct must be specifically defined by the applicable state law, as written or authoritatively construed. A state offense must also be limited to works which, taken as a whole, appeal to the prurient interest in sex, which portray sexual conduct in a patently offensive way, and which, taken as a whole, do not have serious literary, artistic, political, or scientific value.

The basic guidelines for the trier of fact must be: (a) whether "the average person, applying contemporary community standards" would find that the work, taken as a whole, appeals to the prurient interest, *Kois v. Wisconsin, supra*, at 230, quoting *Roth v. United States, supra*, at 489; (b) whether the work depicts or describes, in a patently offensive way, sexual conduct specifically defined by the applicable state law; and (c) whether the work, taken as a whole, lacks serious literary, artistic, political, or scientific value. We do not adopt as a constitutional standard the *"utterly* without redeeming social value" test of *Memoirs v. Massachusetts*, 383 U.S., at 419; that concept has never commanded the adherence of more than three Justices at one time. See *supra*, at 21.

PARIS ADULT THEATRE I v. SLATON
413 U.S. 49 (1973)

MR. CHIEF JUSTICE BURGER delivered the opinion of the Court.

Petitioners are two Atlanta, Georgia, movie theaters and their owners and managers, operating in the style of "adult" theaters. On December 28, 1970, respondents, the local state district attorney and the solicitor for the local state trial court, filed civil complaints in the court alleging that petitioners were exhibiting to the public for paid admission two allegedly obscene films, contrary to Georgia Code Ann. § 26–2101. The two films in question, "Magic Mirror," and "It All Comes Out in the End," depict sexual conduct characterized by the Georgia Supreme Court as "hard core pornography" leaving "little to the imagination."

Respondents' complaints, made on behalf of the State of Georgia, demanded that the two films be declared obscene and that petitioners be enjoined from exhibiting the films. The exhibition of the films was not enjoined, but a temporary injunction was granted *ex parte* by the local trial court, restraining petitioners from destroying the films or removing them from the jurisdiction. Petitioners were further ordered to have one print each of the films in court on January 13, 1971, together with the proper viewing equipment.

On January 13, 1971, 15 days after the proceedings began, the films were produced by petitioners at a jury-waived trial. Certain photographs, also produced at trial, were stipulated to portray the single entrance to both Paris Adult Theatre I and Paris Adult Theatre II as it appeared at the time of the complaints. These photographs show a conventional, inoffensive theater entrance, without any pictures, but with signs indicating that the theaters exhibit "Atlanta's Finest Mature Feature Films." On the door itself is a sign saying: "Adult Theatre—You must be 21 and able to prove it. If viewing the nude body offends you, Please Do Not Enter."

The two films were exhibited to the trial court. The only other state evidence was testimony by criminal investigators that they had paid admission to see the films and that nothing on the outside of the theater indicated the full nature of what was shown. In particular, nothing indicated that the films depicted—as they did—scenes of simulated fellatio, cunnilingus, and group sex intercourse. There was no evidence presented that minors had ever entered the theaters. Nor was there evidence presented that petitioners had a systematic policy of barring minors, apart from posting signs at the entrance. On April 12, 1971, the trial judge dismissed respondents' complaints. He assumed "that obscenity is established," but stated:

> "It appears to the Court that the display of these films in a commercial theatre, when surrounded by requisite notice to the public of their nature and by reasonable protection against the exposure of these films to minors, is constitutionally permissible."

On appeal, the Georgia Supreme Court unanimously reversed. It assumed that the adult theaters in question barred minors and gave a full warning to the general public of the nature of the films shown, but held that the films were without protection under the First Amendment. Citing the opinion of this Court in *United States v. Reidel*, 402 U.S. 351 (1971), the Georgia court stated that "the sale and delivery of obscene material to willing adults is not protected under the first amendment." The Georgia court also held *Stanley v. Georgia*, 394 U.S. 557 (1969), to be inapposite since it did not deal with "the commercial distribution of pornography, but with the right of Stanley to possess, in the privacy of his home, pornographic films." 228 Ga. 343, 345, 185 S.E.2d 768, 769 (1971). After viewing the films, the Georgia Supreme Court held that their exhibition should have been enjoined, stating:

> "The films in this case leave little to the imagination. It is plain what they purport to depict, that is, conduct of the most salacious character. We hold that these films are also hard core pornography, and the showing of such films should have been enjoined since their exhibition is not protected by the first amendment." *Id.*, at 347, 185 S.E.2d, at 770. . . .

We categorically disapprove the theory, apparently adopted by the trial judge, that obscene, pornographic films acquire constitutional immunity from state regulation simply because they are exhibited for consenting adults only. This holding was properly rejected by the Georgia Supreme Court. Although we have often recognized the high importance of the state interest in regulating the exposure of obscene materials to juveniles and unconsenting adults, see *Miller v. California, ante*, at 18–20; *Stanley v. Georgia*, 394 U.S., at 567; *Redrup v. New York*, 386 U.S. 767, 769 (1967), this Court has never declared these to be the only legitimate state interests permitting regulation of obscene material.

Dissenting Opinion   MR. JUSTICE DOUGLAS, dissenting.

My Brother Brennan is to be commended for seeking a new path through the thicket which the Court entered when it undertook to sustain the constitutionality of obscenity laws and to place limits on their application. I have expressed on numerous occasions my disagreement with the basic decision that held that "obscenity" was not protected by the First Amendment. I disagreed also with the definitions that evolved. Art and literature reflect tastes; and tastes, like musical appreciation, are hardly reducible to precise definitions. That is one reason I have always felt that "obscenity" was not an exception to the First Amendment. For matters of taste, like matters of belief, turn on the idiosyncrasies of individuals. They are too personal to define and too emotional and vague to apply, as witness the prison term for Ralph Ginzburg, *Ginzburg v. United States*, 383 U.S. 463, not for what he printed but for the sexy manner in which he advertised his creations.

The other reason I could not bring myself to conclude that "obscenity" was not covered by the First Amendment was that prior to the adoption of our Constitution and Bill of Rights the Colonies had no law excluding "obscenity" from the regime of freedom of expression and press that then existed. I could find no such laws; and more important, our leading colonial expert, Julius Goebel, could find none, J. Goebel, Development of Legal Institutions (1946); J. Goebel, Felony and Misdemeanor (1937). So I became convinced that the creation of the "obscenity" exception to the First Amendment was a legislative and judicial *tour de force*; that if we were to have such a regime of censorship and punishment, it should be done by constitutional amendment.

People are, of course, offended by many offerings made by merchants in this area. They are also offended by political pronouncements, sociological themes, and by stories of official misconduct. The list of activities and publications and pronouncements that offend someone is endless. Some of it goes on in private; some of it is inescapably public, as when a government official generates crime, becomes a blatant offender of the moral sensibilities of the people, engages in burglary, or breaches the privacy of the telephone, the conference room, or the home. Life in this crowded modern technological world creates many offensive statements and many offensive deeds. There is no protection against offensive ideas, only against offensive conduct.

"Obscenity" at most is the expression of offensive ideas. There are regimes in the world where ideas "offensive" to the majority (or at least to those who control the majority) are suppressed. There life proceeds at a monotonous pace. Most of us would find that world offensive. One of the most offensive experiences in my life was a visit to a nation where bookstalls were filled only with books on mathematics and books on religion. . . .

When man was first in the jungle he took care of himself. When he entered a societal group, controls were necessarily imposed. But our society—unlike most in the world—presupposes that freedom and liberty are in a frame of reference that makes the individual, not government, the keeper of his tastes, beliefs, and ideas. That is the philosophy of the First Amendment; and it is the article of faith that sets us apart from most nations in the world.

Dissenting Opinion   MR. JUSTICE BRENNAN, with whom MR. JUSTICE STEWART and MR. JUSTICE MARSHALL join, dissenting.

This case requires the Court to confront once again the vexing problem of reconciling state efforts to suppress sexually oriented expression with the protections of the First Amendment, as applied to the States through the Fourteenth Amendment. No other aspect of the First Amendment has, in recent years, demanded so substantial a commitment of our time, generated such disharmony of views, and remained so resistant to the formulation of stable and manageable standards. I am convinced that the approach initiated 16 years ago in *Roth v. United States,* 354 U.S. 476 (1957), and culminating in the Court's decision today, cannot bring stability to this area of the law without jeopardizing fundamental First Amendment values, and I have concluded that the time has come to make a significant departure from that approach. . . .

In *Roth v. United States,* 354 U.S. 476 (1957), the Court held that obscenity, although expression, falls outside the area of speech or press constitutionally protected under the First and Fourteenth Amendments against state or federal infringement. But at the same time we emphasized in *Roth* that "sex and obscenity are not synonymous," *id.,* at 487, and that matter which is sexually oriented but not obscene is fully protected by the Constitution. For we recognized that "[s]ex, a great and mysterious motive force in human life, has indisputably been a subject of absorbing interest to mankind through the ages; it is one of the vital problems of human interest and public concern." *Ibid. Roth* rested, in other words, on what has been termed a two-level approach to the question of obscenity. While much criticized, that approach has been endorsed by all but two members of this Court who have addressed the question since *Roth.* Yet our efforts to implement that approach demonstrate that agreement on the existence of something called "obscenity" is still a long and painful step from agreement on a workable definition of the term.

Recognizing that "the freedoms of expression . . . are vulnerable to gravely damaging yet barely visible encroachments," *Bantam Books, Inc. v. Sullivan,* 372 U.S. 58, 66 (1963), we have demanded that "sensitive tools" be used to carry out the "separation of legitimate from illegitimate speech." *Speiser v. Randall,* 357 U.S. 513, 525 (1958). The essence of our problem in the obscenity area is that we have been unable to provide "sensitive tools" to separate obscenity from other sexually oriented but constitutionally protected speech, so that efforts to suppress the former do not spill over into the suppression of the latter. The attempt, as the late Mr. Justice Harlan observed, has only "produced a variety of views among the members of the Court unmatched in any other course of constitutional adjudication." *Interstate Circuit, Inc. v. Dallas,* 390 U.S. 676, 704–705 (1968) (separate opinion).

To be sure, five members of the Court did agree in *Roth* that obscenity could be determined by asking "whether to the average person, applying contemporary community standards, the dominant theme of the material taken as a whole appeals to prurient interest." 354 U.S., at 489. But agreement on that test—achieved in the abstract and without reference to the particular material before the Court, see *id.*, at 481 n. 8—was, to say the least, short lived. By 1967 the following views had emerged: Mr. Justice Black and Mr. Justice Douglas consistently maintained that government is wholly powerless to regulate any sexually oriented matter on the ground of its obscenity. See, *e.g. Ginzburg v. United States*, 383 U.S. 463, 476, 482 (1966) (dissenting opinions); *Jacobellis v. Ohio*, 378 U.S. 184, 196 (1964) (concurring opinion); *Roth v. United States*, supra, at 508 (dissenting opinion). Mr. Justice Harlan, on the other hand, believed that the Federal Government in the exercise of its enumerated powers could control the distribution of "hard core" pornography, while the States were afforded more latitude to "[ban] any material which, taken as a whole, has been reasonably found in state judicial proceedings to treat with sex in a fundamentally offensive manner, under rationally established criteria for judging such material." *Jacobellis v. Ohio, supra*, at 204 (dissenting opinion). See also, *e.g.*, *Ginzburg v. United States, supra*, at 493 (dissenting opinion); *A Quantity of Books v. Kansas*, 378 U.S. 205, 215 (1964) (dissenting opinion joined by Clark, J.); *Roth, supra*, at 496 (separate opinion). Mr. Justice Stewart regarded "hard core" pornography as the limit of both federal and state power. See, *e.g.*, *Ginzburg v. United States, supra*, at 497 (dissenting opinion); *Jacobellis v. Ohio, supra*, at 197 (concurring opinion). . . .

In the face of this divergence of opinion the Court began the practice in *Redrup v. New York*, 386 U.S. 767 (1967), of *per curiam* reversals of convictions for the dissemination of materials that at least five members of the Court, applying their separate tests, deemed not to be obscene. This approach capped the attempt in *Roth* to separate all forms of sexually oriented expression into two categories—the one subject to full governmental suppression and the other beyond the reach of governmental regulation to the same extent as any other protected form of speech or press. Today a majority of the Court offers a slightly altered formulation of the basic *Roth* test, while leaving entirely unchanged the underlying approach. . . .

Any effort to draw a constitutionally acceptable boundary on state power must resort to such indefinite concepts as "prurient interest," "patent offensiveness," "serious literary value," and the like. The meaning of these concepts necessarily varies with the experience, outlook, and even idiosyncrasies of the person defining them. Although we have assumed that obscenity does exist and that we "know it when [we] see it," *Jacobellis v. Ohio, supra*, at 197 (Stewart, J., concurring), we are manifestly unable to describe it in advance except by reference to concepts so elusive that they fail to distinguish clearly between protected and unprotected speech. . . .

Our experience since *Roth* requires us not only to abandon the effort to pick out obscene materials on a case-by-case basis, but also to reconsider a fundamental postulate of *Roth*: that there exists a definable class of sexually oriented expression that may be totally suppressed by the Federal and State Governments. Assuming that such a class of expression does in fact exist, I am forced to conclude that the concept of "obscenity" cannot be defined with sufficient specificity and clarity to provide fair notice to persons who create and distribute sexually oriented materials, to prevent substantial erosion of protected speech as a byproduct of the attempt to suppress unprotected speech, and to avoid very costly institutional harms. Given these inevitable side effects of state efforts to suppress what is assumed to be *unprotected* speech, we must scrutinize with care the state interest that is asserted to justify the suppression. For in the absence of some very substantial interest in suppressing such speech, we can hardly condone the ill effects that seem to flow inevitably from the effort. . . .

The opinions of *Redrup* and *Stanley* reflected our emerging view that the state interests in protecting children and in protecting unconsenting adults may stand on a different footing from the other asserted state interests. . . .

It is surely the duty of this Court, as expounder of the Constitution, to provide a remedy for the present unsatisfactory state of affairs. I do not pretend to have found a complete and infallible answer to what Mr. Justice Harlan called "the intractable obscenity problem." *Interstate Circuit, Inc. v. Dallas*, 390 U.S. at 704 (separate opinion). See also *Memoirs v. Massachusetts*, 383 U.S., at 456 (dissenting opinion). Difficult questions must still be faced, notably in the areas of distribution to juveniles and offensive exposure to unconsenting adults. Whatever the extent of state power to regulate in those areas, it should be clear that the view I espouse today would introduce a large measure of clarity to this troubled area, would reduce the institutional pressure on this Court and the rest of the State and Federal Judiciary, and would guarantee fuller freedom of expression while leaving room for the protection of legitimate governmental interests. Since the Supreme Court of Georgia erroneously concluded that the State has power to suppress sexually oriented material even in the absence of distribution to juveniles or exposure to unconsenting adults, I would reverse that judgment and remand the case to that court for further proceedings not inconsistent with this opinion.

JENKINS v. GEORGIA
418 U.S. 153 (1974)

MR. JUSTICE REHNQUIST delivered the opinion of the Court. . .

There is little to be found in the record about the film "Carnal Knowledge" other than the film itself. However, appellant has supplied a variety of information and critical commentary, the authenticity of which appellee does not dispute. The film appeared on many "Ten Best" lists for 1971, the year in which it was released. Many but not all of the reviews were favorable. We believe that the following passage from a review which appeared in the Saturday Review is a reasonably accurate description of the film:

> "[It is basically a story] of two young college men, roommates and lifelong friends forever preoccupied with their sex lives. Both are first met as virgins. Nicholson is the most knowledgeable and attractive of the two; speaking colloquially, he is a burgeoning bastard. Art Garfunkel is his friend, the nice but troubled guy straight out of those early Feiffer cartoons, but real. He falls in love with the lovely Susan (Candice Bergen) and unknowingly shares her with his college buddy. As the 'safer' one of the two, he is selected by Susan for marriage.
>
> "The time changes. Both men are in their thirties, pursuing successful careers in New York. Nicholson has been running through an average of a dozen women a year but has never managed to meet the right one, the one with the full bosom, the good legs, the properly rounded bottom. More than that, each and every one is a threat to his malehood and peace of mind, until at last, in a bar, he finds Ann-Margret, an aging bachelor girl with striking cleavage and, quite obviously, something of a past. 'Why don't we shack up?' she suggests. They do and a horrendous relationship ensues, complicated mainly by her paranoidal desire to marry. Meanwhile, what of Garfunkel? The sparks have gone out of his marriage, the sex has lost its savor, and Garfunkel tries once more. And later, even more foolishly, again."

Appellee contends essentially that under Miller the obscenity vel non of the film "Carnal Knowledge" was a question for the jury, and that the jury having resolved the question against appellant, and there being some evidence to support its findings, the judgment of conviction should be affirmed. We turn to the language of Miller to evaluate appellee's contention.

Miller states that the questions of what appeals to the "prurient interest" and what is "patently offensive" under the obscenity test which it formulates are "essentially questions of fact." 413 U.S., at 30. "When triers of fact are asked to decide whether 'the average person, applying contemporary community standards' would consider certain materials 'prurient' it would be unrealistic to require that the answer be based on some abstract formulation. . . . To require a State to structure obscenity proceedings around evidence of a *national* 'community standard' would be an exercise in futility. *Ibid.* We held in *Paris Adult Theatre I v. Slaton*, 413 U.S. 49 (1973), decided on the same day, that expert testimony as to obscenity is not necessary when the films at issue are themselves placed in evidence. *Id.*, at 56.

But all of this does not lead us to agree with the Supreme Court of Georgia's apparent conclusion that the jury's verdict against appellant virtually precluded all further appellate review of appellant's assertion that his exhibition of the film was protected by the First and Fourteenth Amendments. Even though questions of appeal to the "prurient interest" or of patent offensiveness are "essentially questions of fact," it would be a serious misreading of *Miller* to conclude that juries have unbridled discretion in determining what is "patently offensive." Not only did we there say that "the First Amendment values applicable to the States through the Fourteenth Amendment are adequately protected by the ultimate power of appellate courts to conduct an independent review of constitutional claims when necessary," 413 U.S., at 25, but we made it plain that under that holding "no one will be subject to prosecution for the sale or exposure of obscene materials unless these materials depict or describe patently offensive 'hard core' sexual conduct. . . ." *Id.*, at 27.

We also took pains in *Miller* to "give a few plain examples of what a state statute could define for regulation under part (b) of the standard announced," that is, the requirement of patent offensiveness. *Id.*, at 25. These examples included "representations of descriptions of ultimate sexual acts, normal or perverted, actual or simulated," and "representations or descriptions of masturbation, excretory functions, and lewd exhibition of the genitals." *Ibid.* While this did not purport to be an exhaustive catalog of what juries might find patently offensive, it was certainly intended to fix substantive constitutional limitations, deriving from the First Amendment, on the type of material subject to such a determination. It would be wholly at odds with this aspect of *Miller* to uphold an obscenity conviction based upon a defendant's depiction of a woman with a bare midriff, even though a properly charged jury unanimously agreed on a verdict of guilty.

Our own viewing of the film satisfies us that "Carnal Knowledge" could not be found under the *Miller* standards to depict sexual conduct in a patently offensive way. Nothing in the movie falls within either of the two examples given in *Miller* of material which may constitutionally be found to meet the "patently offensive" element of those standards, nor is there anything sufficiently similar to such material to justify similar treatment. While the subject matter of the picture is, in a broader sense, sex, and there are scenes in which sexual conduct including "ultimate sexual acts" is to be understood to be taking place, the camera does not focus on the bodies of the actors at such times. There is no exhibition whatever of the actors' genitals, lewd or other-wise, during these scenes. There are occasional scenes of nudity, but nudity alone is not enough to make material legally obscene under the *Miller* standards.

Appellant's showing of the film "Carnal Knowledge" is simply not the "public portrayal of hard core sexual conduct for its own sake, and for the ensuing commercial gain" which we said was punishable in *Miller*. *Id.*, at 35. We hold that the film could not, as a matter of constitutional law, be found to depict sexual conduct in a patently offensive way, and that it is therefore not outside the protection of the First and Fourteenth Amendments because it is obscene. No other basis appearing in the record upon which the judgment of conviction can be sustained, we reverse the judgment of the Supreme Court of Georgia.

Reversed.

.... DISCUSSION QUESTIONS ....

1. The current definition of obscenity says that written descriptions of obscene acts are just as obscene as pictures and movies. Do you think that such written descriptions are worthy of more protection by the First Amendment than pictures and movies, or is the Court right to treat them equally?
2. Does it bother you that two part-time clerks were sent to prison for selling obscene magazines? Why?
3. If you were asked to write a definition of obscenity that most people could understand, what would you say?
4. Is nude dancing a form of speech? The justices of the Supreme Court think so. Why do they think so? Do you agree with them?
5. Art is apparently protected by the First Amendment. What is art?
6. Justice Douglas argued throughout his years on the Supreme Court that adults should be allowed to read and see anything they want to. Do you agree? What arguments can you come up with to counter him? What arguments can you come up with to support him? Do you think John Stuart Mill would agree with Justice Douglas?

CHAPTER
six

❀ ❀ ❀ ❀ ❀ ❀ ❀ ❀

Commercial Speech

.... DISCUSSION ....

For the first half of the twentieth century the Supreme Court seemed to implicitly accept the idea that the First Amendment protected only speech about important topics such as politics and religion and that it did not protect unimportant speech such as mere "commercial speech." Over time, the Court realized that commercial speech could be political and could play an important informational role in a democracy. As a result, the Court gradually expanded the right of free speech to include commercial speech.

BOYCOTTS AND FREE SPEECH

In the 1911 case of *Gompers v. Bucks Stove & Range Co.* (see p. 87), the Court reviewed the sentencing of Samuel Gompers, president of the American Federation of Labor, to one year in prison for contempt of court. As president of the AFL, Gompers was considered to be the publisher of its magazine, the *American Federationist*. A regular feature of this labor union publication was a list of companies that union members should not patronize. Companies got on this list by doing things that the AFL did not like, such as refusing to bargain with it over wages and hours. One company that found itself on the list, the Bucks Stove & Range Company, sued Gompers and convinced a judge to order him to take its name off the list. When Bucks Stove & Range Company discovered it had not been taken off the list, it asked the judge to find Gompers in contempt of court for refusing to obey the judge's order. The judge agreed and sentenced Gompers to one year in prison for contempt of court. Gompers appealed to the U.S. Supreme Court, arguing that all Americans, even union leaders, have a right of free speech that includes the right to speak to their fellow citizens, in this case fellow union members, about companies that are unfair to labor. A unanimous Supreme Court disagreed. The justices could not find anything in the First Amendment that protected the right to encourage people to boycott a company. The Court did overturn Gompers's conviction on a technicality, however, and ordered him to be retried.

COMMERCIAL SPEECH VS. POLITICAL AND RELIGIOUS SPEECH

In the 1942 case of *Valentine v. Chrestensen*, the Court was faced with a city ordinance that outlawed the distribution of leaflets with commercial advertising. While the Court had upheld the right of people to pass out leaflets discussing political or religious issues, a unanimous Supreme Court declared in this case that the First Amendment did not protect mere "commercial speech." Cities were free to prohibit the distribution of commercial leaflets if they chose to do so.

In 1951 the Court ruled that it was acceptable for the city of Alexandria, Louisiana, to make it illegal to sell magazine subscriptions door to door (*Breard v. Alexandria*). While the Court had gone a long way in the 1940s to protect the right of political and religious speakers to go door to door in order to spread their messages, sell literature, and ask for contributions, the Court was not willing to extend the same right to people who were simply trying to sell something. Three justices dissented. They were bothered by having to draw a line between the *Watchtower*, a religious publication the sale of which the Court had protected on several occasions, and various news magazines. They thought that the sale of magazines was different from the sale of other products and should enjoy some protection from the First Amendment.

CHANGING VIEWS OF COMMERCIAL SPEECH

The Court's view of commercial speech began to change in 1975 with the case of *Bigelow v. Virginia*. It was a violation of Virginia law to encourage abortions. A group in New York put an advertisement in a Virginia newspaper telling people who wanted abortions that there was help for them in New York. Seven justices believed that the prosecution of these people was an unconstitutional interference with the right of free speech. They pointed out that this advertisement was more than just a "commercial advertisement." They also thought that Virginia's desire to interfere with the right of women to obtain abortions was not entitled to much weight when balanced against the rights of the New York group to speak out on this important issue. The members of the Court began to see the problems that were going to come up if it persisted in limiting the right of free speech to noncommercial speech.

In 1976 the Court decided to expand the reach of the First Amendment to include commercial speech. The case involved a Virginia law that made it illegal for pharmacies to advertise the price of drugs (*Virginia Pharmacy Bd. v. Consumer Council*). The Court accepted the argument that society in general, and consumers in particular, has a right to the "free flow of information." While recognizing that commercial speech would be subject to more government regulation than other types of speech, the Court was willing to bring this type of speech under the protection of the First Amendment. The Court specifically overruled the decisions handed down in 1942 and 1951 that allowed cities and states to outlaw the passing out of commercial leaflets and the door to door sale of magazine subscriptions. The Court did not mention the *Gompers* case. Only Justice Rehnquist dissented from this decision.

Once the door was open, many kinds of advertising that had been outlawed suddenly became legal. In the 1977 case of *Linmark Associates Inc. v. Willingboro*, a unanimous Court overturned a city ordinance that outlawed the placing of "For Sale" or "Sold" signs in the front yards of houses. The city said that its goal was to stop the flow of white people out of the neighborhood. The Court did not think this was a good enough reason to justify the limitation of the right of free speech. People have a right to put signs in their front yards, even if they are commercial signs telling the world that their house is for sale.

PROFESSIONS AND ADVERTISING

Also in 1977 the Court started down a long road when it decided, in a five-to-four decision, that lawyers and other professionals have a constitutional right to advertise under the First Amendment (*Bates v. State Bar of Arizona*). A series of decisions followed that outlined which regulations of attorney advertising were acceptable and which violated the First Amendment. For example, the Court ruled in 1982 that states could not prevent attorneys from sending out notices to the general public announcing the opening of a new office (*In Re R.M.J.*). In 1985 the Court ruled that attorneys have a right to place advertisements in newspapers telling people with particular types of legal problems that they are interested in those kinds of cases (*Zauderer v. Office of Disciplinary Counsel*). In 1988 the Court ruled that attorneys have a right to send out advertisements through the mail to potential clients (*Shapero v. Kentucky Bar Association*). In 1990 the Court ruled that attorneys have a right to say in their advertisements that they have been certified by national training programs (*Peel v. Attorney Disciplinary Comm.*). Finally, in 1993, the Court ruled that certified public accountants have a constitutional right to solicit potential clients in person (*Edenfield v. Fane*).

BUSINESSES AND FREE SPEECH

Other decisions were of more interest to the general business community. In 1978 the Court ruled, with a five-to-four decision, that Massachusetts could not limit the ability of business corporations to buy advertising in order to influence the outcome of a referendum (*First Nat. Bank of Boston v. Bellotti*). The five-member majority believed that corporations have the right under the First Amendment to speak out on both political and commercial issues. They pointed out that the goal of the First Amendment is to protect the public's right to hear as well as other people's right to speak. These justices thought that the public has a right to hear what large corporations think about issues put to a public vote, and that the marketplace of ideas has room for the opinions of large corporations. The four dissenting justices were an unusual group: three liberals and the most conservative justice. The three liberals, Justices White, Brennan, and Marshall, thought that the real question in this case was whether or not a state could prevent corporate management from using the corporate treasury to propagate views having no connection with the corporation's business. They argued that the function of the First Amendment is to protect the right of free speech in order to allow individual self-fulfillment; corporations are not individuals and do not achieve self-fulfillment. The conservative Justice Rehnquist argued that corporations are not people, but artificial creatures created by state governments, and those state governments should be allowed to regulate and control the creatures they create. In his opinion, the rights in the Bill of Rights are "individual rights" and should not be extended to corporations. The majority of justices clearly did not want to get into a situation where an individual business owner would be allowed to spend money on speech activities while a corporation would not. They did not think the "form" of the business should have anything to do with whether or not speech was protected.

In 1980 the Court ruled that states could not prevent electric utility companies from encouraging the use of electricity (*Central Hudson Gas & Elec. v. Public Service Comm.*). The Court ruled that business has a right to speak out and encourage people to engage in lawful activities as long as the advertisements are not misleading. If government wants to limit this kind of speech, it must have a very good reason; the Court thought that the desire to conserve energy was not a good enough reason in this case. Essentially, the Court said what John Stuart Mill had said in 1859: the answer to speech the government does not like is not the suppression of speech, but more speech. The government is free to speak out in a variety of ways in order to encourage people to stop using energy. In fact, the government can take action, such as raising electric rates or placing high taxes on energy, to discourage the use of energy. What the government cannot do is stop others, including public utilities, from speaking out on the issue.

BOYCOTTS REVISITED

In 1982 the Court finally returned to the boycott question with a case involving a boycott of white merchants in Claiborne County, Mississippi, by the National Association for the Advancement of Colored People (*NAACP v. Claiborne Hardware Co.* [see p. 88]). In order to force political change, the NAACP had sent small children to stand in front of white-owned stores with signs reminding black people not to shop there. It had also sent individuals wearing black hats to take down the names of any black people seen patronizing white-owned stores; those names were then published in a black-owned newspaper. The NAACP also had published a list of the white-owned stores that were the target of the boycott. The question in this case was whether the NAACP could be made to pay damages because a few individuals resorted to violence. The Court ruled that it could not, given the facts of this case. All the activities engaged in by the NAACP were protected by the First Amendment. For the first time, the Court ruled, with a unanimous decision, that the act of speaking about and engaging in a boycott is protected by the First Amendment. At the same time, the Court made it clear that threats and violence are not protected.

CONCLUSION

The story of commercial speech illustrates how much the right of free speech has expanded during the twentieth century. As the years passed, the Court came to see the functions of the right of free speech as many and important. While the right of free speech had been seen early in the twentieth century as simply an adjunct to the need to have an effective and efficient democracy, it came to be seen as a positive good in its own right. Not only did voters have a right to hear about candidates, but consumers had a right to hear about products and services. The Court discovered that even commercial speech has a political element, whether it is speech about abortion or racial integration.

The Court also came to see the right of free speech as more than just the right to speak. The right of free speech includes the right of consumers to be informed about drug prices or electricity use. It also includes the right of victims to hear from an attorney and the right of businesses to speak out on important public issues, even if the businesses are corporations or public utilities. More and more the Court thought that the safe decision in difficult cases was the decision that would expand the right of free speech, not the decision that would limit information in the marketplace of ideas.

John Stuart Mill had said in *On Liberty* that governments that wished to improve their citizens were within their rights to remonstrate with them, reason with them, persuade them, or entreat them, but not to compel them.

Mill believed that the answer to speech is more speech, not the suppression of speech. Today the Supreme Court agrees with the central point of Mill's book. Educated and free citizens can be allowed to make both the mundane and the fundamental decisions that affect their lives if society provides them with enough information. Toward that end, the right of free speech becomes more and more central for a society made up of such people.

CASE DECISIONS

In 1911 a unanimous Court ruled that the First Amendment did not protect those seeking to encourage the boycott of a company. Justice Lamar wrote the opinion in *Gompers v. Bucks Stove & Range Co.*, which is included here.

Seventy years later, in 1981, another unanimous Court held in *NAACP v. Claiborne Hardware Co.*, that the First Amendment does protect the right to speak about a boycott. Justice Stevens wrote the opinion for the Court, which is included here. Following are excerpts from the case decisions.

❋ ❋ ❋ ❋ ❋ ❋ ❋ ❋ ❋

GOMPERS v. BUCKS STOVE & RANGE CO.
221 U.S. 418 (1911)

MR. JUSTICE LAMAR . . . delivered the opinion of the court.

The defendants, Samuel Gompers, John Mitchell and Frank Morrison, were found guilty of contempt of court in making certain publications prohibited by an injunction from the Supreme Court of the District of Columbia. They were sentenced to imprisonment for twelve, nine and six months respectively, and this proceeding is prosecuted to reverse that judgment.

The order alleged to have been violated was granted in the equity suit of the "*Bucks Stove & Range Company v. The American Federation of Labor and others*," in which the court issued an injunction restraining all the defendants from boycotting the complainant, or from publishing or otherwise making any statement that the Bucks Stove & Range Company was, or had been, on the "Unfair" or "We don't patronize" lists. Some months later the complainant filed a petition in the cause, alleging that the three defendants above-named, parties to the original cause, in contempt of court and in violation of its order, had disobeyed the injunction by publishing statements which either directly or indirectly called attention to the fact that the Bucks Stove & Range Company was on the "Unfair" list, and that they had thereby continued the boycott which had been enjoined.

The defendants filed separate answers under oath, and, each denied: (1) That they had been in contempt or disregard of the court's orders: (2) That the statements complained of constituted any violation of the order; and, on the argument, (3) contended that if the publication should be construed to amount to a violation of the injunction they could not be punished therefor, because the court must not only possess jurisdiction of the parties and the subject-matter, but must have authority to render the particular judgment. Insisting, therefore, that the court could not abridge the liberty of speech or freedom of the press, the defendants claim that the injunction as a whole was a nullity, and that no contempt proceeding could be maintained for any disobedience of any of its provisions, general or special.

If this last proposition were sound it would be unnecessary to go further into an examination of the case or to determine whether the defendants had in fact disobeyed the prohibitions contained in the injunction. *Ex parte Rowland*, 104 U.S. 612. But we will not enter upon a discussion of the constitutional question raised, for the general provisions of the injunction did not, in terms, restrain any form of publication. The defendants' attack on this part of the injunction raises no question as to an abridgment of free speech, but involves the power of a court of equity to enjoin the defendants from continuing a boycott which, by words and signals, printed or spoken, caused or threatened irreparable damage.

Courts differ as to what constitutes a boycott that may be enjoined. All hold that there must be a conspiracy causing irreparable damage to the business or property of the complainant. Some hold that a boycott against the complainant, by a combination of persons not immediately connected with him in business, can be restrained. Others hold that the secondary boycott can be enjoined, where the conspiracy extends not only to injuring the complainant, but secondarily coerces or attempts to coerce his customers to refrain from dealing with him by threats that unless they do they themselves will be boycotted. Others hold that no boycott can be enjoined unless there are acts of physical violence, or intimidation caused by threats of physical violence.

But whatever the requirement of the particular jurisdiction, as to the conditions on which the injunction against a boycott may issue; when these facts exist, the strong current of authority is that the publication and use of letters, circulars and printed matter may constitute a means whereby a boycott is unlawfully continued, and their use for such purpose may amount to a violation of the order of injunction.

NAACP v. CLAIBORNE HARDWARE CO.
458 U.S. 886 (1982)

JUSTICE STEVENS delivered the opinion of the Court.

The term "concerted action" encompasses unlawful conspiracies and constitutionally protected assemblies. The "looseness and pliability" of legal doctrine applicable to concerted action led Justice Jackson to note that certain joint activities have a "chameleon-like" character. The boycott of white merchants in Claiborne County, Miss., that gave rise to this litigation had such a character; it included elements of criminality and elements of majesty. Evidence that fear of reprisals caused some black citizens to withhold their patronage from respondents' businesses convinced the Supreme Court of Mississippi that the entire boycott was unlawful and that each of the 92 petitioners was liable for all of its economic consequences. Evidence that persuasive rhetoric, determination to remedy past injustices, and a host of voluntary decisions by free citizens were the critical factors in the boycott's success presents us with the question whether the state court's judgment is consistent with the Constitution of the United States.

In March 1966, black citizens of Port Gibson, Miss., and other areas of Claiborne County presented white elected officials with a list of particularized demands for racial equality and integration. The complainants did not receive a satisfactory response and, at a local National Association for the Advancement of Colored People (NAACP) meeting at the First Baptist Church, several hundred black persons voted to place a boycott on white merchants in the area. On October 31, 1969, several of the merchants filed suit in state court to recover losses caused by the boycott and to enjoin future boycott activity. . . .

In late 1965 or early 1966, Charles Evers, the Field Secretary of the NAACP, helped organize the Claiborne County Branch of the NAACP. The pastor of the First Baptist Church, James Dorsey, was elected president of the Branch; regular meetings were conducted each Tuesday evening at the church. At about the same time, a group of black citizens formed a Human Relations Committee and presented a petition for redress of grievances to civic and business leaders of the white community. In response, a biracial committee—including five of the petitioners and several of the respondents—was organized and held a series of unproductive meetings.

The black members of the committee then prepared a further petition entitled "Demands for Racial Justice." This petition was presented for approval at the local NAACP meeting conducted on the first Tuesday evening in March. As described by the chancellor, "the approximately 500 people present voted their approval unanimously." On March 14, 1966, the petition was presented to public officials of Port Gibson and Claiborne County.

The petition included 19 specific demands. It called for the desegregation of all public schools and public facilities, the hiring of black policemen, public improvements in black residential areas, selection of blacks for jury duty, integration of bus stations so that blacks could use all facilities, and an end to verbal abuse by law enforcement officers. It stated that "Negroes are not to be addressed by terms as 'boy,' 'girl,' 'shine,' 'uncle,' or any other offensive term, but as 'Mr.,' 'Mrs.,' or 'Miss,' as is the case with other citizens." As described by the chancellor, the purpose of the demands "was to gain equal rights and opportunities for Negro citizens." The petition further provided that black leaders hoped it would not be necessary to resort to the "selective buying campaigns" that had been used in other communities. On March 23, two demands that had been omitted from the original petition were added, one of which provided: "All stores must employ Negro clerks and cashiers." This supplemental petition stated that a response was expected by April 1.

A favorable response was not received. On April 1, 1966, the Claiborne County NAACP conducted another meeting at the First Baptist Church. As described by the chancellor:

> "Several hundred black people attended the meeting, and the purpose was to decide what action should be taken relative to the twenty-one demands. Speeches were made by Evers and others, and a vote was taken. It was the unanimous vote of those present, without dissent, to place a boycott on the white merchants of Port Gibson and Claiborne County." App. to Pet. for Cert. 15b.

The boycott was underway. . . .

The boycott of white merchants at issue in this case took many forms. The boycott was launched at a meeting of a local branch of the NAACP attended by several hundred persons. Its acknowledged purpose was to secure compliance by both civic and business leaders with a lengthy list of demands for equality and racial justice. The boycott was supported by speeches and nonviolent picketing. Participants repeatedly encouraged others to join in its cause.

Each of these elements of the boycott is a form of speech or conduct that is ordinarily entitled to protection under the First and Fourteenth Amendments. The black citizens named as defendants in this action banded together and collectively expressed their dissatisfaction with a social structure that had denied them rights to equal treatment and respect. As we so recently acknowledged in *Citizens Against Rent Control/Coalition for Fair Housing v. Berkeley*, 454 U.S. 290, 294, "the practice of persons sharing common views banding together to achieve a common end is deeply embedded in the American political process." We recognized that "by collective effort individuals can make their views known, when, individually, their voices would be faint or lost." *Ibid.* In emphasizing "the importance of freedom of association in guaranteeing the right of people to make their voices heard on public issues," *id.*, at 295, we noted the words of Justice Harlan, writing for the Court in *NAACP v. Alabama ex rel. Patterson*, 357 U.S. 449, 460:

"Effective advocacy of both public and private points of view, particularly controversial ones, is undeniably enhanced by group association, as this Court has more than once recognized by remarking upon the close nexus between the freedoms of speech and assembly."

The Chief Justice stated for the Court in *Citizens Against Rent Control*: "There are, of course, some activities, legal if engaged in by one, yet illegal if performed in concert with others, but political expression is not one of them." 454 U.S., at 296. . . .

Speech itself also was used to further the aims of the boycott. Nonparticipants repeatedly were urged to join the common cause, both through public address and through personal solicitation. These elements of the boycott involve speech in its most direct form. In addition, names of boycott violators were read aloud at meetings at the First Baptist Church and published in a local black newspaper. Petitioners admittedly sought to persuade others to join the boycott through social pressure and the "threat" of social ostracism. Speech does not lose its protected character, however, simply because it may embarrass others or coerce them into action. As Justice Rutledge, in describing the protection afforded by the First Amendment, explained:

"It extends to more than abstract discussion, unrelated to action. The First Amendment is a charter for government, not for an institution of learning. 'Free trade in ideas' means free trade in the opportunity to persuade to action, not merely to describe facts." *Thomas v. Collins*, 323 U.S. 516, 537. . . .

In litigation of this kind the stakes are high. Concerted action is a powerful weapon. History teaches that special dangers are associated with conspiratorial activity. And yet one of the foundations of our society is the right of individuals to combine with other persons in pursuit of a common goal by lawful means.

At times the difference between lawful and unlawful collective action may be identified easily by reference to its purpose. In this case, however, petitioners' ultimate objectives were unquestionably legitimate. The charge of illegality—like the claim of constitutional protection—derives from the means employed by the participants to achieve those goals. The use of speeches, marches, and threats of social ostracism cannot provide the basis for a damages award. But violent conduct is beyond the pale of constitutional protection.

The taint of violence colored the conduct of some of the petitioners. They, of course, may be held liable for the consequences of their violent deeds. The burden of demonstrating that it colored the entire collective effort, however, is not satisfied by evidence that violence occurred or even that violence contributed to the success of the boycott. A massive and prolonged effort tc change the social, political, and economic structure of a local environment cannot be characterized as a violent conspiracy simply by reference to the ephemeral consequences of relatively few violent acts. Such a characteriza-tion must be supported by findings that adequately disclose the evidentiary basis for concluding that specific parties agreed to use unlawful means, that carefully identify the impact of such unlawful conduct, and that recognize the importance of avoiding the imposition of punishment for constitutionally protected activity. The burden of demonstrating that fear rather than pro-tected conduct was the dominant force in the movement is heavy. A court must be wary of a claim that the true color of a forest is better revealed by reptiles hidden in the weeds than by the foliage of the countless freestanding trees. The findings of the chancellor, framed largely in the light of two legal theories rejected by the Mississippi Supreme Court, are constitutionally insufficient to support the judgment that all petitioners are liable for all losses resulting from the boycott.

The judgment is reversed. The case is remanded for further proceedings not inconsistent with this opinion.

It is so ordered.

DISCUSSION QUESTIONS

1. Why should we protect commercial speech?
2. The fact that many people throw leaflets on the ground is not a good enough reason to justify interfering with the passing out of political leaflets. Is it a good enough reason to prevent the passing out of commercial leaflets?
3. What reasons could a state put forward to justify limiting speech concerned with boycotts?
4. If a group of white consumers organized a boycott of black-owned businesses, would that be protected by the First Amendment?
5. Cities have been allowed to control the use of commercial signs in order to protect the aesthetics of the city. How far do you think a city can go in limiting commercial signs for this reason?

CHAPTER
seven
❖ ❖ ❖ ❖ ❖ ❖ ❖ ❖

The Rights of a Free Press

One of the consistent features of the twentieth century has been a certain amount of conflict between the press and public officials, particularly judges, at all levels of government. The press has wanted to know things the judges have not wanted it to know. The press has wanted to attend meetings and hearings that public officials have not wanted it to attend. The press has wanted to criticize public officials, including judges, in ways that were not appreciated. Over time, the justices on the Supreme Court have granted the press the right to do some of these things, always mindful that they themselves are judges and that judges must be allowed to maintain judicial integrity and guarantee criminal defendants a fair trial. The Court has also had to weigh the right to privacy against the right to a free press.

CRITICISM OF PUBLIC OFFICIALS

The first free speech case ever heard by the Supreme Court, *Patterson v. Colorado*, concerned this issue. This 1907 case involved a Colorado newspaper that had printed articles and cartoons suggesting that some members of the Colorado Supreme Court were less than upstanding public servants. The articles alleged that the members of the Colorado Supreme Court had been party to a scheme to put a Republican into the Colorado Governor's Mansion instead of the Democrat who had been elected by the people of Colorado. The newspaper also suggested that some members of the Colorado Supreme Court were politically motivated and were not making decisions based on the legal merits of each case. The Colorado Supreme Court held the publisher of the newspaper in contempt of court without even holding a trial. The majority decision, written by Justice Holmes, upheld the Colorado Supreme Court's action. Only Justice Harlan dissented, arguing that the right of a free press guaranteed by the First Amendment had been violated. He believed the right to have a free press should protect the right of the press to criticize public officials, even judges. A majority of the justices did not think the right to have a free press had been violated in this case. In 1907 the Court was not ready to acknowledge that the rights of free speech and free press protected criticism of public officials.

In the 1931 case of *Near v. Minnesota,* the Court was faced with a Minnesota law that allowed officials to close down a newspaper if it was proven that the paper had made a "public nuisance" of itself by publishing "malicious, scandalous and defamatory" material. The particular newspaper in question, *The Saturday Press,* had published articles charging that a "Jewish gangster was in control of gambling, bootlegging and racketeering in Minneapolis, and that law enforcement officers and agencies were not energetically performing their duties." The chief of police was a favorite target of this particular newspaper. A state court found the newspaper to be a nuisance and ordered the publisher to stop publishing and to never publish a newspaper in Minnesota again. The publisher had not even been allowed to present evidence at the trial that what he had published was true.

Chief Justice Hughes wrote the opinion for the five-justice majority. He pointed to a letter written by the Continental Congress to the citizens of the city of Quebec urging them to join in the revolution against England. In the letter, the Continental Congress pointed to the need to establish a free press that would advance "science, morality and the arts" and would "shame oppressive officers" into performing their duty. The Court majority thought that it was one thing to allow public officials who believed they had been the victims of libel to sue as individuals in civil court, but quite another to shut down a newspaper by order of the state. The newspaper argued that it had a right to publish anything as long as it was true, but the Court did not agree with that argument either. The thought of newspapers printing the sailing time of troop transports in time of war suggested that there were some "truths" that the press should not be free to publish. At the same time, the press should be free to publish the kind of stories *The Saturday Press* had published in this case. The chief justice pointed out that if this had been a case involving obscenity or national security, things might have been different, but it was not. It was simply a case of a newspaper criticizing public officials for not doing their job. A majority of the justices thought that if the right of a free press protected anything, it should protect that.

JUDGES AS TARGETS OF CRITICISM

In 1941, the Supreme Court again faced the issue of the right of a free press. In this case, *Bridges v. California* (see p. 103), the Court overturned the 1907 *Patterson v. Colorado* decision by a vote of five to four. Not only would newspapers be allowed to criticize public officials, they would also be allowed to criticize judges. Justice Black wrote the opinion for the majority. The case was very similar to *Patterson v. Colorado*. A newspaper had been found in contempt of court for making derogatory comments about some judicial actions. Justice Black quoted Justice Holmes in the *Schenck* (see p. 54) case when he said that speech may only be suppressed if there is a "clear and present danger" of some evil. There was none in this case. Justice Black quoted Justice Brandeis's concurring opinion in the *Whitney* case where he had said that the founders of the nation intended the rights of free speech and free press to be the foundations of American liberty. Justice Black also quoted the more recent decisions on the free speech issue which had said that speech may only be punished if it poses a "substantial" threat to the workings of the government. He argued that in this case the statements by the press were a "mere inconvenience" for the judges. An inconvenience was not a good enough reason to limit the rights of free speech and of free press.

The four dissenting justices pointed to the power British judges had always had to control the trial process and the press coverage of that process. Justice Black responded that the whole purpose of the American Bill of Rights was to guarantee rights to the people of the United States that the people of Great Britain did not enjoy. Justice Frankfurter in his dissenting opinion argued that newspapers should not be allowed to intimidate judges charged with making important decisions while the particular case is pending before the judge. In Justice Frankfurter's opinion, the press was within its rights when it criticized other public officials, but judges were different from other public officials. The majority of Supreme Court justices did not agree. Judges would have to get used to the criticism of the press just like every other public official.

By 1946 the concept that the right of a free press included the right to criticize judicial procedure seemed more natural to the members of the Supreme Court. A unanimous Supreme Court overturned the contempt conviction of a newspaper in the *Pennekamp v. Florida* case. The newspaper had run a report that commented on the attitude of the judges, but not on the evidence in the case, so the Court believed that there was no danger that potential jurors would be biased by the report. The danger to a fair judicial process must be "clear and immediate," the Court ruled, before judges would be allowed to close the door on comments by the press. Justice Frankfurter, who had dissented in the 1941 *Bridges v. California* case, wrote a concurring opinion in *Pennekamp v. Florida*. He pointed out that a free press is "vital to a free society," and that what the press publishes must be a significant threat to the judicial process before the press can be silenced.

PRIVATE LIBEL LAWSUITS

In 1964, in *New York Times Co. v. Sullivan* (see p. 109), the Court began to alter the ancient rules of private libel lawsuits in order to protect the right of a free press to criticize public officials. This case involved a lawsuit by the police commissioner of Montgomery, Alabama, L. B. Sullivan, who sued the *New York Times* for libel in Alabama and was awarded half a million dollars in damages by an Alabama jury. A unanimous Supreme Court threw out the Alabama verdict in a decision written by Justice Brennan. What had the *New York Times* done? It had published a full-page advertisement, paid for just like any other advertisement, to raise money for the Committee to Defend Martin Luther King. The ad charged that civil rights demonstrators were being subjected to a "wave of terror" in Alabama. Sullivan argued that some of the statements made in the ad about the police in Montgomery were inaccurate and other statements were misleading. For example, the ad said that Martin Luther King had been arrested seven times when he had only been arrested four times. Commissioner Sullivan was not mentioned by name in the advertisement, but he argued that his reputation had been tarnished because he supervised the police and they had been unfairly criticized.

With this case, the Supreme Court had to come to grips with the fact that private libel actions could be just as devastating as criminal prosecutions for libel if they put the newspaper out of business because of the size of the damage award. While the judge in a civil case would not be able to order the newspaper to close down, as the judge in the *Near* case had done, a large damage award would have the same effect. The Court ruled that the libel laws could not be used by a public official to punish a newspaper for criticizing his official conduct in this way. Sullivan pointed out that the Court had consistently said that the First Amendment does not protect libel. Justice Brennan responded that the Court had not considered the use of the libel laws to silence critics of public officials before. He argued that a "rule compelling the critic of official conduct to guarantee the truth of all his factual assertions— and to do so on pain of libel judgments virtually unlimited in amount—leads to" self-censorship. The Court ruled that from then on public officials suing for libel would have to prove that the statement was untrue. Until that time the burden of proving the truth of a statement had been on the defendant. Also, the public official would have to prove that the untrue statement had been made with "actual malice." The Court defined actual malice to be a situation where the newspaper reporter or publisher either knew the statement was false or showed "reckless disregard" for whether or not it was true.

The Court thought that the *New York Times* in this case was, at most, negligent in not investigating the facts of the advertisement, and for that it could not be made to pay damages.

THE RIGHTS OF PUBLIC FIGURES AND THE RIGHTS OF PRIVATE CITIZENS

The 1967 case of *Time, Inc. v. Hill* involved one of the most famous "real life dramas" in American history. The Hill family had become famous because a group of escaped convicts had randomly selected their suburban house as a hide-out. The Hill family had been held hostage for 19 hours. America could not get enough information about this incident. It became the subject of a docu-novel, a docu-movie, and a docu-play, each chronicling the events of those 19 hours. When the play, entitled "The Desperate Hours," opened in New York City, *Life Magazine* published an article entitled "True Crime Inspires Tense Play." The article correctly pointed out that the play had been inspired by the actual events of the Hill family's ordeal, but the article left everyone with the impression that the play was an accurate depiction of those events. It was not. The Hills sued in New York for libel and invasion of privacy and a jury awarded them $30,000. The Supreme Court reversed this decision with a five-to-four vote in favor of *Life Magazine*. Justice Brennan, who wrote the opinion, argued that the Hill family had become "public figures" by virtue of having been held hostage in a famous crime case. Because of this they would be treated the same way public officials are treated. In other words, they would have to prove that the statements made about them in the press were untrue, and that the statements had been made with actual malice as defined in *New York Times Co. v. Sullivan*. The four dissenting justices thought that the right to privacy deserved to be protected as much as the right to a free press, and that the victims of crime should not be put in the same boat with public officials.

For two decades after the decision in *Time Inc. v. Hill*, the Court struggled to draw the line between public figures, who would be treated just like public officials, and private citizens, who would have more of a right to be left alone by the press. In 1988 the Court was finally able to hand down a unanimous decision. The case involved the famous minister Jerry Falwell and the famous adult magazine *Hustler* (*Hustler Magazine v. Falwell*). In the 1980s the Campari liquor company had run a series of advertisements in national magazines in which famous people discussed their "first time." The advertisements were written in such a way that the reader assumed that the famous people were talking about the first time they had sex, but by the end of the advertisement it was clear that they were talking about the first time they had tasted Campari. *Hustler* magazine ran a series of parodies on these advertisements. In one of these parodies it had Jerry Falwell supposedly saying that his "first time" was with his mother in an outhouse. Jerry Falwell knew he could not sue for libel because this was simply a parody with no suggestion to anyone that it was the truth. He sued instead for intentional infliction of emotional distress. The jury awarded damages and *Hustler* magazine appealed the case to the Supreme Court.

Chief Justice Rehnquist, who wrote the opinion for the Court, pointed out that the fake advertisement was listed in the table of contents under "fiction." The Court reversed the lower court's decision, ruling that public figures such as Jerry Falwell could not use "intentional infliction of emotional distress" to get around the rules the Court had developed to deal with libel and invasion of privacy. Instead, public figures would have to sue for libel and prove that what was said was untrue; that it purported to be a statement of fact, not fiction; and that it was made with "actual malice." In other words, Jerry Falwell did not receive damages in this case because the magazine had never suggested that what it was saying about him was true.

LIMITATIONS ON THE RIGHT OF A FREE PRESS

The idea that the press should be free to report and comment on public officials and public figures became easier and easier for the Court to accept. At the same time, the press argued that the right of a free press included certain rights that the Court was not willing to grant. For example, in the 1972 case of *Branzburg v. Hayes*, a newspaper reporter was put in jail for refusing to testify before a grand jury. The reporter argued that the right of a free press included the right not to reveal how he had obtained information for a story, and that if he could be forced to reveal the source of his information, he would be severely hampered in his ability to gather news. The Supreme Court, with a five-to-four vote, ruled that reporters do not have any special privilege under the First Amendment to refuse to testify before courts or grand juries, and they do not have any special right to keep the source of their information confidential. In 1978 the Court also ruled that the news media does not have any special right to inspect government documents or attend government meetings (*Houchins v. KQED*). In both of these cases the Court refused to find that the right of a "free press" granted any special rights to journalists that average people would not also enjoy under the more general right of "free speech."

People in most states and their state legislators reacted to these decisions by passing laws that do provide reporters with the right to refuse to reveal their sources except in limited circumstances. The people of California amended the free speech article in their constitution to guarantee this right to reporters. Also, most states passed "open records" and "open meetings" laws guaranteeing the press and the general public the right to attend most government meetings and to see most government records. The U.S. Congress passed a "freedom of information" law to apply to federal meetings and records. These statutes spell out in great detail what kinds of meetings may be kept private and which documents may be withheld from the public. Generally, personnel matters and matters of national security may be withheld, along with information that might make it difficult for the government to pursue a pending legal case. These laws usually allow government to withhold information that might jeopardize law enforcement efforts. Also, memorandums concerning policy can be withheld so that public officials will feel free to criticize existing policies and suggest new policies without fear that their words will be read out of context in the morning newspaper.

Many people and the press criticized the Supreme Court for not "finding" a reporter's privilege in the First Amendment and not "stretching" the First Amendment to provide reporters with a right of access to government meetings and government documents. The answer to this criticism is that the issue is not that easy. When we look at the open meetings and open records laws that have been fashioned around the country, we see that many different values had to be weighed. The right of public employees to privacy had to be weighed against the right of the public to receive information about them, such as how much money they make and where they live. The right of law enforcement officers to prevent crime had to be weighed against the need to inform the public about police activity. It simply would have been impossible for the Supreme Court to weigh all of those factors and come up with a set of rules that would apply to every situation. The result is a system of statutes and rules that most people think strikes a proper balance between the public's right to know and government's right to carry out its business.

GAG ORDERS

One of the most difficult issues for the Court has been trying to balance the right of the press and the public to find out about criminal trials against the right of defendants to receive a fair trial. In the 1976 case of *Nebraska Press Assn. v. Stuart*, a unanimous Court overturned a judge's "gag order." A gag order forces everyone involved with a trial to make no public statements about the trial until it is over. The Court ruled that while a judge may be able to "gag" the participants in a trial, he or she generally will not be allowed to gag the press. What the press finds out through legal means it can reveal to the public.

The Court made a similar point with another unanimous decision in 1978 (*Landmark Communications v. Virginia*). This case involved a Virginia law that required that information about state investigations of judicial misconduct not be revealed to the public. The *Virginia Pilot* newspaper reported that a particular judge was under investigation for misconduct, and the state of Virginia fined the newspaper $500 for violating the law. The Supreme Court ruled that the state could punish people involved with the investigation who revealed the information to the press, but it could not punish the press. The press has a right under the First Amendment to reveal the truth about government actions, even investigations of judicial misconduct. The newspaper had not used illegal means to gather the information. Chief Justice Burger, writing the opinion, went on to say that what judges do is of the "utmost public concern" and the press must be allowed to reveal it.

PUBLISHING THE NAMES OF RAPE VICTIMS

One area of concern has been the desire of the press to publish information that the judicial system would like kept secret. In 1975 a broadcasting company was prosecuted for violating a Georgia law that made it a crime to publish the name of a rape victim. The Supreme Court, with one dissent, ruled that this law violated the right of free press guaranteed by the First Amendment (*Cox Broadcasting v. Cohn*). While the Court had said on more than one occasion that the press did not have a right to publish every "truth" it came across, in this case the Court ruled that the press did have a right to publish this fact. The Court made it clear that the right of a free press protected radio and television as well as newspapers. While radio and television are subject to greater government regulation because they use the public airwaves (which are considered to be owned by the federal government), they are still protected by the First Amendment (*FCC v. Pacifica Foundation*).

In 1989 the Court was faced with a similar rape victim-protection law in Florida (*Florida Star v. B.J.F.*). Unlike the Georgia case, in which the state tried to prosecute the newspaper for a criminal violation, this was a private lawsuit by the individual whose name had been revealed. The fact that this was a private lawsuit by the victim did not make a difference to a majority of the justices. This person would not be allowed to sue for invasion of privacy in this case. While the Court again refused to say that the press has a right to publish anything as long as it is the truth, the press had the right under the First Amendment to publish information about crime. The three dissenting justices believed that people's right to privacy should also be protected and that the press was going too far.

PRESS ATTENDANCE AT CRIMINAL TRIALS AND HEARINGS

Another area that has been difficult for the Court is the question of whether or not the press and public have a right to attend criminal trials and the hearings that precede them. In 1979, with a vote of five to four, the Court ruled that the press did not have a right to attend a preliminary hearing in a criminal case (*Gannett Co. v. DePasquale*). The majority of justices thought that the right to a public trial was a right of the defendant, and if the defendant wanted the hearing or trial to be conducted in private, and the prosecution agreed, it was none of the press's or public's business.

The next year the Court began to change its mind on this subject. The *Richmond Newspapers v. Virginia* case involved a prosecutor and defendant who wished to keep the press and public away from an actual trial. A unanimous Supreme Court ruled that the press and public have a right under the First Amendment to attend criminal trials, barring exceptional circumstances. The purpose of this First Amendment right is to guarantee that the criminal process is carried on in a regular way, and only the presence of the press can guarantee that. While defendants have a right to a fair trial, they do not generally have a right to a secret trial.

In 1982 the Court overturned with a six-to-three vote a Massachusetts law that required the judge to exclude the press and public from a rape trial if the victim was under the age of 18 (*Globe Newspaper Co. v. Superior Court*). The state argued that it had a significant interest in protecting the privacy of young rape victims. The majority of justices acknowledged that interest but thought that there was a public interest in having public trials. The Court ruled that judges could close the trial when the individual case warranted, but the state could not make the closing of the trial mandatory. Chief Justice Burger, writing a dissenting opinion for himself and the two other dissenting justices, argued that the need to protect minors justified this Massachusetts law.

In 1986 the Court was ready to overturn the decision it had made in 1979 and rule that the press did have a right to attend preliminary hearings in criminal cases (*Press-Enterprise v. Superior Court*). With a seven-to-two vote, the majority was now ready to acknowledge that exposure of all parts of the criminal process was a positive thing unless the facts of a particular case dictated otherwise. If the only way a particular defendant could receive a fair trial was to limit press access, then judges, using their discretion, could limit access, but they would have to have very good reasons. Only if the judge determined that there was a "substantial probability that the defendant would not get a fair trial" could a trial or preliminary hearing be closed to the press and public.

PUBLISHERS AND THE RIGHT OF A FREE PRESS

Over the years the Court came to the conclusion that the right of a free press means that the publisher of a newspaper decides what goes into that newspaper, not the government or anyone else. This is illustrated by two decisions. In 1974 a unanimous Court overturned a Florida law that required newspapers to allow candidates for public office to reply to editorials critical of them in the newspapers (*Miami Herald v. Tornillo*). Chief Justice Burger, writing for the Court, argued that the right of a free press means that government may not force a newspaper to publish something it does not wish to publish. On the other hand, the Court has ruled that the federal government may require radio and television stations to grant "equal time" to candidates because radio and television broadcasts make use of the publicly owned airwaves (*Red Lion Broadcasting Co. v. FCC*).

In the 1988 case of *Hazelwood School District v. Kuhlmeier* (see p. 113) the Court was faced with an unusual case involving a school newspaper. The principal of the school refused to allow some articles written by student reporters to be published. These articles discussed the problems faced by pregnant students and students living with divorced parents. The six-member majority agreed that the principal had the power to refuse to publish these articles. These justices thought that an official school newspaper belongs to the school district, not to the student reporters who work on the paper. The principal can be seen as the publisher, and he or she must have the final say concerning what does and what does not go into the paper. The dissenting justices believed that these student reporters should have a right to express themselves in their paper. The majority of justices believed, however, that it was not the student reporters' paper; it was the "school's" paper. If these student reporters had wanted to, they could have taken the articles in question, copied them at the local copy center, and passed them out or sold them on the sidewalk in front of the school. What they were not free to do was force the principal, the publisher, to print them in the school's newspaper.

CONCLUSION

Throughout the twentieth century the right of the press to criticize public officials, including judges; cover criminal trials; and control the content of newspapers has increased with each passing decade. In 1907 only one Supreme Court justice believed that the First Amendment protected the right of the press to criticize public officials. By 1931 the Court had begun to change its mind. In 1964 the Court began to change the rules of libel lawsuits in order to allow the press more freedom to criticize public officials and to report on, or even make fun of, people in the news. In 1979 a majority of the justices thought that the press did not have a right under the First Amendment to cover criminal trials or preliminary hearings, but by 1986 the Court had overturned that decision and come to the opposite conclusion. In 1974 and again in 1988 the Court affirmed that the content of newspapers is up to the publisher, not the government or the reporters, even if the reporters are students in a public school and the newspaper is a school newspaper. The right of a free press protects the right of publishers to decide what they will print, not the government or the courts.

John Stuart Mill took for granted in *On Liberty* that a democratic society needs a free press to inform the public about the character and actions of public officials. The U.S. Supreme Court was not willing to interpret the First Amendment to grant the American press such powers early in the twentieth century. However, as time passed, and as the Court expanded the reach of the right of free speech in other areas, it came to see the logic of expanding the right of a free press to include the right of the press to report on and criticize public officials, even judges. At the same time, the Court has generally refused to find that the right of a "free press" grants journalists rights not enjoyed by the general public. Both the press and the public have a right to attend criminal trials and to criticize the actions of public officials. There is no special reporter's privilege to attend meetings, view public records, or refuse to reveal sources of information under the First Amendment of the U.S. Constitution.

CASE DECISIONS

In the 1941 case of *Bridges v. California*, the Court ruled that generally judges may not hold people in contempt of court to limit comments about the judicial process by the press. Justice Black's opinion for the five-justice majority is included here. A dissenting opinion by Justice Frankfurter is also included.

In 1964, in *New York Times v. Sullivan*, a unanimous Court ruled that the right of a free press imposed limits on the ability of public officials to sue for libel. Justice Brennan wrote the opinion for the Court, which is included here.

In the 1988 decision of *Hazelwood School District v. Kuhlmeier*, a majority of the justices ruled that a school district may control the content of the school newspaper. Justice White wrote the opinion for the six-justice majority, which is included here. Justice Brennan's dissenting opinion is also included. Following are excerpts from the case decisions.

❋ ❋ ❋ ❋ ❋ ❋ ❋ ❋

BRIDGES v. CALIFORNIA
314 U.S. 252 (1941)

MR. JUSTICE BLACK delivered the opinion of the Court.

These two cases, while growing out of different circumstances and con-cerning different parties, both relate to the scope of our national constitutional policy safeguarding free speech and a free press. All of the petitioners were adjudged guilty and fined for contempt of court by the Superior Court of Los Angeles County. Their conviction rested upon comments pertaining to pending litigation which were published in newspapers. In the Superior Court, and later in the California Supreme Court, petitioners challenged the state's action as an abridgment, prohibited by the Federal Constitution, of freedom of speech and of the press; but the Superior Court overruled this contention, and the Supreme Court affirmed. The importance of the constitutional question prompted us to grant certiorari. 309 U.S. 649; 310 U.S. 623.

In brief, the state courts asserted and exercised a power to punish petitioners for publishing their views concerning cases not in all respects finally determined, upon the following chain of reasoning: California is invested with the power and duty to provide an adequate administration of justice; by virtue of this power and duty, it can take appropriate measures for providing fair judicial trials free from coercion or intimidation; included among such appropriate measures is the common law procedure of punishing certain interferences and obstructions through contempt proceedings; this particular measure, devolving upon the courts of California by reason of their creation as courts, includes the power to punish for publications made outside the court room if they tend to interfere with the fair and orderly administration of justice in a pending case; the trial court having found that the publications had such a tendency, and there being substantial evidence to support the finding, the punishments here imposed were an appropriate exercise of the state's power; in so far as these punishments constitute a restriction on liberty of expression, the public interest in that liberty was properly subordinated to the public interest in judicial impartiality and decorum. . . .

What finally emerges from the "clear and present danger" cases is a working principle that the substantive evil must be extremely serious and the degree of imminence extremely high before utterances can be punished. Those cases do not purport to mark the furthermost constitutional boundaries of protected expression, nor do we here. They do no more than recognize a minimum compulsion of the Bill of Rights. For the First Amendment does not speak equivocally. It prohibits any law "abridging the freedom of speech, or of the press." It must be taken as a command of the broadest scope that explicit language, read in the context of a liberty-loving society, will allow.

Before analyzing the punished utterances and the circumstances surrounding their publication, we must consider an argument which, if valid, would destroy the relevance of the foregoing discussion to this case. In brief, this argument is that the publications here in question belong to a special category marked off by history,—a category to which the criteria of constitutional immunity from punishment used where other types of utterances are concerned are not applicable. For, the argument runs, the power of judges to punish by contempt out-of-court publications tending to obstruct the orderly and fair administration of justice in a pending case was deeply rooted in English common law at the time the Constitution was adopted. That this historical contention is dubious has been persuasively argued elsewhere. Fox, *Contempt of Court, passim, e.g.,* 207. See also Stansbury, *Trial of James H. Peck,* 430. In any event it need not detain us, for to assume that English common law in this field became ours is to deny the generally accepted historical belief that "one of the objects of the Revolution was to get rid of the English common law on liberty of speech and of the press." Schofield, *Freedom of the Press in the United States,* 9 Publications Amer. Sociol. Soc., 67, 76. . . .

We may appropriately begin our discussion of the judgments below by considering how much, as a practical matter, they would affect liberty of expression. It must be recognized that public interest is much more likely to be kindled by a controversial event of the day than by a generalization, however penetrating, of the historian or scientist. Since they punish utterances made during the pendency of a case, the judgments below therefore produce their restrictive results at the precise time when public interest in the matters discussed would naturally be at its height. Moreover, the ban is likely to fall not only at a crucial time but upon the most important topics of discussion. Here, for example, labor controversies were the topics of some of the publications. Experience shows that the more acute labor controversies are, the more likely it is that in some aspect they will get into court. It is therefore the controversies that command most interest that the decisions below would remove from the arena of public discussion.

No suggestion can be found in the Constitution that the freedom there guaranteed for speech and the press bears an inverse ratio to the timeliness and importance of the ideas seeking expression. Yet, it would follow as a practical result of the decisions below that anyone who might wish to give public expression to his views on a pending case involving no matter what problem of public interest, just at the time his audience would be most receptive, would be as effectively discouraged as if a deliberate statutory scheme of censorship had been adopted. Indeed, perhaps more so, because under a legislative specification of the particular kinds of expressions prohibited and the circumstances under which the prohibitions are to operate, the speaker or publisher might at least have an authoritative guide to the permissible scope of comment, instead of being compelled to act at the peril that judges might find in the utterance "a reasonable tendency" to obstruct justice in a pending case.

This unfocused threat is, to be sure, limited in time, terminating as it does upon final disposition of the case. But this does not change its censorial quality. An endless series of moratoria on public discussion, even if each were very short, could hardly be dismissed as an insignificant abridgment of freedom of expression. And to assume that each would be short is to overlook the fact that the "pendency" of a case is frequently a matter of months or even years rather than days or weeks.

For these reasons we are convinced that the judgments below result in a curtailment of expression that cannot be dismissed as insignificant. If they can be justified at all, it must be in terms of some serious substantive evil which they are designed to avert. The substantive evil here sought to be averted has been variously described below. It appears to be double: disrespect for the judiciary; and disorderly and unfair administration of justice. The assumption that respect for the judiciary can be won by shielding judges from published criticism wrongly appraises the character of American public opinion. For it is a prized American privilege to speak one's mind, although not always with perfect good taste, on all public institutions. And an enforced silence, however limited, solely in the name of preserving the dignity of the bench, would probably engender resentment, suspicion, and contempt much more than it would enhance respect.

The other evil feared, disorderly and unfair administration of justice, is more plausibly associated with restricting publications which touch upon pending litigation. The very word "trial" connotes decisions on the evidence and arguments properly advanced in open court. Legal trials are not like elections, to be won through the use of the meeting-hall, the radio, and the newspaper. But we cannot start with the assumption that publications of the kind here involved actually do threaten to change the nature of legal trials, and that to preserve judicial impartiality, it is necessary for judges to have a contempt power by which they can close all channels of public expression to all matters which touch upon pending cases. We must therefore turn to the particular utterances here in question and the circumstances of their publication to determine to what extent the substantive evil of unfair administration of justice was a likely consequence, and whether the degree of likelihood was sufficient to justify summary punishment.

The Los Angeles Times Editorials. The Times-Mirror Company, publisher of the Los Angeles Times, and L. D. Hotchkiss, its managing editor, were cited for contempt for the publication of three editorials. Both found by the trial court to be responsible for one of the editorials, the company and Hotchkiss were each fined $100. The company alone was held responsible for the other two, and was fined $100 more on account of one, and $300 more on account of the other.

The $300 fine presumably marks the most serious offense. The editorial thus distinguished was entitled "Probation for Gorillas?" After vigorously denouncing two members of a labor union who had previously been found guilty of assaulting nonunion truck drivers, it closes with the observation: "Judge A. A. Scott will make a serious mistake if he grants probation to

Matthew Shannon and Kennan Holmes. This community needs the example of their assignment to the jute mill." Judge Scott had previously set a day (about a month after the publication) for passing upon the application of Shannon and Holmes for probation and for pronouncing sentence.

The basis for punishing the publication as contempt was by the trial court said to be its "inherent tendency" and by the Supreme Court its "reasonable tendency" to interfere with the orderly administration of justice in an action then before a court for consideration. In accordance with what we have said on the "clear and present danger" cases, neither "inherent tendency" nor "reasonable tendency" is enough to justify a restriction of free expression. But even if they were appropriate measures, we should find exaggeration in the use of those phrases to describe the facts here. . . .

The Bridges Telegram. While a motion for a new trial was pending in a case involving a dispute between an A. F. of L. union and a C. I. O. union of which Bridges was an officer, he either caused to be published or acquiesced in the publication of a telegram which he had sent to the Secretary of Labor. The telegram referred to the judge's decision as "outrageous"; said that attempted enforcement of it would tie up the port of Los Angeles and involve the entire Pacific Coast; and concluded with the announcement that the C. I. O. union, representing some twelve thousand members, did "not intend to allow state courts to override the majority vote of members in choosing its officers and representatives and to override the National Labor Relations Board." . . .

Let us assume that the telegram could be construed as an announcement of Bridges' intention to call a strike, something which, it is admitted, neither the general law of California nor the court's decree prohibited. With an eye on the realities of the situation, we cannot assume that Judge Schmidt was unaware of the possibility of a strike as a consequence of his decision. If he was not intimidated by the facts themselves, we do not believe that the most explicit statement of them could have sidetracked the course of justice. Again, we find exaggeration in the conclusion that the utterance even "tended" to interfere with justice. If there was electricity in the atmosphere, it was generated by the facts; the charge added by the Bridges telegram can be dismissed as negligible. The words of Mr. Justice Holmes, spoken in reference to very different facts, seem entirely applicable here: "I confess that I cannot find in all this or in the evidence in the case anything that would have affected a mind of reasonable fortitude, and still less can I find there anything that obstructed the administration of justice in any sense that I possibly can give to those words." *Toledo Newspaper Co. v. United States, supra,* 247 U.S. at 425.

Reversed.

Dissenting Opinion   MR. JUSTICE FRANKFURTER, with whom concurred the CHIEF JUSTICE, MR. JUSTICE ROBERTS and MR. JUSTICE BYRNES, dissenting.

Our whole history repels the view that it is an exercise of one of the civil liberties secured by the Bill of Rights for a leader of a large following or for a powerful metropolitan newspaper to attempt to overawe a judge in a matter immediately pending before him. The view of the majority deprives California of means for securing to its citizens justice according to law—means which, since the Union was founded, have been the possession, hitherto unchallenged, of all the states. This sudden break with the uninterrupted course of constitutional history has no constitutional warrant. To find justification for such deprivation of the historic powers of the states is to misconceive the idea of freedom of thought and speech as guaranteed by the Constitution.

Deeming it more important than ever before to enforce civil liberties with a generous outlook, but deeming it no less essential for the assurance of civil liberties that the federal system founded upon the Constitution be maintained, we believe that the careful ambiguities and silences of the majority opinion call for a full exposition of the issues in these cases.

While the immediate question is that of determining the power of the courts of California to deal with attempts to coerce their judgments in litigation immediately before them, the consequence of the Court's ruling today is a denial to the people of the forty-eight states of a right which they have always regarded as essential for the effective exercise of the judicial process, as well as a denial to the Congress of powers which were exercised from the very beginning even by the framers of the Constitution themselves. To be sure, the majority do not in so many words hold that trial by newspapers has constitutional sanctity. But the atmosphere of their opinion and several of its phrases mean that or they mean nothing. Certainly, the opinion is devoid of any frank recognition of the right of courts to deal with utterances calculated to intimidate the fair course of justice—a right which hitherto all the states have from time to time seen fit to confer upon their courts and which Congress conferred upon the federal courts in the Judiciary Act of 1789. . . .

Of course freedom of speech and of the press are essential to the enlightenment of a free people and in restraining those who wield power. Particularly should this freedom be employed in comment upon the work of courts, who are without many influences ordinarily making for humor and humility, twin antidotes to the corrosion of power. But the Bill of Rights is not self-destructive. Freedom of expression can hardly carry implications that nullify the guarantees of impartial trials. And since courts are the ultimate resorts for vindicating the Bill of Rights, a state may surely authorize appropriate historic means to assure that the process for such vindication be not wrenched from its rational tracks into the more primitive mêlée of passion and pressure. The need is great that courts be criticized, but just as great that they be allowed to do their duty.

NEW YORK TIMES CO. v. SULLIVAN
376 U.S. 254 (1964)

MR. JUSTICE BRENNAN delivered the opinion of the Court.

We are required in this case to determine for the first time the extent to which the constitutional protections for speech and press limit a State's power to award damages in a libel action brought by a public official against critics of his official conduct.

Respondent L. B. Sullivan is one of the three elected Commissioners of the City of Montgomery, Alabama. He testified that he was "Commissioner of Public Affairs and the duties are supervision of the Police Department, Fire Department, Department of Cemetery and Department of Scales." He brought this civil libel action against the four individual petitioners, who are Negroes and Alabama clergymen, and against petitioner the New York Times Company, a New York corporation which publishes the New York Times, a daily newspaper. A jury in the Circuit Court of Montgomery County awarded him damages of $500,000, the full amount claimed, against all the petitioners, and the Supreme Court of Alabama affirmed. 273 Ala. 656, 144 So. 2d 25.

Respondent's complaint alleged that he had been libeled by statements in a full-page advertisement that was carried in the New York Times on March 29, 1960. Entitled "Heed Their Rising Voices," the advertisement began by stating that "As the whole world knows by now, thousands of Southern Negro students are engaged in widespread non-violent demonstrations in positive affirmation of the right to live in human dignity as guaranteed by the U.S. Constitution and the Bill of Rights." It went on to charge that "in their efforts to uphold these guarantees, they are being met by an unprecedented wave of terror by those who would deny and negate that document which the whole world looks upon as setting the pattern for modern freedom. . . ." Succeeding paragraphs purported to illustrate the "wave of terror" by describing certain alleged events. The text concluded with an appeal for funds for three purposes: support of the student movement, "the struggle for the right-to-vote," and the legal defense of Dr. Martin Luther King, Jr., leader of the movement, against a perjury indictment then pending in Montgomery.

The text appeared over the names of 64 persons, many widely known for their activities in public affairs, religion, trade unions, and the performing arts. Below these names, and under a line reading "We in the south who are struggling daily for dignity and freedom warmly endorse this appeal," appeared the names of the four individual petitioners and of 16 other persons, all but two of whom were identified as clergymen in various Southern cities. The advertisement was signed at the bottom of the page by the "Committee to Defend Martin Luther King and the Struggle for Freedom in the South," and the officers of the Committee were listed.

Of the 10 paragraphs of text in the advertisement, the third and a portion of the sixth were the basis of respondent's claim of libel. They read as follows:

Third paragraph:

> "In Montgomery, Alabama, after students sang 'My Country, 'Tis of Thee' on the State Capitol steps, their leaders were expelled from school, and truckloads of police armed with shotguns and tear-gas ringed the Alabama State College Campus. When the entire student body protested to state authorities by refusing to re-register, their dining hall was pad-locked in an attempt to starve them into submission."

Sixth paragraph:

> "Again and again the Southern violators have answered Dr. King's peaceful protests with intimidation and violence. They have bombed his home almost killing his wife and child. They have assaulted his person. They have arrested him seven times—for 'speeding,' 'loitering' and similar 'offenses.' And now they have charged him with 'perjury'—a *felony* under which they could imprison him for *ten years.* . . ."

Although neither of these statements mentions respondent by name, he contended that the word "police" in the third paragraph referred to him as the Montgomery Commissioner who supervised the Police Department, so that he was being accused of "ringing" the campus with police. He further claimed that the paragraph would be read as imputing to the police, and hence to him, the padlocking of the dining hall in order to starve the students into submission. As to the sixth paragraph, he contended that since arrests are ordinarily made by the police, the statement "They have arrested [Dr. King] seven times" would be read as referring to him; he further contended that the "They" who did the arresting would be equated with the "They" who committed the other described acts and with the "Southern violators." Thus, he argued, the paragraph would be read as accusing the Montgomery police, and hence him, of answering Dr. King's protests with "intimidation and violence," bombing his home, assaulting his person, and charging him with perjury. Respondent and six other Montgomery residents testified that they read some or all of the statements as referring to him in his capacity as Commissioner.

It is uncontroverted that some of the statements contained in the two paragraphs were not accurate descriptions of events which occurred in Montgomery. Although Negro students staged a demonstration on the State Capitol steps, they sang the National Anthem and not "My Country, 'Tis of Thee." Although nine students were expelled by the State Board of Education, this was not for leading the demonstration at the Capitol, but for demanding service at a lunch counter in the Montgomery County Courthouse on another day. Not the entire student body, but most of it, had protested the expulsion, not by refusing to register, but by boycotting classes on a single day; virtually all the students did register for the ensuing semester. The campus dining hall was not padlocked on any occasion, and the only students who may have been barred from eating there were the few who had neither signed a preregistration application nor requested temporary meal tickets. Although the police were deployed near the campus in large numbers on three occasions, they did not at any time "ring" the campus, and they were not called to the campus in connection with the demonstration on the State Capitol steps, as the third paragraph implied. Dr. King had not been arrested seven times, but only four; and although he claimed to have been assaulted some years earlier in connection with his arrest for loitering outside a courtroom, one of the officers who made the arrest denied that there was such an assault.

On the premise that the charges in the sixth paragraph could be read as referring to him, respondent was allowed to prove that he had not participated in the events described. Although Dr. King's home had in fact been bombed twice when his wife and child were there, both of these occasions antedated respondent's tenure as Commissioner, and the police were not only not implicated in the bombings, but had made every effort to apprehend those who were. Three of Dr. King's four arrests took place before respondent became Commissioner. Although Dr. King had in fact been indicted (he was subsequently acquitted) on two counts of perjury, each of which carried a possible five-year sentence, respondent had nothing to do with procuring the indictment.

Respondent made no effort to prove that he suffered actual pecuniary loss as a result of the alleged libel. One of his witnesses, a former employer, testified that if he had believed the statements, he doubted whether he "would want to be associated with anybody who would be a party to such things that are stated in that ad," and that he would not re-employ respondent if he believed "that he allowed the Police Department to do the things that the paper say he did." But neither this witness nor any of the others testified that he had actually believed the statements in their supposed reference to respondent. . . .

Under Alabama law as applied in this case, a publication is "libelous per se" if the words "tend to injure a person . . . in his reputation" or to "bring [him] into public contempt"; the trial court stated that the standard was met if the words are such as to "injure him in his public office, or impute misconduct to him in his office, or want of official integrity, or want of fidelity to a public trust. . . ." The jury must find that the words were published "of and concerning" the plaintiff, but where the plaintiff is a public official his place in the governmental hierarchy is sufficient evidence to support a finding that his reputation has been affected by statements that reflect upon the agency of which he is in charge. Once "libel per se" has been established, the defendant has no defense as to stated facts unless he can persuade the jury that they were true in all their particulars. . . .

The question before us is whether this rule of liability, as applied to an action brought by a public official against critics of his official conduct, abridges the freedom of speech and of the press that is guaranteed by the First and Fourteenth Amendments.

Respondent relies heavily, as did the Alabama courts, on statements of this Court to the effect that the Constitution does not protect libelous publications. Those statements do not foreclose our inquiry here. None of the cases sustained the use of libel laws to impose sanctions upon expression critical of the official conduct of public officials. . . .

Thus we consider this case against the background of a profound national commitment to the principle that debate on public issues should be uninhibited, robust, and wide-open, and that it may well include vehement, caustic, and sometimes unpleasantly sharp attacks on government and public officials. See *Terminiello v. Chicago*, 337 U.S. 1, 4; *De Jonge v. Oregon*, 299 U.S. 353, 365. The present advertisement, as an expression of grievance and protest on one of the major public issues of our time, would seem clearly to qualify for the constitutional protection. The question is whether it forfeits that protection by the falsity of some of its factual statements and by its alleged defamation of respondent.

Authoritative interpretations of the First Amendment guarantees have consistently refused to recognize an exception for any test of truth—whether administered by judges, juries, or administrative officials—and especially one that puts the burden of proving truth on the speaker. Cf. *Speiser v. Randall*, 357 U.S. 513, 525–526. The constitutional protection does not turn upon "the truth, popularity, or social utility of the ideas and beliefs which are offered." *N.A.A.C.P. v. Button*, 371 U.S. 415, 445. As Madison said, "Some degree of abuse is inseparable from the proper use of every thing; and in no instance is this more true than in that of the press." 4 Elliot's Debates on the Federal Constitution (1876), p. 571. . . .

Injury to official reputation affords no more warrant for repressing speech that would otherwise be free than does factual error. Where judicial officers are involved, this Court has held that concern for the dignity and reputation of the courts does not justify the punishment as criminal contempt of criticism of the judge or his decision. *Bridges v. California*, 314 U.S. 252. This is true even though the utterance contains "half-truths" and "misinformation." *Pennekamp v. Florida*, 328 U.S. 331, 342, 343, n. 5, 345. Such repression can be justified, if at all, only by a clear and present danger of the obstruction of justice. See also *Craig v. Harney*, 331 U.S. 367; *Wood v. Georgia*, 370 U.S. 375. If judges are to be treated as "men of fortitude, able to thrive in a hardy climate," *Craig v. Harney, supra,* 331 U.S., at 376, surely the same must be true of other government officials, such as elected city commissioners. Criticism of their official conduct does not lose its constitutional protection merely because it is effective criticism and hence diminishes their official reputations. . . .

A rule compelling the critic of official conduct to guarantee the truth of all his factual assertions—and to do so on pain of libel judgments virtually unlimited in amount—leads to a comparable "self-censorship." Allowance of the defense of truth, with the burden of proving it on the defendant, does not mean that only false speech will be deterred. Even courts accepting this defense as an adequate safeguard have recognized the difficulties of adducing legal proofs that the alleged libel was true in all its factual particulars. See, *e.g.,* *Post Publishing Co. v. Hallam,* 59 F. 530, 540 (C. A. 6th Cir. 1893); see also Noel, Defamation of Public Officers and Candidates, 49 Col. L. Rev. 875, 892 (1949). Under such a rule, would-be critics of official conduct may be deterred from voicing their criticism, even though it is believed to be true and even though it is in fact true, because of doubt whether it can be proved in court or fear of the expense of having to do so. They tend to make only statements which "steer far wider of the unlawful zone." *Speiser v. Randall, supra,* 357 U.S., at 526. The rule thus dampens the vigor and limits the variety of public debate. It is inconsistent with the First and Fourteenth Amendments.

The constitutional guarantees require, we think, a federal rule that prohibits a public official from recovering damages for a defamatory falsehood relating to his official conduct unless he proves that the statement was made with "actual malice"—that is, with knowledge that it was false or with reckless disregard of whether it was false or not.

HAZELWOOD SCHOOL DISTRICT v. KUHLMEIER
484 U.S. 260 (1988)

JUSTICE WHITE delivered the opinion of the Court.

This case concerns the extent to which educators may exercise editorial control over the contents of a high school newspaper produced as part of the school's journalism curriculum.

Petitioners are the Hazelwood School District in St. Louis County, Missouri; various school officials; Robert Eugene Reynolds, the principal of Hazelwood East High School; and Howard Emerson, a teacher in the school district. Respondents are three former Hazelwood East students who were staff members of Spectrum, the school newspaper. They contend that school officials violated their First Amendment rights by deleting two pages of articles from the May 13, 1983, issue of Spectrum.

Spectrum was written and edited by the Journalism II class at Hazelwood East. The newspaper was published every three weeks or so during the 1982–1983 school year. More than 4,500 copies of the newspaper were distributed during that year to students, school personnel, and members of the community.

The Board of Education allocated funds from its annual budget for the printing of Spectrum. These funds were supplemented by proceeds from sales of the newspaper. The printing expenses during the 1982–1983 school year totaled $4,668.50; revenue from sales was $1,166.84. The other costs associated with the newspaper—such as supplies, textbooks, and a portion of the journalism teacher's salary—were borne entirely by the Board.

The Journalism II course was taught by Robert Stergos for most of the 1982–1983 academic year. Stergos left Hazelwood East to take a job in private industry on April 29, 1983, when the May 13 edition of Spectrum was nearing completion, and petitioner Emerson took his place as newspaper adviser for the remaining weeks of the term.

The practice at Hazelwood East during the spring 1983 semester was for the journalism teacher to submit page proofs of each Spectrum issue to Principal Reynolds for his review prior to publication. On May 10, Emerson delivered the proofs of the May 13 edition to Reynolds, who objected to two of the articles scheduled to appear in that edition. One of the stories described three Hazelwood East students' experiences with pregnancy; the other discussed the impact of divorce on students at the school.

Reynolds was concerned that, although the pregnancy story used false names "to keep the identity of these girls a secret," the pregnant students still might be identifiable from the text. He also believed that the article's references to sexual activity and birth control were inappropriate for some of the younger students at the school. In addition, Reynolds was concerned that a student identified by name in the divorce story had complained that her father "wasn't spending enough time with my mom, my sister and I" prior to the divorce, "was always out of town on business or out late playing cards with the guys," and "always argued about everything" with her mother. App. to Pet. for Cert. 38. Reynolds believed that the student's parents should have been given an opportunity to respond to these remarks or to consent to their publication. He was unaware that Emerson had deleted the student's name from the final version of the article.

Reynolds believed that there was no time to make the necessary changes in the stories before the scheduled press run and that the newspaper would not appear before the end of the school year if printing were delayed to any significant extent. He concluded that his only options under the circumstances were to publish a four-page newspaper instead of the planned six-page newspaper, eliminating the two pages on which the offending stories appeared, or to publish no newspaper at all. Accordingly, he directed Emerson to withhold from publication the two pages containing the stories on pregnancy and divorce. He informed his superiors of the decision, and they concurred.

Respondents subsequently commence this action in the United States District Court for the Eastern District of Missouri seeking a declaration that their First Amendment rights had been violated, injunctive relief, and monetary damages. After a bench trial, the District Court denied an injunction, holding that no First Amendment violation had occurred. 607 F. Supp. 1450 (1985). . . .

The question whether the First Amendment requires a school to tolerate particular student speech—the question that we addressed in *Tinker*—is different from the question whether the First Amendment requires a school affirmatively to promote particular student speech. The former question addresses educators' ability to silence a student's personal expression that happens to occur on the school premises. The latter question concerns educators' authority over school-sponsored publications, theatrical productions, and other expressive activities that students, parents, and members of the public might reasonably perceive to bear the imprimatur of the school. These activities may fairly be characterized as part of the school curriculum, whether or not they occur in a traditional classroom setting, so long as they are supervised by faculty members and designed to impart particular knowledge or skills to student participants and audiences.

Educators are entitled to exercise greater control over this second form of student expression to assure that participants learn whatever lessons the activity is designed to teach, that readers or listeners are not exposed to material that may be inappropriate for their level of maturity, and that the views of the individual speaker are not erroneously attributed to the school. Hence, a school may in its capacity as publisher of a school newspaper or producer of a school play "disassociate itself," *Fraser*, 478 U.S., at 685, not only from speech that would "substantially interfere with [its] work . . . or impinge upon the rights of other students," *Tinker*, 393 U.S., at 509, but also from speech that is, for example, ungrammatical, poorly written, inadequately researched, biased or prejudiced, vulgar or profane, or unsuitable for immature audiences. A school must be able to set high standards for the student speech that is disseminated under its auspices—standards that may be higher than those demanded by some newspaper publishers or theatrical producers in the "real" world—and may refuse to disseminate student speech that does not meet those standards. In addition, a school must be able to take into account the emotional maturity of the intended audience in determining whether to disseminate student speech on potentially sensitive topics, which might range from the existence of Santa Claus in an elementary school setting to the particulars of teenage sexual activity in a high school setting. A school must also retain the authority to refuse to sponsor student speech that might reasonably be perceived to advocate drug or alcohol use, irresponsible sex, or conduct otherwise inconsistent with "the shared values of a civilized social order," *Fraser, supra*, at 683, or to associate the school with any position other than neutrality on matters of political controversy. Otherwise, the schools would be unduly constrained from fulfilling their role as "a principal instrument in awakening the child to cultural values, in preparing him for later professional training, and in helping him to adjust normally to his environment." *Brown v. Board of Education*, 347 U.S. 483, 493 (1954).

Accordingly, we conclude that the standard articulated in *Tinker* for determining when a school may punish student expression need not also be the standard for determining when a school may refuse to lend its name and resources to the dissemination of student expression. Instead, we hold that educators do not offend the First Amendment by exercising editorial control over the style and content of student speech in school-sponsored expressive activities so long as their actions are reasonably related to legitimate pedagogical concerns.

Dissenting Opinion   JUSTICE BRENNAN, with whom JUSTICE MARSHALL and JUSTICE BLACKMUN join, dissenting.

When the young men and women of Hazelwood East High School registered for Journalism II, they expected a civics lesson. Spectrum, a newspaper they were to publish, "was not just a class exercise in which students learned to prepare papers and hone writing skills, it was a . . . forum established to give students an opportunity to express their views while gaining an appreciation of their rights and responsibilities under the First Amendment to the United States Constitution. . . ." 795 F.2d 1368, 1373 (CA8 1986). "[A]t the beginning of each school year," *id.*, at 1372, the student journalists published a Statement of Policy—tacitly approved each year by school authorities—announcing their expectation that "*Spectrum*, as a student-press publication, accepts all rights implied by the First Amendment. . . . Only speech that 'materially and substantially interferes with the requirements of appropriate discipline' can be found unacceptable and therefore prohibited." App. 26 (quoting *Tinker v. Des Moines Independent Community School Dist.*, 393 U.S. 503, 513 (1969)). The school board itself affirmatively guaranteed the students of Journalism II an atmosphere conducive to fostering such an appreciation and exercising the full panoply of rights associated with a free student press. "School sponsored student publications," it vowed, "will not restrict free expression or diverse viewpoints within the rules of responsible journalism." App. 22 (Board Policy 348.51).

This case arose when the Hazelwood East administration breached its own promise, dashing its students' expectations. The school principal, without prior consultation or explanation, excised six articles—comprising two full pages—of the May 13, 1983, issue of Spectrum. He did so not because any of the articles would "materially and substantially interfere with the requirements of appropriate discipline," but simply because he considered two of the six "inappropriate, personal, sensitive, and unsuitable" for student consumption. 795 F.2d, at 1371.

In my view the principal broke more than just a promise. He violated the First Amendment's prohibitions against censorship of any student expression that neither disrupts classwork nor invades the rights of others, and against any censorship that is not narrowly tailored to serve its purpose.

DISCUSSION QUESTIONS

1. Judges used to be able to hold reporters and publishers in contempt of court for any derogatory comment made about judges. That is no longer the case. How far do you think the press should be able to go before a judge should be allowed to hold them in contempt of court?

2. Judges can no longer issue "gag orders" to newspapers, but they can order the lawyers and participants in a trial not to talk to the press until the trial is over. Is this a violation of the free speech rights of those participants? What arguments can be made to support allowing judges to continue to issue these kinds of gag orders?

3. The Supreme Court has changed the rules of libel suits to allow the press more room to criticize public officials and report on public figures. Do you think the Court has done the right thing? Libel suits are now so difficult to win in the United States that most people do not even try. Is that a problem for society?

4. In 1972 the Supreme Court ruled that the First Amendment did not give reporters the "privilege" to refuse to reveal their sources. Over the next two decades most states passed laws providing some kind of reporter's privilege. What arguments could you make that it is now time for the Supreme Court to change its mind and provide a basic privilege that would be uniform across the country?

5. As a general rule the Supreme Court has ruled that the press may report the names of people involved in the criminal process, including the names of juvenile delinquents and rape victims. Do you think the Court

has gone too far? If so, where would you draw the line between what the press can and can not report in this area?

6. Generally, publishers control what they print in their newspapers, not the government, reporters, or the general public. What problems does this create for society? If a city wished to allow its citizens to have some way to respond to articles in the local newspaper, what could it do?

CHAPTER
eight

* * * * * * * *

The Right to Assemble and Petition Government

.... DISCUSSION ....

The last thing the First Amendment protects is "the right of the people peaceably to assemble, and to petition the Government for a redress of grievances." While these words have been in the Constitution since 1791, when the Bill of Rights went into effect, the Supreme Court was not called upon to interpret them until 1940. Since then, the Supreme Court has considered such right to assemble issues as picket lines, boycotts, and civil rights and anti-war demonstrations.

PICKET LINES

Thornhill v. Alabama involved an Alabama law that made "loitering" or "picketing" around a place of business a crime. The Supreme Court was faced with the conviction under this statute of eight union members who had gone on strike and formed a picket line around their employer's place of business. There was no violence in this case, just a peaceful union picket line. The Court ruled that this union picket line was protected by the First Amendment's right to peaceably assemble. The Court viewed the main purpose of the picket line as communication. People who saw the picket line would realize that there was a labor dispute and could ask the picketing union members or the business owner what the dispute was about. The Court majority thought that a labor dispute was something the general public had an interest in knowing about. Because a labor dispute is a "matter of public concern," actions and words designed to communicate about a dispute, such as a picket line, are protected by the First Amendment. Police are allowed to prevent this kind of communication only if there is a "clear and present danger" of some "substantive evil." Only Justice McReynolds dissented, pointing to the long history of labor violence and the need to prevent it by banning labor union picketing.

It is important to remember that between the end of the Civil War and the *Thornhill* decision in 1940 it had become common for judges in all sections of the United States to issue court orders to stop most labor picketing because of the "potential" for violence. Also, many states had statutes on the books that made even peaceful union picketing illegal in most situations. With the decision in *Thornhill* the Court began a new era of labor relations and the general right of the people to assemble to communicate their grievances.

LIMITATIONS ON THE RIGHT TO PICKET

The Court soon decided that labor union picketing was a more complex subject than it had first thought in 1940. In 1941 six of the nine justices decided that union members do not have a right to picket anyone they wish at any time. The case involved a dispute between a labor union and a dairy. The dairy was selling milk to people who owned their own milk trucks and then resold the milk to retailers and residential customers (*Drivers Union v. Meadowmoor Co.*). These milk truck owners were independent contractors, not employees, so they could work for less than the union drivers were willing to work for. The driver's union believed its members would soon be out of work if this trend continued, so union members formed picket lines. The dispute resulted in considerable violence, including bomb throwing. A judge issued an order to stop both the violence and the picketing, and a majority of the Supreme Court justices agreed that the judge was within his legal power to issue such an order. The three dissenters, Justices Black, Douglas, and Reed, argued that while the judge was certainly free to order a stop to the violence, he was not free to stop peaceful picketing. The dissenters thought that peaceful picketing was protected by the First Amendment, or at least that is what they thought the Court had decided the year before in the *Thornhill* case.

In 1942, in *Carpenters Union v. Ritter's Cafe*, five members of the Court agreed that another judge could issue another order to stop union picketing even without violence or the threat of violence. This case involved a dispute between several labor unions and the owner of Ritter's Cafe. The owner of the cafe had hired a contractor to build a new building, and the contractor had hired some employees who did not belong to a union. The carpenter's union picketed the cafe. As a result, the employees of the cafe went on strike and most delivery-truck drivers refused to cross the picket line. This put Ritter's Cafe out of business. Again, given the complex nature of this dispute, a majority of the justices thought that the First Amendment did not protect this kind of "assembly" under these circumstances. These justices believed the carpenter's union had a right to picket the contractor, but not the person who had hired the contractor. The four dissenting justices, Justices Black, Douglas, Murphy, and Reed, argued that the decision in *Thornhill* should have settled this question.

Also in 1942 the Court ruled, with a unanimous decision in *Bakery Driver's Local v. Wohl*, that a union had a constitutional right to picket an employer with whom it did have a direct labor dispute. The case involved bakeries that were replacing their union drivers with independent contractors who signed up to work six days a week and who were not covered by workers compensation or unemployment compensation. The union put two pickets in front of each bakery. The Court said that peaceful picketing of an employer with whom the union had a direct dispute was protected by the First Amendment.

Throughout the next half century the Court struggled with what labor unions did and did not have a right to do under the First Amendment. The general rule the Court developed was that unions have a right to picket only employers with whom they have a direct labor dispute.

PARADES

The argument could be made that a union picket line is not exactly what the authors of the First Amendment had in mind when they guaranteed the people's right to assemble and "petition the government for a redress of grievances." In 1941 the Court began to address that particular right with the case of *Cox v. New Hampshire*, which involved the power of states and cities to control parades. The parade in this case consisted of a group of 20 Jehovah's Witnesses marching single file down the sidewalk of the business district of Manchester, New Hampshire. A unanimous Supreme Court ruled that people have a right under the First Amendment to have a parade. At the same time, a city may require people having parades to get a parade permit and pay a "reasonable" fee designed to cover the city's costs. A city could control the "time, place and manner" of speech, including a parade, in order to maintain order, but it could not prevent parades or issue parade permits based on the "subject" of the parade.

Some might question whether or not a parade can be seen as an attempt to "petition government," but since the *Cox* decision the Supreme Court has accepted the idea that in a democracy the government and the people are one and the same. If people want to assemble in order to communicate with their fellow citizens about almost anything, that is enough to bring them under the protection of the First Amendment's right to assemble.

THE RIGHT TO ASSEMBLE AND VIOLATIONS OF THE LAW

In 1949 the Court voted five to four to protect the right of a group of people to assemble to hear speeches. The case, *Terminiello v. Chicago* (see p. 127), (see p. 127) involved a meeting of the Christian Veterans of America. While 800 people met inside an auditorium in Chicago, about 1,000 people gathered outside to protest what they considered to be a Fascist organization. The main speaker for the night, Father Terminiello, was arrested by Chicago police for "disorderly conduct" and "breach of the peace" because a riot broke out in front of the auditorium. Five members of the Court ruled that the city could not prosecute this speaker and his organization because another group of people chose to break the law and breach the peace. Father Terminiello had not used "fighting words" or said anything that could be seen as directly inciting a riot. The people outside the auditorium simply did not agree with what Father Terminiello had to say. The majority of justices thought that the First Amendment was designed to protect speakers from being silenced by those who disagreed. Justice Douglas, who wrote the majority opinion, argued that one of the functions of speech is to "invite dispute" and that the First Amendment was designed to protect "verbal disputes" as long as they did not become something more. He also thought that to allow Chicago to punish Father Terminiello because some other group violated the law would give any group willing to riot a veto over who could speak on public issues. This, he thought, should never be allowed. Justice Jackson, in his dissenting opinion, argued that Father Terminiello's anti-Jewish rhetoric was a prime cause of the riot and therefore he should be asked to bear some of the blame for the breach of the peace that did occur.

By 1950 a unanimous Court, with an opinion written by Justice Frankfurter, could agree on the broad outlines of what the right to assemble does and does not protect. The case of *Hughes v. Superior Court* involved a picket line around Lucky grocery stores in California by the Progressive Citizens of America. This group believed that Lucky had discriminated against blacks in hiring and they asked management at Lucky to agree to hire only blacks as white employees quit until half of all the employees were black. The group believed that since over half of Lucky's customers were black in the stores they had targeted, half of their employees should also be black. A California judge had issued an order to stop the picketing. The judge thought that the Progressive Citizens were asking Lucky stores to discriminate on the basis of race in hiring, which would violate California laws against race discrimination. A unanimous Supreme Court agreed that "picketing" is more than just speech and can be stopped for a good reason. The desire to stop this group from trying to pressure Lucky to violate the law was a good enough reason in this case.

During the 1940s the Court concluded that one rule simply protecting the right to "assemble" would not work. A union picket line is different from a political picket line, which is different from a parade, which is different from a group in a meeting hall listening to speeches, which is different from a small group passing out leaflets. In each of these situations the right to assemble must be weighed against the need to maintain order and to avoid a variety of evils that cities and states have a right to avoid, if possible. While the Court was able to say that everyone has a right to go door to door to pass out leaflets on any subject, the same did not apply to the right to picket or march. The Court spent the next four decades trying to explain what the rules were for these different situations.

CIVIL RIGHTS DEMONSTRATIONS

Most right to assemble cases in the 1940s involved labor unions and religious groups. By the 1960s most right to assemble cases involved civil rights groups and anti-war demonstrators. In 1963 the Court was faced with 187 "Negro high school and college students" who gathered at the steps of the state capitol in Columbia, South Carolina, to protest racial discrimination (*Edwards v. South Carolina*). When told to disperse they refused and sang protest songs instead. The students were then arrested for breach of the peace, even though there had been no violence or threat of violence. The Court, with one dissent, ruled that these convictions violated the right to assemble protected by the First Amendment. The Court ruled that a state may not "make criminal the peaceful expression of unpopular views." The lone dissenter, Justice Clark, argued that disorder was imminent when the police led the demonstrators away and the police must have the power to prevent violence in these kinds of situations.

In 1966 five justices overturned the breach of the peace convictions of several black students who staged a sit-in demonstration in a public library in Louisiana to protest the fact that blacks were not allowed in public libraries in Louisiana (*Brown v. Louisiana*). The five-justice majority thought that even though this was a sit-in, it had been peaceful and the action had been intended to convey a message. Therefore, it was a kind of assembly protected by the First Amendment. The four dissenting justices thought that a sit-in in a public building could not be seen as speech and could be punished without violating the First Amendment.

In 1969 a unanimous Court overturned the conviction of a group of demonstrators who marched from city hall to the mayor's residence in Chicago to protest the lack of integration in Chicago public schools (*Gregory v. Chicago*). When a group of bystanders became unruly, the police ordered the demonstrators to disperse, but they refused. The convictions were overturned because the trial judge's interpretation of the law could have led the members of the jury to believe that they could send these people to jail simply for the act of demonstrating which was not true. The demonstrators could have been sent to jail for refusal to disperse, but that is not what they had been convicted of.

In 1969 a unanimous Court overturned a permit ordinance in Birmingham, Alabama (*Shuttlesworth v. Birmingham*). The city had refused to give a permit to anyone wishing to hold a parade or demonstration protesting the lack of racial integration in Alabama. The Court ruled that while a city may have a permit law if it is narrowly drawn to regulate the "time, place and manner" of a demonstration, a city could not refuse to issue permits based on the content of the speech in question. The Birmingham ordinance gave total discretion to the city manager to refuse to issue permits for any reason. This was not acceptable. What about the demonstrators who were arrested? The Court said that anyone faced with an unconstitutional law may ignore it and, if punished, seek the protection of the federal courts.

In the 1970s the Court made it clear that laws that attempt to control free speech and assembly had to be clear and reasonable. In *Coates v. Cincinnati*, the Court threw out a Cincinnati, Ohio, ordinance that made it a crime for three or more people to assemble and "conduct themselves in a way annoying to persons passing by." The Court found this ordinance to be too vague. How can anyone know in advance what might be "annoying"? On the other hand, the Court upheld an ordinance in Rockford, Illinois, that made it a crime to make noise near a school while the school was in session (*Grayned v. Rockford*). The Court thought that this ordinance was not vague and was reasonable given its purpose, which was to allow schools to perform their educational function.

PARADE OF THE AMERICAN NAZI PARTY

In 1977 and 1978 a series of decisions were handed down that showed just how far the Court had come in deciding that the right of free speech and assembly is entitled to protection. The case involved the American Nazi Party (National Socialist Party), which wanted to stage a parade through Skokie, Illinois, knowing full well that many of the survivors of the Holocaust lived in Skokie. This case went to the Supreme Court several times. Throughout the long process of appeals, the Nazi Party was represented by a Jewish attorney who believed the right to assemble protected everyone, even Nazis. In 1977 the Court issued a per curiam decision lifting the court order by an Illinois judge that had prevented the parade (*National Socialist Party v. Skokie*). A per curiam decision means the Court did not hear formal arguments in the case; the Court simply read the information supplied in the petition asking the Court to take the case and decided the case on the basis of that information. Faced with a possible Nazi parade, the town of Skokie enacted three ordinances. The first required people to obtain $300,000 in liability insurance and

$50,000 in property damage insurance before they could receive a parade permit. The second outlawed the distribution of any materials that might incite racial hatred. The third prohibited public demonstrations by any political party whose members intended to wear military-style uniforms during the parade. A federal judge threw out these ordinances, finding them a violation of the right to speak and the right to assemble protected by the First Amendment. The judge said that "it is better to allow those who preach racial hatred to expend their venom in rhetoric rather than to be panicked into embarking on the dangerous course of permitting the government to decide what its citizens may say and hear" (*Collin v. Smith*). In 1978 the Supreme Court refused to review this decision (*Smith v. Collin*). Several justices objected to the process used throughout this case. They thought that the Court should have heard formal arguments and made a formal decision, but a majority of justices refused to take that approach. Apparently they believed that their past decisions were enough to affirm that even Nazis have a right to hold a parade in America. After winning their case, the Nazis decided to march in Chicago instead. On July 9, 1978, 25 Nazis held a rally in a Chicago park. There was no violence.

ANTI-ABORTION PROTESTS

By the late 1980s the major issue in right to assemble cases was not civil rights or anti-war demonstrations, but anti-abortion protests by right-to-life groups. One of the tactics of these groups was to picket the homes of doctors who performed abortions. In 1988, in *Frisby v. Schultz* (see p. 131), the Court ruled that cities and states could pass laws that prohibited picketing in front of a particular residence. The protesters in this case wanted to form a picket line around the home of a doctor in Brookfield, Wisconsin, but a city ordinance made residential picketing illegal. Justice O'Connor, writing for the majority, interpreted this ordinance to prohibit picketing in front of a particular residence and ruled that this was permissible under the First Amendment. The right of privacy and the need to maintain public safety were enough to justify this limitation on the right to assemble. She also interpreted this ordinance to allow picketers to march through the residential area, as long as they did not focus on one particular house. Justice O'Connor pointed out that these demonstrators did not wish to "inform" the public about their views. Instead, they wished to "intrude" on the privacy of a doctor who performed legal abortions in an effort to force the doctor to stop doing so. The three dissenters thought that Justice O'Connor had taken great liberties in "interpreting" this ordinance in order to save it from being declared unconstitutional.

PARADE FEES

In 1992 the Court came back to an issue it had just briefly touched on in 1941 with its decision in *Cox v. New Hampshire*. In *Cox* the Court had ruled that a city may require someone wishing to have a parade to pay a fee based on the reasonable expected cost of supervising the parade. In 1992 five justices voted to overturn an ordinance that did just that in *Forsyth County v. Nationalist Movement*. The ordinance allowed a fee of up to $1,000 to be charged based on the expected cost of the parade. The majority of justices believed that this ordinance allowed officials to raise or lower the fee based on whether or not they agreed with the content of the speech to be expressed during the parade. This kind of discretion could not be allowed. The power to vary the fee could be used to discourage some groups and encourage others. The Court ruled that variable parade fees must be based on definite standards set out in the ordinance and cannot be based in any way on the content of the speech involved. The four dissenting justices, Chief Justice Rehnquist and Justices White, Scalia, and Thomas, argued that this issue had been decided in 1941 in the *Cox* decision and there was no reason to change the Court's mind on this issue.

What went unsaid in this 1992 decision is that a lot had changed in the half century that separated these two decisions. The Court had expanded its protection of the right of free speech, including the right to "peaceably assemble." Federal courts had protected civil rights demonstrators and the Ku Klux Klan; the Christian Veterans of America, Nazis, and anti-war demonstrators; and pro-choice and pro-life advocates. The right to assemble to express unpopular views received the same protection as the right to assemble to express popular views.

CONCLUSION

In 1940 the Court set out to remove unreasonable obstacles to peaceful assembly, and by the 1990s it had done just that. Gone are the unreasonable permit requirements, insurance requirements, and parade fees. Gone are the broadly written and vague laws against disorderly conduct and breach of the peace. While states and cities may control the "time, place and manner" of the assembly to achieve legitimate goals such as controlling traffic flow, they may not prevent assemblies based on the subject to be discussed. The fact that some group may not approve of the assembly and violence may result will not generally justify withholding a parade permit or limiting the right of free speech.

The Court has continued to recognize that a large group of demonstrators is different from a lone individual passing out leaflets or carrying a sign. The potential for violence is greater with a large group, and cities and states need some freedom to act when violence is imminent. The Court now requires, however, that the possibility of violence be real and imminent before police may act to limit the right of free speech and assembly guaranteed by the First Amendment.

............................CASE DECISIONS............................

In the 1949 case of *Terminiello v. Chicago*, a majority of justices ruled that a city could not punish a speaker just because a riot broke out near the auditorium in which he was speaking. The Court based its decision on the definition of "breach of the peace" that was given to the jury in the case. Justice Douglas wrote the opinion for the five-justice majority, which is included here. Dissenting opinions by Chief Justice Vinson and Justice Jackson are also included. Justice Frankfurter's dissenting opinion is not included.

In the 1988 decision of *Frisby v. Schultz*, the Court upheld the constitutionality of an ordinance that limited the right to picket in front of a private residence. The majority opinion, written by Justice O'Connor for the six-justice majority, is included here. Justice White's concurring opinion is not included. Dissenting opinions by Justices Brennan and Stevens are included. Following are excerpts from the case decisions.

❀ ❀ ❀ ❀ ❀ ❀ ❀ ❀

TERMINIELLO v. CHICAGO
337 U.S. 1 (1949)

MR. JUSTICE DOUGLAS delivered the opinion of the Court.

Petitioner after jury trial was found guilty of disorderly conduct in violation of a city ordinance of Chicago and fined. The case grew out of an address he delivered in an auditorium in Chicago under the auspices of the Christian Veterans of America. The meeting commanded considerable public attention. The auditorium was filled to capacity with over eight hundred persons present. Others were turned away. Outside of the auditorium a crowd of about one thousand persons gathered to protest against the meeting. A cordon of policemen was assigned to the meeting to maintain order; but they were not able to prevent several disturbances. The crowd outside was angry and turbulent.

Petitioner in his speech condemned the conduct of the crowd outside and vigorously, if not viciously, criticized various political and racial groups whose activities he denounced as inimical to the nation's welfare.

The trial court charged that "breach of the peace" consists of any "misbehavior which violates the public peace and decorum"; and that the "misbehavior may constitute a breach of the peace if it stirs the public to anger, invites dispute, brings about a condition of unrest, or creates a disturbance, or if it molests the inhabitants in the enjoyment of peace and quiet by arousing alarm." Petitioner did not take exception to that instruction. But he maintained at all times that the ordinance as applied to his conduct violated his right of free speech under the Federal Constitution. The judgment of conviction was affirmed by the Illinois Appellate Court (332 Ill. App. 17, 74 N.E.2d 45) and by the Illinois Supreme Court. 396 Ill. 41, 71 N.E.2d 2; 400 Ill. 23, 79 N.E.2d 39. The case is here on a petition for certiorari which we granted because of the importance of the question presented.

The argument here has been focused on the issue of whether the content of petitioner's speech was composed of derisive, fighting words, which carried it outside the scope of the constitutional guarantees. See *Chaplinsky v. New Hampshire*, 315 U.S. 568; *Cantwell v. Connecticut*, 310 U.S. 296, 310. We do not reach that question, for there is a preliminary question that is dispositive of the case.

As we have noted, the statutory words "breach of the peace" were defined in instructions to the jury to include speech which "stirs the public to anger, invites dispute, brings about a condition of unrest, or creates a disturbance. . . ." That construction of the ordinance is a ruling on a question of state law that is as binding on us as though the precise words had been written into the ordinance. See *Hebert v. Louisiana*, 272 U.S. 312, 317; *Winters v. New York*, 333 U.S. 507, 514.

The vitality of civil and political institutions in our society depends on free discussion. As Chief Justice Hughes wrote in *De Jonge v. Oregon*, 299 U.S. 353, 365, it is only through free debate and free exchange of ideas that government remains responsive to the will of the people and peaceful change is effected. The right to speak freely and to promote diversity of ideas and programs is therefore one of the chief distinctions that sets us apart from totalitarian regimes.

Accordingly a function of free speech under our system of government is to invite dispute. It may indeed best serve its high purpose when it induces a condition of unrest, creates dissatisfaction with conditions as they are, or even stirs people to anger. Speech is often provocative and challenging. It may strike at prejudices and preconceptions and have profound unsettling effects as it presses for acceptance of an idea. That is why freedom of speech, though not absolute, *Chaplinsky v. New Hampshire*, *supra*, pp. 571–572, is nevertheless protected against censorship or punishment, unless shown likely to produce a clear and present danger of a serious substantive evil that rises far above public inconvenience, annoyance, or unrest. See *Bridges v. California*, 314 U.S. 252, 262; *Craig v. Harney*, 331 U.S. 367, 373. There is no room under our Constitution for a more restrictive view. For the alternative would lead to standardization of ideas either by legislatures, courts, or dominant political or community groups.

The ordinance as construed by the trial court seriously invaded this province. It permitted conviction of petitioner if his speech stirred people to anger, invited public dispute, or brought about a condition of unrest. A conviction resting on any of those grounds may not stand.

Dissenting Opinion   MR. CHIEF JUSTICE VINSON, dissenting.

I dissent. The Court today reverses the Supreme Court of Illinois because it discovers in the record one sentence in the trial court's instructions which permitted the jury to convict on an unconstitutional basis. The offending sentence had heretofore gone completely undetected. It apparently was not even noticed, much less excepted to, by the petitioner's counsel at the trial. No objection was made to it in the two Illinois appellate tribunals which reviewed the case. Nor was it mentioned in the petition for certiorari or the briefs in this Court. In short, the offending sentence in the charge to the jury was no part of the case until this Court's independent research ferreted it out of a lengthy and somewhat confused record. I think it too plain for argument that a reversal on such a basis does not accord with any principle governing review of state court decisions heretofore announced by this Court.

Dissenting Opinion   MR. JUSTICE JACKSON, dissenting.

The Court reverses this conviction by reiterating generalized approbations of freedom of speech with which, in the abstract, no one will disagree. Doubts as to their applicability are lulled by avoidance of more than passing reference to the circumstances of Terminiello's speech and judging it as if he had spoken to persons as dispassionate as empty benches, or like a modern Demosthenes practicing his Philippics on a lonely seashore.

But the local court that tried Terminiello was not indulging in theory. It was dealing with a riot and with a speech that provoked a hostile mob and incited a friendly one, and threatened violence between the two. When the trial judge instructed the jury that it might find Terminiello guilty of inducing a breach of the peace if his behavior stirred the public to anger, invited dispute, brought about unrest, created a disturbance or molested peace and quiet by arousing alarm, he was not speaking of these as harmless or abstract conditions. He was addressing his words to the concrete behavior and specific consequences disclosed by the evidence. He was saying to the jury, in effect, that if this particular speech added fuel to the situation already so inflamed as to threaten to get beyond police control, it could be punished as inducing a breach of peace. When the light of the evidence not recited by the Court is thrown upon the Court's opinion, it discloses that underneath a little issue of Terminiello and his hundred-dollar fine lurk some of the most far-reaching constitutional questions that can confront a people who value both liberty and order. This Court seems to regard these as enemies of each other and to be of the view that we must forego order to achieve liberty. So it fixes its eyes on a conception of freedom of speech so rigid as to tolerate no concession to society's need for public order. . . .

The street mob, on the other hand, included some who deny being communists, but Terminiello testified and offered to prove that the demonstration was communist-organized and communist-led. He offered literature of left-wing organizations calling members to meet and "mobilize" for instruction as pickets and exhorting followers: "All out to fight Fascist Smith."

As this case declares a nation-wide rule that disables local and state authorities from punishing conduct which produces conflicts of this kind, it is unrealistic not to take account of the nature, methods and objectives of the forces involved. This was not an isolated, spontaneous and unintended collision of political, racial or ideological adversaries. It was a local manifestation of a world-wide and standing conflict between two organized groups of revolutionary fanatics, each of which has imported to this country the strong-arm technique developed in the struggle by which their kind has devastated Europe. Increasingly, American cities have to cope with it. One faction organizes a mass meeting, the other organizes pickets to harass it; each organizes squads to counteract the other's pickets; parade is met with counterparade. Each of these mass demonstrations has the potentiality, and more than a few the purpose, of disorder and violence. This technique appeals not to reason but to fears and mob spirit; each is a show of force designed to bully adversaries and to overawe the indifferent. We need not resort to speculation as to the purposes for which these tactics are calculated nor as to their consequences. Recent European history demonstrates both. . . .

This drive by totalitarian groups to undermine the prestige and effectiveness of local democratic governments is advanced whenever either of them can win from this Court a ruling which paralyzes the power of these officials. This is such a case. The group of which Terminiello is a part claims that his behavior, because it involved a speech, is above the reach of local authorities. If the mild action those authorities have taken is forbidden, it is plain that hereafter there is nothing effective left that they can do. If they can do nothing as to him, they are equally powerless as to rival totalitarian groups. Terminiello's victory today certainly fulfills the most extravagant hopes of both right and left totalitarian groups, who want nothing so much as to paralyze and discredit the only democratic authority that can curb them in their battle for the streets. . . .

This Court has gone far toward accepting the doctrine that civil liberty means the removal of all restraints from these crowds and that all local attempts to maintain order are impairments of the liberty of the citizen. The choice is not between order and liberty. It is between liberty with order and anarchy without either. There is danger that, if the Court does not temper its doctrinaire logic with a little practical wisdom, it will convert the constitutional Bill of Rights into a suicide pact.

I would affirm the conviction.

MR. JUSTICE BURTON joins in this opinion.

FRISBY v. SCHULTZ
487 U.S. 474 (1988)

JUSTICE O'CONNOR delivered the opinion of the Court.

Brookfield, Wisconsin, has adopted an ordinance that completely bans picketing "before or about" any residence. This case presents a facial First Amendment challenge to that ordinance.

Brookfield, Wisconsin, is a residential suburb of Milwaukee with a population of approximately 4,300. The appellees, Sandra C. Schultz and Robert C. Braun, are individuals strongly opposed to abortion and wish to express their views on the subject by picketing on a public street outside the Brookfield residence of a doctor who apparently performs abortions at two clinics in neighboring towns. Appellees and others engaged in precisely that activity, assembling outside the doctor's home on at least six occasions between April 20, 1985, and May 20, 1985, for periods ranging from one to one and a half hours. The size of the group varied from 11 to more than 40. The picketing was generally orderly and peaceful; the town never had occasion to invoke any of its various ordinances prohibiting obstruction of the streets, loud and unnecessary noises, or disorderly conduct. Nonetheless, the picketing generated substantial controversy and numerous complaints.

The Town Board therefore resolved to enact an ordinance to restrict the picketing. On May 7, 1985, the town passed an ordinance that prohibited all picketing in residential neighborhoods except for labor picketing. But after reviewing this Court's decision in *Carey v. Brown*, 447 U.S. 455 (1980), which invalidated a similar ordinance as a violation of the Equal Protection Clause, the town attorney instructed the police not to enforce the new ordinance and advised the Town Board that the ordinance's labor picketing exception likely rendered it unconstitutional. This ordinance was repealed on May 15, 1985, and replaced with the following flat ban on all residential picketing:

"It is unlawful for any person to engage in picketing before or about the residence or dwelling of any individual in the Town of Brookfield." App. to Juris. Statement A–28.

The ordinance itself recites the primary purpose of this ban: "the protection and preservation of the home" through assurance "that members of the community enjoy in their homes and dwellings a feeling of well-being, tranquility, and privacy." *Id.*, at A–26. The Town Board believed that a ban was necessary because it determined that "the practice of picketing before or about residences and dwellings causes emotional disturbance and distress to the occupants . . . [and] has as its object the harassing of such occupants." *Id.*, at A–26–A–27. The ordinance also evinces a concern for public safety, noting that picketing obstructs and interferes with "the free use of public sidewalks and public ways of travel." *Id.*, at A–27.

On May 18, 1985, appellees were informed by the town attorney that enforcement of the new, revised ordinance would begin on May 21, 1985. Faced with this threat of arrest and prosecution, appellees ceased picketing in Brookfield and filed this lawsuit in the United States District Court for the Eastern District of Wisconsin. The complaint was brought under 42 U. S. C. § 1983 and sought declaratory as well as preliminary and permanent injunctive relief on the grounds that the ordinance violated the First Amendment. Appellees named appellants—the three members of the Town Board, the Chief of Police, the town attorney, and the town itself—as defendants. . . .

The antipicketing ordinance operates at the core of the First Amendment by prohibiting appellees from engaging in picketing on an issue of public concern. Because of the importance of "uninhibited, robust, and wide-open" debate on public issues, *New York Times Co. v. Sullivan*, 376 U.S. 254, 270 (1964), we have traditionally subjected restrictions on public issue picketing to careful scrutiny. See, *e.g., Boos v. Barry*, 485 U.S. 312, 318 (1988); *United States v. Grace*, 461 U.S. 171 (1983); *Carey v. Brown*, 447 U.S. 455 (1980). Of course, "[e]ven protected speech is not equally permissible in all places and at all times." *Cornelius v. NAACP Legal Defense & Educational Fund, Inc.*, 473 U.S. 788, 799 (1985).

To ascertain what limits, if any, may be placed on protected speech, we have often focused on the "place" of that speech, considering the nature of the forum the speaker seeks to employ. Our cases have recognized that the standards by which limitations on speech must be evaluated "differ depending on the character of the property at issue." *Perry Education Assn. v. Perry Local Educators' Assn.*, 460 U.S. 37, 44 (1983). Specifically, we have identified three types of fora: "the traditional public forum, the public forum created by government designation, and the nonpublic forum." *Cornelius, supra*, at 802.

The relevant forum here may be easily identified: appellees wish to picket on the public streets of Brookfield. Ordinarily, a determination of the nature of the forum would follow automatically from this identification; we have repeatedly referred to public streets as the archetype of a traditional public forum. See, e.g., *Boos v. Barry, supra*, at 318; *Cornelius, supra*, at 802; *Perry,* 460 U.S., at 45. "[T]ime out of mind" public streets and sidewalks have been used for public assembly and debate, the hallmarks of a traditional public forum. See *ibid.; Hague v. CIO,* 307 U.S. 496, 515 (1939) (Roberts, J.). Appellants, however, urge us to disregard these "clichés." Tr. of Oral Arg. 16. They argue that the streets of Brookfield should be considered a nonpublic forum. Pointing to the physical narrowness of Brookfield's streets as well as to their residential character, appellants contend that such streets have not by tradition or designation been held open for public communication. See Brief for Appellants 23 (citing *Perry, supra,* at 46).

We reject this suggestion. Our prior holdings make clear that a public street does not lose its status as a traditional public forum simply because it runs through a residential neighborhood. In *Carey v. Brown*—which considered a statute similar to the one at issue here, ultimately striking it down as a violation of the Equal Protection Clause because it included an exception for labor picketing—we expressly recognized that "public streets and sidewalks in residential neighborhoods," were "public for[a]." 447 U.S., at 460–461. This rather ready identification virtually forecloses appellants' argument. See also *Perry, supra,* at 54–55 (noting the "key" to *Carey* "was the presence of a public forum").

In short, our decisions identifying public streets and sidewalks as traditional public fora are not accidental invocations of a "cliché," but recognition that "[w]herever the title of streets and parks may rest, they have immemorially been held in trust for the use of the public." *Hague v. CIO, supra,* at 515 (Roberts, J.). No particularized inquiry into the precise nature of a specific street is necessary; all public streets are held in the public trust and are properly considered traditional public fora. Accordingly, the streets of Brookfield are traditional public fora. . . .

The precise scope of the ban is not further described within the text of the ordinance, but in our view the ordinance is readily subject to a narrowing construction that avoids constitutional difficulties. Specifically, the use of the singular form of the words "residence" and "dwelling" suggests that the ordinance is intended to prohibit only picketing focused on, and taking place in front of, a particular residence. . . . This narrow reading is supported by the representations of counsel for the town at oral argument, which indicate that the town takes, and will enforce, a limited view of the "picketing" proscribed in the ordinance. Thus, generally speaking, "picketing would be having the picket proceed on a definite course or route in front of a home." Tr. of Oral Arg. 8. The picket need not be carrying a sign, *id.* at 14, but in order to fall within the scope of the ordinance the picketing must be directed at a single residence, *id.*, at 9. General marching through residential neighborhoods, or even walking a route in front of an entire block of houses, is not prohibited by this ordinance. *Id.*, at 15. Accordingly, we construe the ban to be a limited one; only focused picketing taking place solely in front of a particular residence is prohibited.

So narrowed, the ordinance permits the more general dissemination of a message. As appellants explain, the limited nature of the prohibition makes it virtually self-evident that ample alternatives remain:

> "Protestors have not been barred from residential neighborhoods. They may enter such neighborhoods, alone or in groups, even marching. . . . They may go door-to-door to proselytize their views. They may distribute literature in this manner . . . or through the mails. They may contact residents by telephone, short of harassment." Brief for Appellants 41–42 (citations omitted).

We readily agree that the ordinance preserves ample alternative channels of communication and thus move on to inquire whether the ordinance serves a significant government interest. We find that such an interest is identified within the text of the ordinance itself: the protection of residential privacy. See App. to Juris. Statement A–26.

"The State's interest in protecting the well-being, tranquility, and privacy of the home is certainly of the highest order in a free and civilized society." *Carey v. Brown*, 447 U.S., at 471. Our prior decisions have often remarked on the unique nature of the home, "the last citadel of the tired, the weary, and the sick," *Gregory v. Chicago*, 394 U.S. 111, 125 (1969) (Black, J., concurring), and have recognized that "[p]reserving the sanctity of the home, the one retreat to which men and women can repair to escape from the tribulations of their daily pursuits, is surely an important value." *Carey, supra,* at 471.

One important aspect of residential privacy is protection of the unwilling listener. Although in many locations, we expect individuals simply to avoid speech they do not want to hear, cf. *Erznoznik v. City of Jacksonville, supra,* at 210–211; *Cohen v. California*, 403 U.S. 15, 21–22 (1971), the home is different. "That we are often 'captives' outside the sanctuary of the home and subject to objectionable speech . . . does not mean we must be captives everywhere." *Rowan v. Post Office Dept.*, 397 U.S. 728, 738 (1970). Instead, a special benefit of the privacy all citizens enjoy within their own walls, which the State may legislate to protect, is an ability to avoid intrusions. Thus, we have repeatedly held that individuals are not required to welcome unwanted speech into their own homes and that the government may protect this freedom. See, *e.g., FCC v. Pacifica Foundation*, 438 U.S. 726, 748–749 (1978) (offensive radio broadcasts); *id.*, at 759–760 (Powell, J., concurring in part and concurring in judgment) (same); *Rowan, supra* (offensive mailings); *Kovacs v. Cooper*, 336 U.S. 77, 86–87 (1949) (sound trucks). . . .

Because the picketing prohibited by the Brookfield ordinance is speech directed primarily at those who are presumptively unwilling to receive it, the State has a substantial and justifiable interest in banning it. The nature and scope of this interest make the ban narrowly tailored. The ordinance also leaves open ample alternative channels of communication and is content neutral. Thus, largely because of its narrow scope, the facial challenge to the ordinance must fail. The contrary judgment of the Court of Appeals is

Reversed.

Dissenting Opinion JUSTICE BRENNAN, with whom JUSTICE MARSHALL joins, dissenting.

The Court today sets out the appropriate legal tests and standards governing the question presented, and proceeds to apply most of them correctly. Regrettably, though, the Court errs in the final step of its analysis, and approves an ordinance banning significantly more speech than is necessary to achieve the government's substantial and legitimate goal. Accordingly, I must dissent.

The ordinance before us absolutely prohibits picketing "before or about" any residence in the town of Brookfield, thereby restricting a manner of speech in a traditional public forum. Consequently, as the Court correctly states, the ordinance is subject to the well-settled time, place, and manner test: the restriction must be content and viewpoint neutral, leave open ample alternative channels of communication, and be narrowly tailored to further a substantial governmental interest. *Ante*, at 482; *Perry Education Assn. v. Perry Local Educators' Assn.*, 460 U.S. 37, 45 (1983).

Assuming one construes the ordinance as the Court does, I agree that the regulation reserves ample alternative channels of communication. *Ante*, at 482–484. I also agree with the Court that the town has a substantial interest in protecting its residents' right to be left alone in their homes. *Ante*, at 484–485; *Carey v. Brown*, 447 U.S. 455, 470–471 (1980). It is, however, critical to specify the precise scope of this interest. The mere fact that speech takes place in a residential neighborhood does not automatically implicate a residential privacy interest. It is the intrusion of speech into the home or the unduly coercive nature of a particular manner of speech around the home that is subject to more exacting regulation. Thus, the intrusion into the home of an unwelcome solicitor, *Martin v. Struthers*, 319 U.S. 141 (1943), or unwanted mail, *Rowan v. Post Office*, 397 U.S. 728 (1970), may be forbidden. Similarly, the government may forbid the intrusion of excessive noise into the home, *Kovacs v. Cooper*, 336 U.S. 77 (1949), or, in appropriate circumstances, perhaps even radio waves, *FCC v. Pacifica Foundation*, 438 U.S. 726 (1978).

Similarly, the government may prohibit unduly coercive conduct around the home, even though it involves expressive elements. A crowd of protesters need not be permitted virtually to imprison a person in his or her own house merely because they shout slogans or carry signs. But so long as the speech remains outside the home and does not unduly coerce the occupant, the government's heightened interest in protecting residential privacy is not implicated. See *Organization for a Better Austin v. Keefe*, 402 U.S. 415, 420 (1971). . . .

Without question there are many aspects of residential picketing that, if unregulated, might easily become intrusive or unduly coercive. Indeed, some of these aspects are illustrated by this very case. As the District Court found, before the ordinance took effect up to 40 sign-carrying, slogan-shouting protesters regularly converged on Dr. Victoria's home and, in addition to protesting, warned young children not to go near the house because Dr. Victoria was a "baby killer." Further, the throng repeatedly trespassed onto the Victorias' property and at least once blocked the exits to their home. 619 F. Supp. 792, 795 (ED Wis. 1985). Surely it is within the government's power to enact regulations as necessary to prevent such intrusive and coercive abuses. Thus, for example, the government could constitutionally regulate the number of residential picketers, the hours during which a residential picket may take place, or the noise level of such a picket. In short, substantial regulation is permitted to neutralize the intrusive or unduly coercive aspects of picketing around the home. But to say that picketing may be substantially regulated is not to say that it may be prohibited in its entirety. Once size, time, volume, and the like have been controlled to ensure that the picket is no longer intrusive or coercive, only the speech itself remains, conveyed perhaps by a lone, silent individual, walking back and forth with a sign. Cf *NLRB v. Retail Store Employees*, 447 U.S. 607, 618 (1980) (Stevens, J., concurring in part and concurring in result). Such speech, which no longer implicates the heightened governmental interest in residential privacy, is nevertheless banned by the Brookfield law. Therefore, the ordinance is not narrowly tailored. . . .

A valid time, place, or manner law neutrally regulates speech only to the extent necessary to achieve a substantial governmental interest, and no further. Because the Court is unwilling to examine the Brookfield ordinance in light of the precise governmental interest at issue, it condones a law that suppresses substantially more speech than is necessary. I dissent.

Dissenting Opinion   JUSTICE STEVENS, dissenting.
"GET WELL CHARLIE—OUR TEAM NEEDS YOU."
In Brookfield, Wisconsin, it is unlawful for a fifth grader to carry such a sign in front of a residence for the period of time necessary to convey its friendly message to its intended audience.

The Court's analysis of the question whether Brookfield's ban on picketing is constitutional begins with an acknowledgment that the ordinance "operates at the core of the First Amendment," *ante*, at 479, and that the streets of Brookfield are a "traditional public forum," *ante*, at 480. It concludes, however, that the total ban on residential picketing is "narrowly tailored" to protect "only unwilling recipients of the communications." *Ante*, at 485. The plain language of the ordinance, however, applies to communications to willing and indifferent recipients as well as to the unwilling. . . .

The picketing that gave rise to the ordinance enacted in this case was obviously intended to do more than convey a message of opposition to the character of the doctor's practice; it was intended to cause him and his family substantial psychological distress. As the record reveals, the picketers' message was repeatedly redelivered by a relatively large group—in essence, increasing the volume and intrusiveness of the same message with each repeated assertion, cf. *Kovacs v. Cooper*, 336 U.S. 77 (1949). As is often the function of picketing, during the periods of protest the doctor's home was held under a virtual siege. I do not believe that picketing for the sole purpose of imposing psychological harm on a family in the shelter of their home is constitutionally protected. I do believe, however, that the picketers have a right to communicate their strong opposition to abortion to the doctor, but after they have had a fair opportunity to communicate that message, I see little justification for allowing them to remain in front of his home and repeat it over and over again simply to harm the doctor and his family. Thus, I agree that the ordinance may be constitutionally applied to the kind of picketing that gave rise to its enactment.

On the other hand, the ordinance is unquestionably "overbroad" in that it prohibits some communication that is protected by the First Amendment. The question, then, is whether to apply the overbreadth doctrine's "strong medicine," see *Broadrick v. Oklahoma*, 413 U.S. 601, 613 (1973), or to put that approach aside "and await further developments," see *ante*, at 491 (White, J., concurring in judgment). In *Broadrick*, the Court framed the inquiry thusly:

"To put the matter another way, particularly where conduct and not merely speech is involved, we believe that the overbreadth of a statute must not only be real, but substantial as well, judged in relation to the statute's plainly legitimate sweep." 413 U.S., at 615.

In this case the overbreadth is unquestionably "real." Whether or not it is "substantial" in relation to the "plainly legitimate sweep" of the ordinance is a more difficult question. My hunch is that the town will probably not enforce its ban against friendly, innocuous, or even brief unfriendly picketing, and the Court may be right in concluding that its legitimate sweep makes its overbreadth insubstantial. But there are two countervailing considerations that are persuasive to me. The scope of the ordinance gives the town officials far too much discretion in making enforcement decisions; while we sit by and await further developments, potential picketers must act at their peril. Second, it is a simple matter for the town to amend its ordinance and to limit the ban to conduct that unreasonably interferes with the privacy of the home and does not serve a reasonable communicative purpose. Accordingly, I respectfully dissent.

DISCUSSION QUESTIONS

1. In an effort to prevent right-to-life protesters from targeting the homes of doctors who perform abortions, one city passed an ordinance forbidding all picketing and demonstrating within 300 feet of any residence. Is that ordinance constitutional?

2. The Supreme Court has on several occasions said that government may not have one set of rules for union picketing and another set for everyone else. Yet the Supreme Court has done just that by creating one set of rules for unions and another for everyone else. How can we explain this apparent inconsistency?

3. The justification for "special rules" for union picketing has been that they are needed to control violence. The response has been that violence is already illegal, so why punish all picketers for the actions of a few? Do you think today's Supreme Court would be more susceptible to this argument?

4. The Supreme Court did not allow a city to charge different parade permit fees based on the expected cost of the parade. Could a city charge a uniform fee? What if the uniform fee was $10,000? What if the city could prove that the average parade cost the city significantly more than $10,000 to supervise?

5. The general rule is that one group should not be allowed to use the threat of violence to stop speech by another group. Can you imagine a set of circumstances where you would be willing to stop speech in the face of such a threat? Do you think you could convince the Supreme Court that you did not violate the First Amendment?

CHAPTER
nine

❋ ❋ ❋ ❋ ❋ ❋ ❋ ❋

Freedom of Speech, Press, and Assembly Today

For people living in the United States today, the concept of almost unbridled free speech seems very natural, while the concept of government censorship seems very foreign. However, not so long ago in the United States, free speech was not so free. In 1911 a unanimous Supreme Court ruled that Americans had no right to speak to each other about boycotting businesses, and that decision was not overturned until 1982. A unanimous Supreme Court ruled in 1915 that movies were not protected by the First Amendment. That decision was not overturned until 1952. In 1919 a unanimous Supreme Court upheld the conviction of Eugene V. Debs for making a speech critical of U.S. foreign policy at a political convention. As recently as the 1950s officials in New York City were banning movies because they were sacrilegious, and risqué books were being banned in Boston as late as the 1960s.

When we look back on the twentieth century we see a remarkable story of the expansion of the rights of free speech, press, and assembly. In no other area has the Court changed its collective mind so many times, and each time it has been in order to expand these rights. In 1919 a unanimous Court sent people to prison for speech that might tend to interfere with the recruitment of soldiers in time of war. In 1970 a unanimous Court overturned the convictions of anti-Vietnam War demonstrators who had staged a sit-in at a recruiting station because the jury that convicted them might have based the conviction on the content of their speech. In 1907 only one justice could see a constitutional problem with judges holding a newspaper in contempt of court for criticizing their decisions. In 1941 the Court ruled that the rights of free speech and free press protected the right to criticize government officials, even judges. In 1940 the Court ruled that schoolchildren could be expelled for refusing to say the Pledge of Allegiance to the American flag. By 1943 the

Court had changed its collective mind and found that the right to speak included the right not to speak, at least under these circumstances.

Early on the Court tried to list types of speech that were not protected by the First Amendment. The list was long and included obscenity, libel, fighting words, and words that might, at some time, result in revolution or violence. The list included speech about commerce and speech designed primarily to entertain. With each passing decade this list has gotten shorter and shorter; today the only speech not entitled to at least some protection is speech that is likely to lead to immediate violence, what the Court calls "fighting words." All other speech is entitled to some protection from the First Amendment.

How could the Supreme Court change its mind so many times and still argue that it follows the doctrine of stare decisis? The answer lies in the Court's conception of its role in the U.S. legal system. Once the Court has interpreted a federal statute, it almost never changes its mind. The argument is that if the Court has misinterpreted the statute, Congress is always free to amend the statute, to correct the Court's misinterpretation. This happens from time to time. When it comes to interpreting the Constitution, however, only the Supreme Court can say what the Constitution means, and only a later Court can overturn an interpretation by an earlier Court. Because of this, the Court has been more willing to change its mind when interpreting the Constitution. Also, the Court has generally considered decisions that expand the rights of Americans to be fundamentally different from decisions that contract those rights. A majority of justices have been comfortable expanding rights to deal with new situations, even if previous Supreme Courts were not ready to do so. An early Supreme Court did not think movies fell under the umbrella of the right of free speech. A later Court, more familiar with what movies are capable of conveying, came to a different conclusion. An early Court did not see how protecting commercial speech could improve the marketplace of ideas. A later Court realized that even commercial speech can have political implications and redrew the line to bring commercial speech under the protection of the First Amendment. Each expansion of the right of free speech seemed reasonable, almost natural, by the time the Court was ready to make it. It is only when we stand back and look at the Court's decisions over time that the amount of change becomes apparent.

The kinds of speech subject to protection expanded so significantly because with each passing decade the Court accepted the philosophers' argument that the right of free speech was intended to do more than just protect political debate. Early on, the right of free speech combined with the right to freely exercise religion came to protect religious speech. In 1948 the Court expanded the right of free speech to protect all kinds of entertainment speech, including "true crime" magazines. Eventually this right would even protect the right of nude dancers to dance for tips in a nightclub. The right of consumers to receive information about commercial products and even the right of businesses to "pass out leaflets" on the sidewalk eventually fell under the protection of the First Amendment. In 1979 the Court ruled that the press did not have a right to attend criminal trials or hearings. By 1982 that idea had been completely rejected by the Court.

Early in the twentieth century, Justice Oliver Wendell Holmes developed the idea that speech could be limited if it posed a "clear and present danger" of a substantive evil. Over the years, the danger had to be more clear and the evil had to be more substantial to outweigh the right of free speech. Justice Brandeis expanded the thinking of the Court when he argued that the right of free speech was intended to protect the right of "free men to develop their faculties" as well as the right to discover political truth. Chief Justice Stone pointed out that the right to have and express one's own personal beliefs is paramount, and that the right to speak or not to speak, free from government interference, is a significant part of the right to believe. In decision after decision Justice Douglas argued for the greatest expansion of the rights of speech, press, and assembly. He could find very little that would justify the suppression of these rights by government.

Gradually the Court came to accept John Stuart Mill's argument that the correct response to "bad speech" is "good speech," not the suppression of speech; that the answer to "wrong speech" is more speech not less speech; that the right of a free press to criticize public officials is paramount to the workings of a democracy. John Stuart Mill recognized that speech that might result in mob violence could be controlled. That was the only specific exception he discussed in his book On Liberty, and it is now the only major limitation to the right of free speech in the United States. The Supreme Court has taken over a century to do it, but it has brought the actual right of free speech into line with what John Stuart Mill imagined it could be in 1859. In the process the Court has reflected, and helped to create, a nation dedicated to the ideal of the right of free speech. While many people in America objected to the flag-burning decisions, many others rejoiced that they lived in a country where they, as free citizens, even had the right to burn the national flag to make a political point.

Such an unlimited right of free speech is not without its price. Today, home owners often find themselves summoned to the door to discuss politics, religion, or commerce with someone they do not know. They find their mailboxes filled with information they do not have the time to wade through. They cannot walk anywhere without being asked for money or a signature on a petition. At times the amount of information circulating in the "marketplace of ideas" seems so overwhelming as to be beyond digesting or comprehending. Justice Jackson said in 1944 that "the price of freedom of religion or of speech or of the press is that we must put up with, and even pay for, a good deal of rubbish" (*United States v. Ballard*). One has to wonder what Justice Jackson would think if he were alive today to see just how the "rubbish" has multiplied since his time.

The right of free speech was purchased at a price. When we look back, it is striking how often the price of expanding the right of free speech was paid by the children of the United States. In the 1930s and 1940s it was the refusal of the Jehovah's Witnesses children to speak when that speech violated their religious beliefs that expanded the right to speak to include the right not to speak. In the 1970s and 1980s it was college students protesting the Vietnam War and other social problems that expanded the concept of what could be done in the name of speech, from burning flags to blocking recruiting stations. Black children in Birmingham, Alabama, were attacked by dogs and knocked down by blasts of water from high-powered fire hoses because they dared to march for civil rights from the 16th Street Baptist Church. Hundreds of those children filled jail cells in Birmingham, and four children were killed when the 16th Street Baptist Church was blown up in September 1963.

Those who cried out that American society would be destroyed if this or that group was not silenced have been proven wrong. Words and speeches can be hurtful, but they are not the equivalent of armed revolution or mob violence. People who are given a peaceful and legal outlet for their ideas do seem less prone to throw bombs and plot revolution.

Nude dancers and foreign films have not brought an end to morality. The use of zoning laws to control "adult entertainment" and the invention of cable television and the VCR seem to have allowed American society to adjust to new concepts of art and entertainment without the need for an official censor. The idea that at one time, not too long ago, judges could declare a book to be obscene now seems ridiculous. The movies that were subjected to censorship just two or three decades ago seem so tame by today's standards as to make the whole movie censorship process seem silly in retrospect.

At the same time the Court and society still recognize that at its core the right of free speech was intended to allow for a full debate about political personalities and public policy. This idea did not keep some communists, socialists, and anarchists from going to prison during the first half of the twentieth century but would protect them today. Only in the United States do Nazis find themselves represented by a Jewish lawyer arguing that they have a Constitutional right to march through a Jewish neighborhood to proclaim their hatred of Jews.

The steady expansion of the rights of free speech, press, and assembly is even more impressive when we realize that the makeup of the Court has changed drastically over the years. A group of conservative Republican justices was replaced by a group of liberal Democrat justices that was in turn replaced by another group of conservative Republicans. Throughout this process the evolution of the right of free speech has moved forward as if driven by some powerful internal logic. Justice Holmes began his book *The Common Law* with the line "The life of the law has not been logic; it has been experience." This is nowhere more true than in the area of free speech. Each decade the Court has experimented successfully with allowing greater freedom of speech. The feared revolution did not come, the social fabric did not tear apart, and the threatened violence did not erupt. Instead, American society was able to absorb new ideas and new lifestyles and go on. Millions of Americans have been called upon to fight for freedom in every corner of the globe. In the process Americans have come to see the right of free speech as the first freedom, the fundamental freedom, without which all other freedoms and democracy itself would be empty.

In 1919 Justice Holmes wrote a famous dissenting opinion in the case of *Abrams v. United States,* in which an "unknown man" was sentenced to 20 years in prison for passing out a "silly leaflet" protesting the presence of American troops in Russia. Holmes said:

> But when men have realized that time has upset many fighting faiths, they may come to believe even more than they believe the very foundation of their own conduct that the ultimate good desired is better reached by free trade in ideas—that the best test of truth is the power of the thought to get itself accepted in the competition of the market and that truth is the only ground upon which their wishes safely can be carried out. That at any rate is the theory of our Constitution. It is an experiment, as all life is an experiment. Every year, if not every day, we have to wager our salvation upon some prophecy based upon imperfect knowledge. While the experiment is part of our system I think that we should be eternally vigilant against attempts to check the expression of opinions that we loathe and believe to be fraught with death, unless they so imminently threaten immediate interference with the lawful and pressing purposes of the law that an immediate check is required to save the country.

In many ways the United States of America has indeed been an experiment. It has been an experiment with democracy and an experiment with freedom. The most radical experiment has been in the area of free speech. Can a society really prosper if it allows a "free marketplace of ideas" to flourish? Can a nation remain united while every sector of the nation is allowed to express its differences? The answer appears to be yes.

GLOSSARY OF
LEGAL TERMS

❋ ❋ ❋ ❋ ❋ ❋ ❋ ❋

A fortiori: Latin, meaning literally "from the stronger." It is used by judges to mean that if one fact exists, another fact must follow from it. If someone is alive, then we know *a fortiori* that he or she is breathing.

Allegation: A statement of fact that has not yet been proven. In a criminal case we would say that allegations have been made against the defendant which the prosecutor will attempt to prove.

Amicus curiae: Latin, meaning literally "a friend of the Court." In some cases, especially in cases that have been appealed, other people besides those people directly involved in a case may have an interest in the outcome. In an effort to influence the justices, these people will file briefs as "friends of the Court," suggesting why the decision should come out one way or the other. When people file *amicus curiae* briefs, they are usually arguing that the court's decision will have an impact on them or on society in general which the court should consider when making its decision.

Analogy: A way of thinking about an issue that relates a particular situation to another situation by identifying similarities. People involved in a case often argue that their case is analogous (or similar) to another case because they know what the court decided in the other case and they would like the court to make the same decision in their case.

Appeal: A request to a higher court to review the decision of a lower court. When a trial is over, the losing party may appeal the decision to an appeals court.

Appellant/Appellee: The appellant is the person who appeals a case to a higher court; the appellee is the person who has to respond to the appeal.

Atheist: A person who does not believe in the existence of a God.

Bill of attainder: A law passed by a legislature declaring that a particular person or a group of persons is guilty of a crime. The person, or group of persons, to whom the bill of attainder applies has not received a trial.

Brief: A written document given to a judge to support a particular legal opinion. When a case is appealed to a higher court, each side will file a brief explaining why it should win the case. Other people may also file briefs as "friends of the Court" (*amicus curiae* briefs), pointing out the effects a decision may have on them or on society in general.

Certiorari: Latin, meaning literally "to be certain." In American law, when someone wants to appeal his or her case to the U.S. Supreme Court, he or she usually asks for a writ of certiorari. If the Court agrees to hear the case, it issues a writ of certiorari which orders the parties in the case to bring the case before the court.

Circuit Court of Appeals: In the federal judicial system, the district court conducts the trial and the Supreme Court hears cases on appeal. There is an appeals court between the district court and the Supreme Court, called the circuit court. Generally a case must be appealed to the circuit court before it can go on to the Supreme Court.

Citizen: Someone who is a full legal member of a nation. In the United States, only a citizen can vote and hold some public offices.

Civil: In American law, most cases are either civil or criminal. In a civil case, one person sues another person. In a criminal case, the government claims that someone has broken the law and should pay a fine or go to jail.

Common law: Common law is law made by judges as opposed to statutes passed by legislatures. In ancient times, people were subject to the laws of their tribe. After his conquest of England in 1066 A.D., William I decided that there should be one law for all of the subjects in his kingdom. This law was developed mainly by the king's judges, as they made decisions and then based later decisions on their decisions in earlier cases. Over the centuries the English judges developed many legal principles that became the basis for most of their decisions in civil cases. These principles became the common law for England and her colonies. The United States inherited this common law. It has been modified by the judges in each state over the centuries, so that today each state is considered to have its own unique common law. The main exception to this is Louisiana, which bases its law on French and Spanish law, not the English common law.

Conscientious objector: A person who, for reasons of conscience, objects to fighting in a war. To qualify as a true "conscientious objector," the person must believe that war is objectionable in general, and not just object to a particular war.

Constitution: In the United States, the Constitution is a written document that forms the supreme law and organization of the government. Governments may exercise only those powers granted to them by the Constitution and they are limited by the rights reserved for the individual citizens.

Criminal: *See* **Civil.**

De minimis: The short form of the Latin phrase *de minimis non curat lex,* which means the law does not care about very "minimal" or small things. If a legal violation is technically a violation of the law but so small as to be not worth the court's time, the judge may dismiss the case as *de minimis.*

Defendant: A defendant is someone who is being sued or is charged with committing a crime.

Dicta: From the Latin, meaning statements of opinion by a judge that are not directly relevant to the decision of the case. Dicta are general statements concerning a particular judge's definition of the law but that do not directly relate to the case before the court.

Dissent: When a group of judges is making a decision and some of the judges do not agree with the majority, they will "dissent" from the majority opinion. To dissent simply means to disagree. They may state their dissent, or they may write a dissenting opinion explaining why they disagree. On some occasions a dissenting opinion has convinced the group to reverse its opinion about a decision.

District court: In the federal judicial system, trial of a case is held at the district court. A case may then be appealed to the circuit court, and from there to the Supreme Court. It is the district court that determines the facts of the case.

Ex post facto law: A law passed after an act has been committed. Conviction on the basis of an ex post facto law is not allowed in the United States; a person may only be convicted of acts for which laws were actually on the books when the act was committed.

Holding: The decision of the court and the reason for that decision. Attorneys generally say that the holding of the case is the reason why the winning party in a case was successful.

Impeachment: Impeachment occurs when a public official is removed from office for having done something illegal or immoral.

In loco parentis: Latin, meaning literally "in the place of the parent." *In loco parentis* is a legal concept that says that if someone, such as a babysitter or a teacher, has been put in charge of a child, then that person has the same power over the child that the child's parent would have.

Infra: Latin, meaning literally "below." If a judge mentions a case briefly that he or she will be discussing in detail later in the decision, then the judge may put the word *infra* after the name of the case. This lets the reader know that the case will be discussed later in more detail.

Injunction: A court order telling a person to do, or not to do, something. People might say that a person has been "injoined" from acting. A restraining order is one kind of injunction.

Interstate commerce: The movement of goods across state lines in the United States. Under the U.S. Constitution, the federal government is given the power to control "interstate commerce" to make sure that goods flow between states with a minimum of disruption.

Jurisdiction: The area over which a particular court has power. For example, the U.S. Supreme Court can only decide cases concerned with federal law and questions of constitutional interpretation. Most issues are within the jurisdiction of state courts, not federal courts.

Mens rea: Latin, meaning literally "guilty mind." Generally, a person cannot be found guilty of a crime unless he or she had a "guilty mind," meaning he or she intended to do harm or to commit a crime.

Naturalization: The process by which a noncitizen becomes a citizen.

Parens patriae: Latin, meaning literally "the parent of the country." In ancient times this term meant that the king was regarded as the ultimate parent for everyone and had the power to act as the parent of any subject in the kingdom if the subject's real parents were not available. In countries without a king, the term means that, if there is no natural parent to deal with a problem, then the government may have to fulfill that function. For example, the government may act as a parent in dealing with a child, with an insane person, or with someone who is not capable of dealing with things for himself or herself.

Per curiam: Latin, meaning literally "by the court." When an opinion has been written by the court as a whole, rather than by one particular judge, it is called a *per curiam* decision.

Petitioner: A person who petitions a judge to make a decision. Someone who files a lawsuit or begins an appeal can be called a petitioner. The person who is being sued or is defending against an appeal is the respondent.

Plaintiff: In a lawsuit, the person who brings the lawsuit is called the plaintiff. The person being sued by the plaintiff is called the defendant. The defendant defends against the charges that have been brought by the plaintiff.

Police power: A concept of U.S. law. Courts in the United States have decided that state constitutions provide state governments with police power, meaning the power to do everything that it is "reasonable" for government to do. Although the U.S. Constitution spells out the powers of the federal government, most state constitutions do not do this. The police power is very broad and includes the power to build roads, fight disease, and put people in jail; however, a court can decide that a particular action by a state legislature is unconstitutional if it is beyond the police power. The problem with this broad concept is that it is very vague and gives courts a great deal of power to declare the actions of legislatures to be unconstitutional as a violation of the state constitution. If a state government takes action beyond its power, the court does not have to ask whether or not any rights protected by the Bill of Rights have been violated. A court may invalidate an action of government either because the action was beyond the power of government or because it violated a right protected by the Bill of Rights.

Precedent: In the U.S. legal system, lower courts are bound by the decisions of courts above them. We say that those higher court decisions serve as precedents for the decisions to be made by the lower courts.

Restraining order: A court order that orders someone not to do something. If a person wants to stop another person from doing something, he or she may ask a judge for a restraining order against that other person.

Scienter: Latin, meaning "knowingly." Generally people cannot be con-victed of crimes unless they acted knowingly, with scienter, meaning that the people knew what they were doing when they committed the crime. They were not acting unconsciously or without knowledge of the facts in the case.

Separation of powers: Generally government is thought of as having three basic powers: the power to make the law (legislative), the power to enforce the law (executive), and the power to decide what the law is (judicial). In the United States, these three powers are separate from each other. That has not always been true in other countries or in the past. In ancient Athens, for example, the legislature was also the supreme court.

Standing: In the American legal system, people are generally not allowed to complain about a violation of the law or the Constitution unless the violation has injured them personally in some way. Only people who actually have been injured have standing to complain about their injury in a civil or criminal case.

Stare decisis: Latin, meaning literally "the decision must stand." In American law, once a particular court has made a decision, it is expected that the court will not change its ruling. People can then alter their behavior to comply with the decision without fear that it will change in the near future. This concept is particularly important for the U.S. Supreme Court because Supreme Court decisions have such a far-reaching impact on society.

Statute: A law passed by a legislative body, such as a state legislature or the U.S. Congress.

Stipulate: The purpose of a trial is to determine the facts of a particular case. If there are facts on which both sides agree, then both sides will "stipulate" that those facts are true and correct. For the rest of the trial, everyone will assume that those facts are true without having to prove them.

Supra: Latin, meaning literally "above." If a judge has already discussed a case in detail and wishes to mention it briefly again, he or she may put the word *supra* after the name of the case to let the reader know that the case has already been discussed in detail earlier in the decision.

Tort: Comes from the same Latin root as words such as *twist* and *torture*. In American law, if one person has injured another person in some way, we say that a tort has been committed. The injury may be physical, economic, or psychological. When people sue because they have been injured, we say they are "suing in tort."

Ubiquity: The concept that something can be everywhere at the same time, omnipresent. Some believe that God is ubiquitous. We generally conceive that the law and government are ubiquitous, even if there is no government official at a particular place at a particular time.

Writ of habeas corpus: A court order that requires a person who has someone under custody to either bring that person to court or release him or her from custody.

FURTHER READING

∗ ∗ ∗ ∗ ∗ ∗ ∗ ∗ ∗

Adler, Renata. *Reckless Disregard*. New York: Alfred A. Knopf, 1986.
Examines General Westmorland's suit for libel against CBS and General Sharon's suit for libel against *Time* magazine.

Bollinger, Lee C. *The Tolerant Society*. Oxford: Oxford University Press, 1986.
Discusses the protection of extreme speech and develops a theory of tolerance to help understand the Supreme Court's decisions concerning the right of free speech.

Canavan, Francis. *Freedom of Expression*. Durham, NC: Carolina Academic Press, 1984.
Scholarly treatise on the meaning of free speech and the impact of specific philosophers on the concept of free speech.

Dan, Uri. *Blood Libel*. New York: Simon & Schuster, 1987.
Explores the story of the libel suit by General Sharon against *Time* magazine.

de Garzia, Edward. *Girls Lean Back Everywhere*. New York: Random House, 1992.
Presents the history of obscenity law in America as a struggle by artists to gain the right of free expression.

de Garzia, Edward, and Newman, Roger K. *Banned Films*. New York: R. R. Bowker Co., 1982.
Examines the history of movie censorship in America.

Downs, Donald Alexander. *Nazis in Skokie*. Notre Dame, IN: University of Notre Dame Press, 1985.
Examines the case of the Nazis who wished to march through Skokie, Illinois.

Downs, Donald Alexander. *The New Politics of Pornography*. Chicago: University of Chicago Press, 1989.
Examines the desire of some feminists to control pornography and the impact of their ideas on the right of free speech.

Emerson, Thomas I. *The System of Freedom of Expression*. New York: Random House, 1970.
    Classic treatise on the right of free speech.

Hentoff, Nat. *The First Freedom*. New York: Delacorte Press, 1980.
    Presents the "tumultuous" history of the right of free speech in the United States.

Hentoff, Nat. *Free Speech for Me—But Not for Thee*. New York: Harper Collins, 1992.
    Examines the role of free speech in the United States and the forces seeking to limit this right.

Kalven, Harry. *A Worthy Tradition*. New York: Harper & Row, 1988.
    Scholarly treatise on the right of free speech, focusing particularly on the right of free association.

Levy, Leonard W. *Emergence of a Free Press*. Oxford: Oxford University Press, 1985.
    Examines the early history of the right to a free press in the United States.

Lewis, Anthony. *Make No Law*. New York: Random House, 1991.
    Examines the case of *New York Times Co. v. Sullivan*.

Polenberg, Richard. *Fighting Faiths*. New York: Viking, 1987.
    Examines the case of *Abrams v. United States*.

Powe, Lucas A. *American Broadcasting, the First Amendment*. Berkeley, CA: University of California Press, 1987.
    Examines the issue of free speech and the regulation of the broadcast media.

Powe, Lucas A. *The Fourth Estate and the Constitution*. Berkeley, CA: University of California Press, 1991.
    Examines the current state of the right of a free press in the United States.

Radish, Martin H. *Freedom of Expression*. Charlottesville, VA: The Michie Company, 1984.
    Scholarly treatise on the meaning of the right of free speech.

Rember, Charles. *The End of Obscenity*. New York: Random House, 1968.
    The story of the obscenity cases involving the novels *Lady Chatterley's Lover*, *Tropic of Cancer*, and *Fanny Hill*, by the attorney who represented the authors in each case and won.

Shapiro, Martin. *Freedom of Speech*. Englewood Cliffs, NJ: Prentice-Hall, 1966.
    Scholarly treatise on the subject of free speech.

Smolla, Rodney A. *Free Speech in an Open Society*. New York: Alfred A. Knopf, 1992.
    Examines what the limits of free speech should be in the United States today.

Smolla, Rodney A. *Jerry Falwell v. Larry Flynt*. New York: St. Martin's Press, 1988.
    Examines the case of *Hustler Magazine v. Falwell*.

Zerman, Melvyn, *Taking on the Press*. New York: Thomas Y. Crowell, 1986.
    Examines the right of a free press in historical perspective.

APPENDIX A

* * * * * * * *

Constitution of the United States

PREAMBLE

We the People of the United States, in Order to form a more perfect Union, establish Justice, insure domestic Tranquility, provide for the common defence, promote the general Welfare, and secure the Blessings of Liberty to ourselves and our Posterity, do ordain and establish this Constitution for the United States of America.

ARTICLE I

Section 1. All legislative Powers herein granted shall be vested in a Congress of the United States, which shall consist of a Senate and House of Representatives.

Section 2. The House of Representatives shall be composed of Members chosen every second Year by the People of the several States, and the Electors in each State shall have the Qualifications requisite for Electors of the most numerous Branch of the State Legislature.

No Person shall be a Representative who shall not have attained to the age of twenty five Years, and been seven Years a Citizen of the United States, and who shall not, when elected, be an Inhabitant of that State in which he shall be chosen.

Representatives and direct Taxes shall be apportioned among the several States which may be included within this Union, according to their respective Numbers, which shall be determined by adding to the whole Number of free Persons, including those bound to Service for a Term of Years, and excluding Indians not taxed, three fifths of all other Persons. The actual Enumeration shall be made within three Years after the first Meeting of the Congress of the

United States, and within every subsequent Term of ten Years, in such Manner as they shall by Law direct. The Number of Representatives shall not exceed one for every thirty Thousand, but each State shall have at Least one Representative; and until such enumeration shall be made, the State of New Hampshire shall be entitled to chuse three, Massachusetts eight, Rhode-Island and Providence Plantations one, Connecticut five, New-York six, New Jersey four, Pennsylvania eight, Delaware one, Maryland six, Virginia ten, North Carolina five, South Carolina five, and Georgia three.

When vacancies happen in the Representation from any State, the Executive Authority thereof shall issue Writs of Election to fill such Vacancies.

The House of Representatives shall chuse their Speaker and other Officers; and shall have the sole Power of Impeachment.

Section 3. The Senate of the United States shall be composed of two Senators from each State, chosen by the Legislature thereof, for six Years; and each Senator shall have one Vote.

Immediately after they shall be assembled in Consequence of the first Election, they shall be divided as equally as may be into three Classes. The Seats of the Senators of the first Class shall be vacated at the Expiration of the second Year, of the second Class at the Expiration of the fourth Year, and of the third Class at the Expiration of the sixth Year, so that one third may be chosen every second Year; and if Vacancies happen by Resignation, or otherwise, during the Recess of the Legislature of any State the Executive thereof may make temporary Appointments until the next Meeting of the Legislature, which shall then fill such Vacancies.

No Person shall be a Senator who shall not have attained to the Age of thirty Years, and been nine Years a Citizen of the United States, and who shall not, when elected, be an Inhabitant of that State for which he shall be chosen.

The Vice President of the United States shall be President of the Senate, but shall have no Vote, unless they be equally divided.

The Senate shall chuse their other Officers, and also a President pro tempore, in the Absence of the Vice President, or when he shall exercise the Office of President of the United States.

The Senate shall have the sole Power to try all Impeachments. When sitting for that Purpose, they shall be on Oath or Affirmation. When the President of the United States is tried the Chief Justice shall preside: And no Person shall be convicted without the Concurrence of two thirds of the Members present.

Judgment in Cases of Impeachment shall not extend further than to removal from Office, and disqualification to hold and enjoy any Office of honor, Trust or Profit under the United States: but the Party convicted shall nevertheless be liable and subject to Indictment, Trial, Judgment and Punishment, according to Law.

Section 4. The Times, Places and Manner of holding Elections for Senators and Representatives, shall be prescribed in each State by the Legislature thereof; but the Congress may at any time by Law make or alter such Regulations, except as to the Places of chusing Senators.

The Congress shall assemble at least once in every Year, and such Meeting shall be on the first Monday in December, unless they shall by Law appoint a different Day.

Section 5. Each House shall be the Judge of the Elections, Returns and Qualifications of its own Members, and a Majority of each shall constitute a Quorum to do Business; but a smaller Number may adjourn from day to day, and may be authorized to compel the Attendance of absent Members, in such Manner, and under such Penalties as each House may provide.

Each House may determine the Rules of its Proceedings, punish its Members for disorderly Behaviour, and, with the Concurrence of two thirds, expel a Member.

Each House shall keep a Journal of its Proceedings, and from time to time publish the same, excepting such Parts as may in their Judgment require Secrecy; and the Yeas and Nays of the Members of either House on any question shall, at the Desire of one fifth of those Present, be entered on the Journal.

Neither House, during the Session of Congress, shall, without the Consent of the other, adjourn for more than three days, nor to any other Place than that in which the two Houses shall be sitting.

Section 6. The Senators and Representatives shall receive a Compensation for their Services, to be ascertained by Law, and paid out of the Treasury of the United States. They shall in all Cases, except Treason, Felony and Breach of the Peace, be privileged from Arrest during their Attendance at the Session of their respective Houses, and in going to and returning from the same; and for any Speech or Debate in either House, they shall not be questioned in any other Place.

No Senator or Representative shall, during the Time for which he was elected, be appointed to any civil Office under the Authority of the United States, which shall have been created, or the Emoluments whereof shall have been encreased during such time; and no Person holding any Office under the United States, shall be a Member of either House during his Continuance in Office.

Section 7. All Bills of raising Revenue shall originate in the House of Representatives; but the Senate may propose or concur with amendments as on other Bills.

Every Bill which shall have passed the House of Representatives and the Senate, shall, before it become a Law, be presented to the President of the United States; If he approve he shall sign it, but if not he shall return it, with his Objections to that House in which it shall have originated, who shall enter the Objections at large on their Journal, and proceed to reconsider it. If after such Reconsideration two thirds of that House shall agree to pass the Bill, it shall be sent, together with the Objections, to the other House, by which it shall likewise be reconsidered, and if approved by two thirds of that House, it shall become a Law. But in all such Cases the Votes of both Houses shall be determined by yeas and Nays, and the Names of the Persons voting for and against the Bill shall be entered on the Journal of each House respectively. If any Bill shall not be returned by the President within ten Days (Sunday excepted) after it shall have been presented to him, the Same shall be a Law, in like Manner as if he had signed it, unless the Congress by their Adjournment prevent its Return, in which Case it shall not be a Law.

Every Order, Resolution, or Vote to which the Concurrence of the Senate and House of Representatives may be necessary (except on a question of Adjournment) shall be presented to the President of the United States; and before the Same shall take Effect, shall be approved by him, or being disapproved by him, shall be repassed by two thirds of the Senate and House of Representatives, according to the Rules and Limitations prescribed in the Case of a Bill.

Section 8. The Congress shall have Power To lay and collect Taxes, Duties, Imposts and Excises, to pay the Debts and provide for the common Defence and general Welfare of the United States; but all Duties, Imposts and Excises shall be uniform throughout the United States;

To borrow Money on the credit of the United States;

To regulate Commerce with foreign Nations, and among the several States, and with the Indian Tribes;

To establish an uniform Rule of Naturalization, and uniform Laws on the subject of Bankruptcies throughout the United States;

To coin Money, regulate the Value thereof, and of foreign Coin, and fix the Standard of Weights and Measures;

To provide for the Punishment of counterfeiting the Securities and current Coin of the United States;

To establish Post Offices and post Roads;

To promote the Progress of Science and useful Arts, by securing for limited Times to Authors and Inventors the exclusive Right to their respective Writings and Discoveries;

To constitute Tribunals inferior to the supreme Court;

To define and punish Piracies and Felonies commit[t]ed on the high Seas, and Offences against the Law of Nations;

To declare War, grant Letters of Marque and Reprisal, and make Rules concerning Captures on Land and Water;

To raise and support Armies, but no Appropriation of Money to that Use shall be for a longer Term than two Years;

To provide and maintain a Navy;

To make Rules for the Government and Regulation of the land and naval Forces;

To provide for calling forth the Militia to execute the Laws of the Union, suppress Insurrections and repel Invasions;

To provide for organizing, arming, and disciplining the Militia, and for governing such Part of them as may be employed in the Service of the United States, reserving to the States respectively, the Appointment of the Officers, and the Authority of training the Militia according to the discipline prescribed by Congress;

To exercise exclusive Legislation in all Cases whatsoever, over such District (not exceeding ten Miles square) as may, by Cession of Particular States, and the Acceptance of Congress, become the Seat of the Government of the United States, and to exercise like Authority over all Places purchased by the Consent of the Legislature of the State in which the Same shall be, for the Erection of Forts, Magazines, Arsenals, dock-Yards, and other needful Buildings;

—And

To make all Laws which shall be necessary and proper for carrying into Execution the foregoing Powers, and all other Powers vested by this Constitution in the Government of the United States, or in any Department or Officer thereof.

Section 9. The Migration or Importation of such Persons as any of the States now existing shall think proper to admit, shall not be prohibited by the Congress prior to the Year one thousand eight hundred and eight, but a Tax or duty may be imposed on such Importation, not exceeding ten dollars for each Person.

The Privilege of the Writ of Habeas Corpus shall not be suspended, unless when in Cases of Rebellion or Invasion the public Safety may require it.

No Bill of Attainder or ex post facto law shall be passed.

No capitation, or other direct, Tax shall be laid, unless in Proportion to the Census of Enumeration herein before directed to be taken.

No Tax or Duty shall be laid on Articles exported from any State.

No Preference shall be given by any Regulation of Commerce or Revenue to the Ports of one State over those of another; nor shall Vessels bound to, or from, one State, be obliged to enter, clear or pay Duties in another.

No Money shall be drawn from the Treasury, but in Consequence of Appropriations made by Law; and a regular Statement and Account of the

Receipts and Expenditures of all public Money shall be published from time to time.

No Title of Nobility shall be granted by the United States: And no Person holding any Office of Profit or Trust under them, shall without the Consent of the Congress, accept of any present, Emolument, Office, or Title, of any kind whatever, from any King, Prince or foreign State.

Section 10. No State shall enter into any Treaty, Alliance, or Confederation; grant Letters of Marque and Reprisal; coin Money; emit Bills of Credit; make any Thing but gold and silver Coin a Tender in Payment of Debts; pass any Bill of Attainder, ex post facto Law, or Law impairing the Obligation of Contracts, or grant any Title of Nobility.

No State shall, without the Consent of the Congress, lay any Imposts or Duties on Imports or Exports, except what may be absolutely necessary for executing it's inspection Laws: and the net Produce of all Duties and Imposts, laid by any State on Imports or Exports, shall be for the Use of the Treasury of the United States; and all such Laws shall be subject to the Revision and Controul of the Congress.

No State shall, without the Consent of Congress, lay any Duty of Tonnage, keep Troops, or Ships of War in time of Peace, enter into any Agreement or Compact with another State, or with a foreign Power, or engage in War, unless actually invaded, or in such imminent Danger as will not admit of delay.

ARTICLE II

Section 1. The executive Power shall be vested in a President of the United States of America. He shall hold his Office during the Term of four Years, and, together with the Vice President, chosen for the same Term, be elected, as follows.

Each State shall appoint, in such Manner as the Legislature thereof may direct, a Number of Electors, equal to the whole Number of Senators and Representatives to which the State may be entitled in the Congress: but no Senator or Representative, or Person holding an Office of Trust or Profit under the United States, shall be appointed an Elector.

The Electors shall meet in their respective States, and vote by Ballot for two Persons, of whom one at least shall not be an Inhabitant of the same State with themselves. And they shall make a List of all the Persons voted for, and of the Number of Votes for each; which List they shall sign and certify, and transmit sealed to the Seat of the Government of the United States, directed to the President of the Senate. The President of the Senate shall, in the Presence of the Senate and House of Representatives, open all the Certificates, and the Votes shall then be counted. The Person having the greatest Number of Votes shall be the President, if such Number be a Majority of the whole Number of

Electors appointed; and if there be more than one who have such Majority, and have an equal Number of Votes, then the House of Representatives shall immediately chuse by Ballot one of them for President; and if no Person have a Majority, then from the five highest on the list the said House shall in like Manner chuse the President. But in chusing the President, the Votes shall be taken by States, the Representation from each State having one Vote; a quorum for this Purpose shall consist of a Member or Members from two thirds of the States, and a Majority of all the States shall be necessary to a Choice. In every Case, after the Choice of the President, the Person having the greatest Number of Votes of the Electors shall be the Vice President. But if there should remain two or more who have equal Votes, the Senate shall chuse from them by Ballot the Vice President.

The Congress may determine the Time of chusing the Electors, and the Day on which they shall give their Votes; which Day shall be the same throughout the United States.

No Person except a natural born Citizen, or a Citizen of the United States, at the time of the Adoption of this Constitution, shall be eligible to the Office of President; neither shall any Person be eligible to that Office who shall not have attained to the Age of thirty five Years, and been fourteen Years a Resident within the United States.

In Case of the Removal of the President from Office, or of his Death, Resignation, or Inability to discharge the Powers and Duties of the said Office, the Same shall devolve on the Vice President, and the Congress may by Law provide for the Case of Removal, Death, Resignation or Inability, both of the President and Vice President, declaring what Officer shall then act as President, and such Officer shall act accordingly, until the Disability be removed, or a President shall be elected.

The President shall, at stated Times, receive for his Services, a Compensation, which shall neither be encreased nor diminished during the Period for which he shall have been elected, and he shall not receive within that Period any other Emolument from the United States, or any of them.

Before he enter on the Execution of his Office, he shall take the following Oath or Affirmation:—"I do solemnly swear (or affirm) that I will faithfully execute the Office of President of the United States, and will to the best of my Ability, preserve, protect and defend the Constitution of the United States."

Section 2. The President shall be Commander in Chief of the Army and Navy of the United States, and of the Militia of the several States, when called into the actual Service of the United States; he may require the Opinion, in writing, of the principal Officer in each of the executive Departments, upon any Subject relating to the Duties of their respective Offices, and he shall have Power to grant Reprieves and Pardons for Offenses against the United States, except in Cases of Impeachment.

He shall have Power, by and with the Advice and Consent of the Senate, to make Treaties, provided two thirds of the Senators present concur; and he shall nominate, and by and with the Advice and Consent of the Senate, shall appoint Ambassadors, other public Ministers and Consuls, Judges of the supreme Court, and all other Officers of the United States, whose Appointments are not herein otherwise provided for, and which shall be established by Law: but the Congress may by Law vest the Appointment of such inferior Officers, as they think proper, in the President alone, in the Courts of Law, or in the Heads of Departments.

The President shall have Power to fill up all Vacancies that may happen during the Recess of the Senate, by granting Commissions which shall expire at the End of their next Session.

Section 3. He shall from time to time give to the Congress Information of the State of the Union, and recommend to their Consideration such Measures as he shall judge necessary and expedient; he may, on extraordinary Occasions, convene both Houses, or either of them, and in Case of Disagreement between them, with Respect to the Time of Adjournment, he may adjourn them to such Time as he shall think proper; he shall receive Ambassadors and other public Ministers; he shall take Care that the Laws be faithfully executed, and shall Commission all the Officers of the United States.

Section 4. The President, Vice President and all Civil Officers of the United States, shall be removed from office on Impeachment for, and Conviction of, Treason, Bribery, or other high Crimes and Misdemeanors.

ARTICLE III

Section 1. The judicial Power of the United States shall be vested in one supreme Court, and in such inferior Courts as the Congress may from time to time ordain and establish. The Judges, both of the supreme and inferior Courts, shall hold their Offices during good Behaviour, and shall, at stated Times, receive for their Services, a Compensation, which shall not be diminished during their Continuance in Office.

Section 2. The judicial Power shall extend to all Cases, in Law and Equity, arising under this Constitution, the Laws of the United States, and Treaties made, or which shall be made, under their Authority;—to all Cases affecting Ambassadors, other public Ministers and Consuls;—to all Cases of admiralty and maritime Jurisdiction;—to Controversies to which the United States shall be a Party;—to Controversies between two or more States;—between a State and Citizens of another State;—between Citizens of different States;—between Citizens of the same State claiming Lands under Grants of different States, and between a State, or the Citizens thereof, and foreign States, Citizens or Subjects.

In all Cases affecting Ambassadors, other public Ministers and Consuls, and those in which a State shall be Party, the supreme Court shall have original Jurisdiction. In all the other Cases before mentioned, the supreme Court shall have appellate Jurisdiction, both as to Law and Fact, with such Exceptions, and under such Regulations as the Congress shall make.

The Trial of all Crimes, except in cases of Impeachment, shall be by Jury; and such Trial shall be held in the State where the said Crimes shall have been committed; but when not committed within any State, the Trial shall be at such Place or Places as the Congress may by Law have directed.

Section 3. Treason against the United States shall consist only in levying War against them, or in adhering to their Enemies, giving them Aid and Comfort. No Person shall be convicted of Treason unless on the Testimony of two Witnesses to the same overt Act, or on Confession in open Court.

The Congress shall have Power to declare the Punishment of Treason, but no Attainder of Treason shall work Corruption of Blood, or Forfeiture except during the Life of the Person attainted.

ARTICLE IV

Section 1. Full Faith and Credit shall be given in each State to the public Acts, Records, and judicial Proceedings of every other State. And the Congress may by general Laws prescribe the Manner in which such Acts, Records and Proceedings shall be proved, and the Effect thereof.

Section 2. The Citizens of each State shall be entitled to all Privileges and Immunities of Citizens in the several States.

A Person charged in any State with Treason, Felony, or other Crime, who shall flee from Justice, and be found in another State, shall on Demand of the executive Authority of the State from which he fled, be delivered up, to be removed to the State having Jurisdiction of the Crime.

No Person held to Service or Labour in one State, under the Laws thereof, escaping into another, shall, in Consequence of any Law or Regulation therein, be discharged from such Service or Labour, but shall be delivered up on Claim of the Party to whom such Service or Labour may be due.

Section 3. New States may be admitted by the Congress into this Union; but no new State shall be formed or erected within the Jurisdiction of any other State; nor any State be formed by the Junction of two or more States, or Parts of States, without the Consent of the Legislatures of the States concerned as well as of the Congress.

The Congress shall have Power to dispose of and make all needful Rules and Regulations respecting the Territory or other Property belonging to the United States; and nothing in this Constitution shall be so construed as to Prejudice any Claims of the United States, or of any particular State.

Section 4. The United States shall guarantee to every State in this Union a Republican Form of Government, and shall protect each of them against invasion; and on Application of the Legislature, or of the Executive (when the Legislature cannot be convened) against domestic Violence.

ARTICLE V

The Congress, whenever two thirds of both Houses shall deem it necessary, shall propose Amendments to this Constitution, or, on the Application of the Legislatures of two thirds of the several States, shall call a Convention for proposing Amendments, which, in either Case, shall be valid to all Intents and Purposes, as Part of this Constitution, when ratified by the Legislatures of three fourths of the several States, or by Conventions in three fourths thereof, as the one or the other Mode of Ratification may be proposed by the Congress; Provided that no Amendment which may be made prior to the Year One thousand eight hundred and eight shall in any Manner affect the first and fourth Clauses in the Ninth Section of the first Article; and that no State, without its Consent, shall be deprived of its equal Suffrage in the Senate.

ARTICLE VI

All Debts contracted and Engagements entered into, before the Adoption of this Constitution, shall be as valid against the United States under this Constitution, as under the Confederation.

This Constitution, and the Laws of the United States which shall be made in Pursuance thereof; and all Treaties made, or which shall be made, under the Authority of the United States, shall be the supreme Law of the Land; and the Judges in every State shall be the supreme Law of the Land; and the Judges in every State shall be bound thereby, any Thing in the Constitution or Laws or any State to the Contrary notwithstanding.

The Senators and Representatives before mentioned, and the Members of the several State Legislatures, and all executive and judicial Officers, both of the United States and of the several States, shall be bound by Oath or Affirmation, to support this Constitution; but no religious Test shall ever be required as a Qualification to any Office or public Trust under the United States.

ARTICLE VII

The Ratification of the Conventions of nine States, shall be sufficient for the Establishment of this Constitution between the States so ratifying the Same.

AMENDMENTS
Amendment I

Congress shall make no law respecting an establishment of religion, or prohibiting the free exercise thereof; or abridging the freedom of speech, or of the press; or the right of the people peaceably to assemble, and to petition the Government for a redress of grievances.

Amendment II

A well regulated Militia, being necessary to the security of a free State, the right of the people to keep and bear Arms, shall not be infringed.

Amendment III

No Soldier shall, in time of peace be quartered in any house, without the consent of the Owner, nor in time of war, but in a manner to be prescribed by law.

Amendment IV

The right of the people to be secure in their persons, houses, papers, and effects, against unreasonable searches and seizures, shall not be violated, and no Warrants shall issue, but upon probable cause, supported by Oath or affirmation, and particularly describing the place to be searched, and the persons or things to be seized.

Amendment V

No person shall be held to answer for a capital, or otherwise infamous crime, unless on a presentment or indictment of a Grand Jury, except in cases arising in the land or naval forces, or in the Militia, when in actual service in time of War or public danger; nor shall any person be subject for the same offence to be twice put in jeopardy of life or limb; nor shall be compelled in any criminal case to be a witness against himself, nor be deprived of life, liberty, or property, without due process of law; nor shall private property be taken for public use, without just compensation.

Amendment VI

In all criminal prosecutions, the accused shall enjoy the right to a speedy and public trial, by an impartial jury of the State and district wherein the crime shall have been committed, which district shall have been previously ascertained by law, and to be informed of the nature and cause of the accusation; to be confronted with the witnesses against him; to have compulsory process for obtaining witnesses in his favor, and to have the Assistance of Counsel for his defence.

Amendment VII

In Suits at common law, where the value in controversy shall exceed twenty dollars, the right of trial by jury shall be preserved, and no fact tried by a jury, shall be otherwise reexamined in any Court of the United States, than according to the rules of the common law.

Amendment VIII

Excessive bail shall not be required, nor excessive fines imposed, nor cruel and unusual punishments inflicted.

Amendment IX

The enumeration in the Constitution, of certain rights, shall not be construed to deny or disparage others retained by the people.

Amendment X

The powers not delegated to the United States by the Constitution, nor prohibited by it to the States, are reserved to the States respectively, or to the people.

[First 10 amendments ratified 15 December 1791]

Amendment XI

The Judicial power of the United States shall not be construed to extend to any suit in law or equity, commenced or prosecuted against one of the United States by Citizens of another State, or by Citizens or Subjects of any Foreign State.

[Ratified 7 February 1795]

Amendment XII

The Electors shall meet in their respective states and vote by ballot for President and Vice-President, one of whom, at least, shall not be an inhabitant of the same state with themselves; they shall name in their ballots the person voted for as President, and in distinct ballots the person voted for as Vice-President, and they shall make distinct lists of all persons voted for as President, and of all persons voted for as Vice-President, and of the number of votes for each, which lists they shall sign and certify, and transmit sealed to the seat of the government of the United States, directed to the President of the Senate;—The President of the Senate shall, in the presence of the Senate and House of Representatives, open all the certificates and the votes shall then be counted;—The person having the greatest number of votes for President, shall be the President, if such number be a majority of the whole number of Electors appointed; and if no person have such majority, then from the persons having the highest numbers not exceeding three on the list of those voted for as President, the House of Representatives shall chuse immediately, by ballot, the President. But in chusing the President, the votes shall be taken by states, the representation from each state having one vote; a quorum for this purpose shall consist of a member or members from two-thirds of the states, and a majority of all the states shall be necessary to a choice. And if the House of Representatives shall not chuse a President whenever the right of choice shall devolve upon them, before the fourth day of March next following, then the Vice-President shall act as President, as in the case of the death or other constitutional disability of the President—The person having the greatest number of votes as Vice-President, shall be the Vice-President, if such number be a majority of the whole number of Electors appointed, and if no person have a majority, then from the two highest numbers on the list, the Senate shall chuse the Vice-President; a quorum for the purpose shall consist of two-thirds of the whole number of Senators, and a majority of the whole number shall be necessary to a choice. But no person constitutionally ineligible to the office of President shall be eligible to that of Vice-President of the United States.

[Ratified 15 June 1804]

Amendment XIII

Section 1. Neither slavery nor involuntary servitude, except as a punishment for crime whereof the party shall have been duly convicted, shall exist within the United States, or any place subject to their jurisdiction.

Section 2. Congress shall have power to enforce this article by appropriate legislation.

[Ratified 6 December 1865]

Amendment XIV

Section 1. All persons born or naturalized in the United States and subject to the jurisdiction thereof, are citizens of the United States and of the State wherein they reside. No State shall make or enforce any law which shall abridge the privileges or immunities of citizens of the United States; nor shall any State deprive any person of life, liberty, or property, without due process of law; nor deny to any person within its jurisdiction the equal protection of the laws.

Section 2. Representatives shall be apportioned among the several States according to their respective numbers, counting the whole number of persons in each State, excluding Indians not taxed. But when the right to vote at any election for the choice of electors for President and Vice President of the United States, Representatives in Congress, the Executive and Judicial officers of a State, or the members of the Legislature thereof, is denied to any of the male inhabitants of such State, being twenty-one years of age, and citizens of the United States, or in any way abridged, except for participation in rebellion, or other crime, the basis of representation therein shall be reduced in the proportion which the number of such male citizens shall bear to the whole number of male citizens twenty-one years of age in such State.

Section 3. No person shall be a Senator or Representative in Congress, or elector of President and Vice President, or hold any office, civil or military, under the United States, or under any State, who, having previously taken an oath, as a member of Congress, or as an officer of the United States, or as a member of any State legislature, or as an executive or judicial officer of any State, to support the Constitution of the United States, shall have engaged in insurrection or rebellion against the same, or given aid or comfort to the enemies thereof. But Congress may by a vote of two-thirds of each House, remove such disability.

Section 4. The validity of the public debt of the United States, authorized by law, including debts incurred for payment of pensions and bounties for services in suppressing insurrection or rebellion, shall not be questioned. But neither the United States nor any State shall assume or pay any debt or obligation incurred in aid of insurrection or rebellion against the United States, or any claim for the loss or emancipation of any slave; but all such debts, obligations and claims shall be held illegal and void.

Section 5. The Congress shall have power to enforce, by appropriate legislation, the provisions of this article.

[Ratified 9 July 1868]

Amendment XV

Section 1. The right of citizens of the United States to vote shall not be denied or abridged by the United States or by any State on account of race, color, or previous condition of servitude.

Section 2. The Congress shall have power to enforce this article by appropriate legislation.

[Ratified 3 February 1870]

Amendment XVI

The Congress shall have power to lay and collect taxes on incomes, from whatever source derived, without apportionment among the several States, and without regard to any census or enumeration.

[Ratified 3 February 1913]

Amendment XVII

The Senate of the United States shall be composed of two Senators from each State, elected by the people thereof, for six years; and each Senator shall have one vote. The electors in each State shall have the qualifications requisite for electors of the most numerous branch of the State legislatures.

When vacancies happen in the representation of any State in the Senate, the executive authority of such State shall issue writs of election to fill such vacancies: *Provided,* That the legislature of any State may empower the executive thereof to make temporary appointments until the people fill the vacancies by election as the legislature may direct.

This amendment shall not be so construed as to affect the election or term of any Senator chosen before it becomes valid as part of the Constitution.

[Ratified 8 April 1913]

Amendment XVIII

Section 1. After one year from the ratification of this article the manufacture, sale, or transportation of intoxicating liquors within, the importation thereof into, or the exportation thereof from the United States and all territory subject to the jurisdiction thereof for beverage purposes is hereby prohibited.

Section 2. The Congress and the several States shall have concurrent power to enforce this article by appropriate legislation.

Section 3. This article shall be inoperative unless it shall have been ratified as an amendment to the Constitution by the legislatures of the several States, as provided in the Constitution, within seven years from the date of the submission hereof to the States by the Congress.

[Ratified 16 January 1919]

Amendment XIX

The right of citizens of the United States to vote shall not be denied or abridged by the United States or by any State on account of sex.

Congress shall have power to enforce this article by appropriate legislation.

[Ratified 18 August 1920]

Amendment XX

Section 1. The terms of the President and Vice President shall end at noon on the 20th day of January, and the terms of Senators and Representatives at noon on the 3d day of January, of the years in which such terms would have ended if this article had not been ratified; and the terms of their successors shall then begin

Section 2. The Congress shall assemble at least once in every year, and such meeting shall begin at noon on the 3d day of January, unless they shall by law appoint a different day.

Section 3. If, at the time fixed for the beginning of the term of the President, the President elect shall have died, the Vice President elect shall become President. If a President shall not have been chosen before the time fixed for the beginning of his term, or if the President elect shall have failed to qualify, then the Vice President elect shall act as President until a President shall have qualified; and the Congress may by law provide for the case wherein neither a President elect nor a Vice President elect shall have qualified, declaring who shall then act as President, or the manner in which one who is to act shall be selected, and such person shall act accordingly until a President or Vice President shall have qualified.

Section 4. The Congress may by law provide for the case of the death of any of the persons from whom the House of Representatives may choose a President whenever the right of choice shall have devolved upon them, and for the case of the death of any of the persons from whom the Senate may choose a Vice President whenever the right of choice shall have devolved upon them.

Section 5. Sections 1 and 2 shall take effect on the 15th day of October following the ratification of this article.

Section 6. This article shall be inoperative unless it shall have been ratified as an amendment to the Constitution by the legislatures of three-fourths of the several States within seven years from the date of its submission.

[Ratified 23 January 1933]

Amendment XXI

Section 1. The eighteenth article of amendment to the Constitution of the United States is hereby repealed.

Section 2. The transportation or importation into any State, Territory or possession of the United States for delivery or use therein of intoxicating liquors, in violation of the laws thereof, is hereby prohibited.

Section 3. This article shall be inoperative unless it shall have been ratified as an amendment to the Constitution by conventions in the several States, as provided in the Constitution, within seven years from the date of the submission hereof to the States by the Congress.

[Ratified 5 December 1933]

Amendment XXII

Section 1. No person shall be elected to the office of the President more than twice, and no person who has held the office of President, or acted as President, for more than two years of a term to which some other person was elected President shall be elected to the office of the President more than once. But this article shall not apply to any person holding the office of President when this Article was proposed by the Congress, and shall not prevent any person who may be holding the office of President, or acting as President, during the term within which this Article become[s] operative from holding the office of President or acting as President during the remainder of such term.

Section 2. This Article shall be inoperative unless it shall have been ratified as an amendment to the Constitution by the legislatures of three-fourths of the several States within seven years from the date of its submission to the States by the Congress.

[Ratified 27 February 1951]

Amendment XXIII

Section 1. The District constituting the seat of Government of the United States shall appoint in such manner as the Congress may direct:

A number of electors of President and Vice President equal to the whole number of Senators and Representatives in Congress to which the District would be entitled if it were a State, but in no event more than the least populous State; they shall be in addition to those appointed by the States, but they shall be considered, for the purposes of the election of President and Vice President, to be electors appointed by a State; and they shall meet in the District and perform such duties as provided by the twelfth article of amendment.

Section 2. The Congress shall have power to enforce this article by appropriate legislation.

[Ratified 29 March 1961]

Amendment XXIV

Section 1. The right of citizens of the United States to vote in any primary or other election for President or Vice President, for electors for President or Vice President, or for Senator or Representative in Congress, shall not be denied or abridged by the United States or any State by reason of failure to pay any poll tax or other tax.

Section 2. The Congress shall have power to enforce this article by appropriate legislation.

[Ratified 23 January 1964]

Amendment XXV

Section 1. In case of the removal of the President from office or of his death or resignation, the Vice President shall become President.

Section 2. Whenever there is a vacancy in the office of the Vice President, the President shall nominate a Vice President who shall take office upon confirmation by a majority vote of both Houses of Congress.

Section 3. Whenever the President transmits to the President pro tempore of the Senate and the Speaker of the House of Representatives his written declaration that he is unable to discharge the powers and duties of his office, and until he transmits to them a written declaration to the contrary, such powers and duties shall be discharged by the Vice President as Acting President.

Section 4. Whenever the Vice President and a majority of either the principal officers of the executive departments or of such other body as Congress may by law provide, transmit to the President pro tempore of the Senate and the Speaker of the House of Representatives their written declaration that the President is unable to discharge the powers and duties of his office, the Vice President shall immediately assume the powers and duties of the office as Acting President.

Thereafter, when the President transmits to the President pro tempore of the Senate and the Speaker of the House of Representatives his written declaration that no inability exists, he shall resume the powers and duties of his office unless the Vice President and a majority of either the principal officers of the executive department or of such other body as Congress may by law provide, transmit within four days to the President pro tempore of the Senate and the Speaker of the House of Representatives their written declaration that the President is unable to discharge the powers and duties of his office. Thereupon Congress shall decide the issue, assembling within forty-eight hours for that purpose if not in session. If the Congress, within twenty-one days after receipt of the latter written declaration, or, if Congress is not in session, within twenty-one days after Congress is required to assemble, determines by two-thirds vote of both houses that the President is unable to discharge the powers and duties of his office, the Vice President shall continue to discharge the same as Acting President; otherwise, the President shall resume the powers and duties of his office.

[Ratified 10 February 1967]

Amendment XXVI

Section 1. The right of citizens of the United States, who are eighteen years of age or older, to vote shall not be denied or abridged by the United States or by any State on account of age.

Section 2. The Congress shall have power to enforce this article by appropriate legislation.

[Ratified 1 July 1971]

Amendment XXVII

No law, varying the compensation for the services of the Senators and Representatives, shall take effect, until an election of Representatives shall have intervened.

[Ratified 7 May 1992]

APPENDIX
B

❈ ❈ ❈ ❈ ❈ ❈ ❈ ❈

Justices of the Supreme Court

	Tenure	Appointed by	Replaced
JOHN JAY	1789–1795	Washington	
John Rutledge	1789–1791	Washington	
William Cushing	1789–1810	Washington	
James Wilson	1789–1798	Washington	
John Blair	1789–1796	Washington	
James Iredell	1790–1799	Washington	
Thomas Johnson	1791–1793	Washington	Rutledge
William Paterson	1793–1806	Washington	Johnson
JOHN RUTLEDGE	1795	Washington	Jay
Samuel Chase	1796–1811	Washington	Blair
OLIVER ELLSWORTH	1796–1800	Washington	Rutledge
Bushrod Washington	1798–1829	John Adams	Wilson
Alfred Moore	1799–1804	John Adams	Iredell
JOHN MARSHALL	1801–1835	John Adams	Ellsworth
William Johnson	1804–1834	Jefferson	Moore
Brockholst Livingston	1806–1823	Jefferson	Paterson
Thomas Todd	1807–1826	Jefferson	(new judgeship)
Gabriel Duval	1811–1835	Madison	Chase
Joseph Story	1811–1845	Madison	Cushing
Smith Thompson	1823–1843	Monroe	Livingston

Chief justices' names appear in capital letters.

	Tenure	Appointed by	Replaced
Robert Trimble	1826–1828	John Q. Adams	Todd
John McLean	1829–1861	Jackson	Trimble
Henry Baldwin	1830–1844	Jackson	Washington
James Wayne	1835–1867	Jackson	Johnson
ROGER B. TANEY	1836–1864	Jackson	Marshall
Phillip P. Barbour	1836–1841	Jackson	Duval
John Catron	1837–1865	Jackson	(new judgeship)
John McKinley	1837–1852	Van Buren	(new judgeship)
Peter V. Daniel	1841–1860	Van Buren	Barbour
Samuel Nelson	1845–1872	Tyler	Thompson
Levi Woodbury	1846–1851	Polk	Story
Robert C. Grier	1846–1870	Polk	Baldwin
Benjamin R. Curtis	1851–1857	Fillmore	Woodbury
John A. Campbell	1853–1861	Pierce	McKinley
Nathan Clifford	1858–1881	Buchanan	Curtis
Noah H. Swayne	1862–1881	Lincoln	McLean
Samuel F. Miller	1862–1890	Lincoln	Daniel
David Davis	1862–1877	Lincoln	Campbell
Stephen J. Field	1863–1897	Lincoln	(new judgeship)
SALMON CHASE	1864–1873	Lincoln	Taney
William Strong	1870–1880	Grant	Grier
Joseph P. Bradley	1870–1892	Grant	Wayne
Ward Hunt	1872–1882	Grant	Nelson
MORRISON R. WAITE	1874–1888	Grant	Chase
John Marshall Harlan	1877–1911	Hayes	Davis
William B. Woods	1880–1887	Hayes	Strong
Stanley Matthews	1881–1889	Garfield	Swayne
Horace Gray	1881–1902	Arthur	Clifford
Samuel Blatchford	1882–1893	Arthur	Hunt
Lucius Q. C. Lamar	1888–1893	Cleveland	Woods
MELVILLE W. FULLER	1888–1910	Cleveland	Waite
David J. Brewer	1889–1910	Harrison	Matthews
Henry B. Brown	1890–1906	Harrison	Miller
George Shiras, Jr.	1892–1903	Harrison	Bradley
Howell E. Jackson	1893–1895	Harrison	Lamar

	Tenure	Appointed by	Replaced
Edward D. White	1894–1910	Cleveland	Blatchford
Rufus W. Peckham	1895–1909	Cleveland	Jackson
Joseph McKenna	1898–1925	McKinley	Field
Oliver Wendell Holmes	1902–1932	T. Roosevelt	Gray
William R. Day	1903–1922	T. Roosevelt	Shiras
William H. Moody	1906–1910	T. Roosevelt	Brown
Horace H. Lurton	1909–1914	Taft	Peckham
Charles Evans Hughes	1910–1916	Taft	Brewer
EDWARD D. WHITE	1910–1921	Taft	Fuller
Willis Van Devanter	1910–1937	Taft	White
Joseph R. Lamar	1910–1916	Taft	Moody
Mahlon Pitney	1912–1922	Taft	Harlan
James McReynolds	1914–1941	Wilson	Lurton
Louis D. Brandeis	1916–1939	Wilson	Lamar
John H. Clarke	1916–1922	Wilson	Hughes
WILLIAM H. TAFT	1921–1930	Harding	White
George Sutherland	1922–1938	Harding	Clarke
Pierce Butler	1922–1939	Harding	Day
Edward T. Sanford	1923–1930	Harding	Pitney
Harlan F. Stone	1925–1941	Coolidge	McKenna
CHARLES EVANS HUGHES	1930–1941	Hoover	Taft
Owen J. Roberts	1932–1945	Hoover	Sanford
Benjamin N. Cardozo	1932–1938	Hoover	Holmes
Hugo L. Black	1937–1971	F. Roosevelt	Van Devanter
Stanley F. Reed	1938–1957	F. Roosevelt	Sutherland
Felix Frankfurter	1939–1962	F. Roosevelt	Cardozo
William O. Douglas	1939–1975	F. Roosevelt	Brandeis
Frank Murphy	1940–1949	F. Roosevelt	Butler
James F. Byrnes	1941–1942	F. Roosevelt	McReynolds
HARLAN F. STONE	1941–1946	F. Roosevelt	Hughes
Robert H. Jackson	1941–1954	F. Roosevelt	Stone
Wiley B. Rutledge	1943–1949	F. Roosevelt	Byrnes
Harold H. Burton	1945–1958	Truman	Roberts
FRED M. VINSON	1946–1953	Truman	Stone

	Tenure	Appointed by	Replaced
Tom C. Clark	1949–1967	Truman	Murphy
Sherman Minton	1949–1956	Truman	Rutledge
EARL WARREN	1954–1969	Eisenhower	Vinson
John M. Harlan	1955–1971	Eisenhower	Jackson
William J. Brennan	1957–1990	Eisenhower	Minton
Charles E. Whittaker	1957–1962	Eisenhower	Reed
Potter Stewart	1959–1981	Eisenhower	Burton
Byron R. White	1962–1993	Kennedy	Whittaker
Arthur J. Goldberg	1962–1965	Kennedy	Frankfurter
Abe Fortas	1965–1969	Johnson	Goldberg
Thurgood Marshall	1967–1991	Johnson	Clark
WARREN E. BURGER	1969–1986	Nixon	Warren
Harry A. Blackmun	1970–	Nixon	Fortas
Lewis F. Powell	1971–1988	Nixon	Black
William H. Rehnquist	1971–	Nixon	Harlan
John Paul Stevens	1975–	Ford	Douglas
Sandra Day O'Connor	1981–	Reagan	Stewart
WILLIAM H. REHNQUIST	1986–	Reagan	Burger
Antonin Scalia	1986–	Reagan	Rehnquist
Anthony M. Kennedy	1988–	Reagan	Powell
David H. Souter	1990–	Bush	Brennan
Clarence Thomas	1991–	Bush	Marshall
Ruth Bader Ginsburg	1993–	Clinton	White

INDEX

❋ ❋ ❋ ❋ ❋ ❋ ❋ ❋

by David Heiret